Experimental Nations

TRANSLATION I TRANSNATION

SERIES EDITOR **EMILY APTER**

RÉDA BENSMAÏA

Experimental Nations

Or, the Invention of the Maghreb

TRANSLATED BY **ALYSON WATERS**

PRINCETON UNIVERSITY PRESS

PRINCETON AND OXFORD

Copyright © 2003 by Princeton University Press
Published by Princeton University Press, 41 William Street,
Princeton, New Jersey 08540
In the United Kingdom: Princeton University Press,
3 Market Place, Woodstock, Oxfordshire OX20 1SY

Library of Congress Cataloging-in-Publication Data

Bensmaïa, Réda
[Nations expérimentales. English]
Experimental nations : or, the invention of the Maghreb / Réda Bensmaïa ; translated by Alyson
Waters.
p. cm. — (Translation/transnation)
Includes bibliographical reference and index. •
ISBN: 0-691-08936-1 (alk. paper)—ISBN: 0-691-08937-X (pbk. : alk. paper)
1. North African literature (French)—History and criticism. I. Waters, Alyson, 1955–
II. Title. III. Series.
PQ3988.5.N6 B46613 2003
840.9′961—dc21   2002074906

British Library Cataloging-in-Publication Data is available.

This book has been composed in Minion with Gill Sans display.

Printed on acid-free paper. ∞

www.pupress.princeton.edu

Printed in the United States of America

10 9 8 7 6 5 4 3 2 1

CONTENTS

TRANSLATOR'S NOTE

Where a published English version of authors cited was available, I have used it throughout, and made reference to it accordingly. All other translations of citations are my own. Chapter 5, section 1, and chapter 6, section 3, of this book were translated by Jennifer Curtiss Gage.

I would like to thank Réda Bensmaïa for his generous and patient responses to my queries over the course of this translation. I would also like to thank Gwenaël Kerlidou and Roger Celestin for lending me, on occasion, their *génie de la (bi) langue.*

ACKNOWLEDGMENTS

This book is composed of texts that cover more than ten years of work on Francophone literature from the Maghreb. It would never have seen the light of day had it not been for Emily Apter's persistent and persistently friendly offer to include one of my books in the series she edits for Princeton University Press. I owe to her my awareness that these texts, which had each taken shape in specific historical circumstances, together sketched out the map of a "country" that I did not yet know and would only discover at the end of my journey. As I was piecing together the different sections of this map, the experimental nature of the works under study here began to emerge as the discovery of a sui generis virtual reality, that is, of an unknown Maghreb that bore within it a mad, intense hope. And now, at the moment this book is being published, I cannot forget that Algeria is filled with a violence that divides it internally, and separates it from the other countries of the Maghreb as well. This is yet one more reason not to be discouraged and to continue, resolutely, to survey the territory.

There is the map that this book represents—a map that is no doubt partial in both senses of the word: incomplete and biased. But there are also the sections of this map I mentioned above, and whose contours I could not have begun to trace without the help of those explorers who have accompanied me since the start of my work. Only after the fact did I realize how impossible it would have been to travel across such uneven terrain had I not encountered these inspiring pioneers: Françoise Lionnet, Ronnie Scharfman, Danielle Marx-Scouras,

Anne Donadey, Christopher Miller, Anne Smock, Mireille Rosello, Bernard Arésu, Michael Dash, Hafid Gafaiti, Winnie Woodhull, Dana Strand, Marie-Pierre Le Hir, Marie-Claire Ropars-Wuilleumier, Michèle Lagny, Pierre Sorlin, and all those who have contributed to marking out the roads leading to that splendid region of the Francophone world that is the literature of the Maghreb. I thank them warmly here. Because of their work and their support, I never felt myself to be a stranger in a strange land!

Once this original journey had been completed, I had yet to discover new aspects of this region through the *translation* of the texts that make up this book. I am grateful for a preliminary crossing of this veritable zone to the talented and resourceful students Denise Davis, Touria Khannous, Elisa Hartz, and Jennifer Curtiss Gage of Brown University, as well as to friends and colleagues such as Karen Tucker, Whitney Sanford, and Bernard Arésu. In the first English-language incarnation of some of these texts, each of these "smugglers" of language left his or her mark on the transformation of a monolingual landscape into a language where one speaks in tongues; by translating some of the texts found here, they re-created them and gave them a second life and, one could say, a new soul.

But my journey in and through languages did not stop here. When all of these various sections of map had to be joined to form a country, I had to call upon yet another cartographer. It fell to one person to create a whole. And if ever this book has the possibility of leading somewhere and of serving as a guide, it is to Alyson Waters that I owe this possibility. It is to her that fell the most difficult: to translate all the texts anew and to do so in such a way that what could have been a mismatched patchwork became instead the *atlas* of a very recognizable part of the world. I would like to thank her here for having transformed my varied voices into a single voice that, at the time of a translation, was reconciled with itself. Many thanks also to Barbara Coster, who copyedited the manuscript and allowed Alyson and me to put the finishing touches on the present book.

Several institutions have played a crucial role in the conception and the production of the texts that constitute this book. I am referring here to the journals where many of these texts were first published. My thanks go to the editors of *Research in African Literature, Yale French Studies, SubStance, World Literature Today, L'Esprit Créateur,* and *Hors-Cadre* for their early interest in Francophone literature and culture, and the State University of New York Press and Cornell University Press for making it possible to produce numerous important contributions to a better knowledge of Francophone literature and culture and, more generally speaking, "postcolonial studies."

I also want to present my deepest thanks to Fred Appel and Mary Murrell, my editors and mentors at Princeton University Press, who helped me with their advice and provided encouragement and perspective for the production of this book in all its stages. To Maurizia Natali goes my gratitude for her advice, patience, and confidence in me. I am grateful to her for having shared with me the joys of discovery and the anxieties of being en route in these territories. I owe her many of the nuances that color my maps. Last, but not least, I want to thank Rachid Koraïchi, an artist of vision and talent, to whom I owe the sunny embroidered image that shines on the cover of this book as a message of hope.

"Political Geography of Literature," reprinted by permission from *French Cultural Studies: Criticism at the Crossroads,* by Marie-Pierre Le Hir and Dana Strand (eds.), State University of New York Press, © 2000 by State University of New York. All right reserved.

"La Nouba des femmes du Mont Chenoua: Introduction to the Cinematic Fragment," vol. 70, no. 4, Autumn 1996. Reprinted by permission from *World Literature Today,* © 1996 by WLT.

"Multilingualism and National 'Characteristic,' on Khatibi's 'Bi-Langue,' " reprinted by permission from *Algeria in Other's Languages,* by Anne-Emmanuelle Berger (ed.), © 2002 by Cornell University. Used by permission of the publisher, Cornell University Press.

"Alger est-il un 'lieu de mémoire'? En partant de Salut, Cousin de Merzak Allouache," XLI.3, Fall 2001, 114–24. Reprinted by permission from *L'Esprit Créateur,* © 2001 by *L'Esprit Créateur.*

"Postcolonial Nations: Political or Poetic Allegories?" vol. 30, issue 3, Spring 2003. Reprinted by permission from *Research in African Literature,* © 2003 by Indiana University Press.

"Writing Metafiction: On Khatibi's *Le Livre du Sang*," *Sub-Stance* 69, vol. 21, no. 3. Reprinted by permission of the University of Wisconsin Press, © 1992.

"The Exiles of Nabile Farès: Or How to Become a Minority," vol. 2, no. 83, 1993. Reprinted by permission from *Yale French Studies*, © 1993 by *Yale French Studies*.

Experimental Nations

Is an "Experimental" Nation Possible?

For a majority of the French at the time of the Third Republic (1870–1940), Algeria could be summed up by a few clichés from Alphonse Daudet's 1892 *Tartarin de Tarascon,* one of the contemporary classics for elementary school children. During this same period, the vast stretches of Algerian territory began to serve in the imaginary of a decadent elite as a kind of stock of images, animals, and workers where differences could flourish under the protection of the French flag. Perceived as a mix of sensuality and proud purity, of oasis and desert, Algeria became a catalyst for writers wanting to break with Parisian culture. It was, in a sense, a terrain of experimentation. Théophile Gautier, Eugène Fromentin, and Guy de Maupassant traveled to Algeria seeking out novelty, and were followed by Henri de Montherlant and other French writers on the prowl for new, exotic experiences.[1] It was not until 1925 that André Gide would discover (and finally denounce) the "misdeeds" of colonialism, in his *Voyage au Congo.* However, in 1893 it was chiefly pleasure he found in Algeria: its oases gave him a taste for the "fruits of the earth."

During World War II, tired of posing for these exotic portraits, Algerians themselves began actively to enter French literature. They could do so, however, only by resorting to the language of their colonizers. Tunisian writer Albert Memmi described this "linguistic wrenching" as one of the most painful aspects of the alienation suffered by the colonized. Analyzing the colonial situation in *The Colonizer and the Colonized*, he spoke of the "linguistic drama" (108) raging within the colonized person: "His mother tongue is humiliated, crushed. . . . He himself sets about discarding this infirm language, hiding it from strangers' eyes." (107; translation modified) This process of self-mutilation had to come to an end before the struggle for national liberation could succeed. The idea of an Algerian literature written in French was a contradiction in the context of decolonization, and it was believed that political independence would soon be followed by cultural and linguistic independence. And yet, since Algerian independence in 1962, the number of works written in French by Maghrebi authors has continued to multiply. This fact led Memmi to retract his words some thirty years later in the preface to his anthology, *Francophone Writers from the Maghreb* [Écrivains francophones du Maghreb]: "While I have never stopped believing that the Arabic language will ultimately find the place it deserves, I have had to admit that the *inertia of custom* is more powerful than logical or sentimental hope." (11)

In Algeria, this state of affairs reflects a profound linguistic pluralism. Several languages are spoken in addition to classical and dialectic Arabic. This situation predates the French conquest. Kabyle is spoken in the mountains of Kabylia, Touareg in the desert, Mozabit in the oases—and these languages are themselves divided into dialects. Furthermore, illiteracy has been the most serious problem in Algeria— as in most of the African countries that were colonized by France: in 1962, 85 percent of the population not only did not speak French but could not read or write in either Arabic or French, and today a great many Algerians remain illiterate. Algerian writers were therefore obliged to turn to the French language in order to find readers. Prior to Algerian independence, most Algerian writers were teachers who owed their schooling to the colonial educational system. The works of poet Jean Amrouche and novelist Mouloud Feraoun (Feraoun was assassinated in 1962 by the Organisation de l'Armée Secrète [OAS], the French far-right terrorist organization that was desperately trying to sabotage de Gaulle's final recognition of Algerian independence), for example, are emblematic of the contradiction in which Maghrebi literature of that generation was mired—a contradiction that independence did not manage to resolve. In an attempt to revitalize national culture,

Amrouche devoted himself to the systematic translation of Berber popular songs into French. In his introduction to *Chants berbères de Kabylie* (1939), he insisted on the maternal roots of this popular oral poetry: "A man whose life is not separated from the life of the Mother is naturally a poet." (13) And yet it was only by being exiled in the French language that these songs could become literature: in this instance, transcription and translation are part of one and the same gesture of separation and distance. Amrouche's collection is representative of the fate of Algerian literature, a literature born of the severing of what Kateb Yacine would call the "umbilical tie" to the mother tongue. In several chapters in this book—and particularly in the first—I have attempted to show the complexity of the problems posed by the relation to language.

The end of World War II represented a liberation for the French; this was not so for the Algerians. For them the time of experimentation was only beginning. In May 1945, a general uprising was followed by a brutal repression during which tens of thousands of Algerians were killed. Kateb Yacine (1929–89), who was a high school student at the time, took part in these anti-French demonstrations, was imprisoned, and was forbidden access to higher education. In his first novel, *Nedjma*, Kateb interwove his high school memories with those of the uprising that led to the country's liberation from the colonial yoke. In one scene, Lakhdar, a student who was expelled from school after the demonstrations, boards a train to return home. He is the only one in his compartment who can read the names of the station stops, written in French, and he discovers that the educational system from which he has just been excluded has made him betray his linguistic universe: "If we had our own trains . . . [f]irst of all, the farmers would be comfortable. They wouldn't be fidgeting at each station, afraid of missing their stop. They could read. And in Arabic too! I'd have to reeducate myself in our own language. I'd be grandfather's classmate." (84) In this key episode of the novel, French school is no longer presented as a conciliating instrument or an institution designed to lead to assimilation; instead, it is a site where contradictions become visible and explosive. While for Feraoun school was a symbol of compromise, for Kateb it accentuated the sense of an impasse, of loss and betrayal. The most powerful image of the uprising in *Nedjma* is that of the old

Si Mokhtar, who in May 1945 in Constantine "walked through the city alone, past the fascinated police officers, with a gag in his mouth showing two slogans of his own invention which crowds of people engraved in their memory: Vive La France/Les Arabes silence!" (206) This scene stages in miniature what Kateb himself said of his novel when he called it an Algerian work in "Arabic," despite the fact that it was written in French. As the editors of *Nedjma* wrote: "Conceived and written in French, *Nedjma* remains a profoundly Arab work, and we cannot arrive at a valid assessment of it if we isolate it from the tradition to which, *even in its repudiations*, it still belongs." (6; translation modified)

Kateb's second autobiographical novel, *Le polygone étoilé* (1966), also ends on a violent note. The narrator, born into a literate family, recalls that in his childhood, everyone had expected him to become a writer—"Kateb" means writer in Arabic—but a writer who would of course write in Arabic, "like his father, mother, uncles, and grandparents." (179) However, his father, a Muslim magistrate, sends him to French school. This decision leads to the explosion of jealousy on which the novel closes: the mother cannot bear the fact that her son is seeking approval from a French schoolteacher who, she believes, won her son over to a language that she does not even speak. Kateb evokes this moment of dramatic betrayal:

> Never did I cease, even on those days when my teacher praised me, to feel deep inside me a second severing of the umbilical cord, that internal exile that drew the schoolboy closer to his mother only to pull them apart yet again, each time a little more, with the murmur of the blood, the reproachful tremors of a banished tongue, secretly, in an agreement that was broken as soon as it was made. . . . *So I had lost at one and the same time my mother and her language, the only inalienable treasures—that were alienated none the less!* [179–80]

This is the situation that most colonized countries inherited after independence. For Francophone writers, the questions remained the same: to write, of course, but in which language? To write, but *for whom*? The question that Jean-Paul Sartre asked in his *What Is Literature?*

(1947) became a tragic problem in a culture that had no real audience for literature.

Kateb settled in Annaba, near Algiers, with the explicit intention of creating a *public* for literature. *Mohammed prends ta valise* (1971) leaves no doubt regarding the public he decided to address. This play, the first he produced in popular Arabic, was a huge success with the Algerian public both in Algeria and in France. The main character is an immigrant worker, a typical figure in contemporary Algerian life. But around this modern nomad—the uprooted proletarian—multiple echoes of traditional nomadic culture, popular songs, and ancient tales and legends swirl. Unlike rigid, printed language, the language of the stage is more flexible. It more readily reflects the complexity of daily language and the plurality of tongues that coexist in Algeria. It makes it possible to avoid the strict linguistic choices imposed by writing and the printed word, and the uniformity and impoverishment they entail. Kateb, playing among languages, brings to a head the linguistic chaos in which most Algerians still live today. What literature should one promote? Is literature the best medium to use? And what can its contributions be to efforts to build the country, to construct the nation?

Contrary to pessimistic forecasts, Maghrebi literature has continued to be written in French after Kateb. Other writers have appeared on the scene to face the challenges not only of language and identity but also of existence itself. In Morocco, authors such as Abdelatif Laabi, Mohammed Khair-Eddine, Abdelkebir Khatibi, and Tahar Ben Jelloun; in Tunisia, Mohammed Tlili, Hélé Béji, and Abdelwahab Meddeb; and in Algeria again, poets and novelists such as Nabile Farès, Rachid Mimouni, Habib Tengour, and Assia Djebar all have succeeded in showing that this literature carries a message beyond mere revolt, all the while insisting that it is the product of an iniquitous historical situation. What the works of these writers prove is that Maghrebi literature exists. It was not something brilliant and illusory that faded away. In the past, it denounced a system that, by giving it a voice, caused it to lose its language. Today, using a broad variety of styles and themes, Maghrebi literature is producing works in French that contribute to an understanding of the "new world" (Farès) that has come into being since Algerian independence. This literature has also become an indispensable tool for the elaboration—or perlaboration and anamnesis—of something that was believed lost for good: the idiosyncratic nature of indigenous cultures.

This book is a collection of texts each belonging to a different period in my research—periods that are marked by academia's increasing awareness of the importance of so-called postcolonial writers. I begin with the premise that the contribution of these writers to the awakening of what could be called a new literary consciousness has not always been fully recognized. This consciousness very rapidly moved beyond the limits of national boundaries to become open to—as well as to open—a field that is now planetwide.

What has long struck me was the nonchalance with which the work of these writers was analyzed. Whenever these novels were studied, they were almost invariably reduced to anthropological or cultural case studies. Their literariness was rarely taken seriously. And once they were finally integrated into the deconstructed canon of world literature, they were made to serve as tools for political or ideological agendas. This kind of reading resulted more often than not in their being reduced to mere signifiers of other signifiers, with a total disregard for what makes them literary works *in and of themselves.*

The works of Nabile Farès, for example, although they represent one of the most original undertakings of independent Algeria, have not yet been translated into English. And on those rare occasions when they have been studied, they have been reduced to a discussion of ethnic identities! Farès is considered to be a Berberist—a poet of Berber culture and identity—even though he has behind him a body of work that, according to Jacques Godbout, makes use of one of the most courageous and original techniques of the "reappropriation of culture and of the world." Another example: Kateb Yacine, the Algerian writer who is considered to have given Francophone African literature its letters patent of nobility and whose plays have mobilized tens of thousands, if not millions, of immigrant workers throughout the world, has not yet garnered the recognition he deserves in France or elsewhere in Europe and the Americas. As Edouard Glissant recently said, the French do not yet have the ability to assimilate, let alone understand, Kateb. And yet they were, theoretically, in the most logical position to do so.

Examples of this kind of deafness or blindness to writers who have managed to make themselves known to their people without really arousing the interest of academics are rampant. I am thinking of writers such as Tahar Ben Jelloun, Assia Djebar, Patrick Chamoiseau, Yasmina Khadra, and many, many others. They have all succeeded in finding an audience in France and, in some cases, in the United States, Germany, Italy, or Great Britain, but, except in rare instances, they had never really been read or taken seriously until very recently. Nevertheless—and this is the line of questioning followed in this book—I do not think it possible to understand the current climate in contemporary world literature without paying close attention to what is at stake in the works analyzed here. Whether it is the problem of languages or of the nation or the "transnation" (Khatibi's term); whether it is the question of what is happening in the contemporary world—Glissant's "Tout Monde" or Appaduraï's "ethnoscape"; or whether it is a matter of intellectual output in general and the fight against neocolonialism and the avatars of imperialism—few "national" literatures have played as important a role as those called Francophone. As Edward Said has emphasized, "[I]n the decades-long struggle to achieve decolonization and independence from European control, *literature has played a crucial role in the reestablishment of national cultural heritage, in the reinstatement of native idioms, in the reimagining and refiguring of local histories, geographies, communities. As such, then, literature not only mobilized active resistance to incursions from the outside but also contributed massively as the shaper, creator, agent of illumination within the realm of the colonized.*"[2]

This book is dedicated to bringing to light the originality of the *literary* strategies deployed by postcolonial Maghrebi writers to reappropriate their national cultural heritage, to regain their idioms, and to reconfigure their history, territory, and community. Whether in Assia Djebar's cinema, Khatibi's prose poems or critical essays, or the novels and poems of Farès, Dib, Meddeb, Béji, Bouraroui, or Djaout, it has always been a matter of raising the veil that hid the intrinsic richness of these works from the eyes of even the most attentive readers. That is to say, this book does not simply examine the way Francophone writers from the Maghreb have dealt with their nation. It also attempts to show how they were constantly opening up their nation to what was escaping it on all sides. And in this sense, what lies at the heart of this work, what unifies it, is not so much a theme as a problematic. This problematic allows us to see that there may be more affinities between an Algerian writer and an African American writer today than there were between this same writer and another writer from his or her own country in the past. Under today's postmodern conditions, it is not geographical or even political boundaries that determine identities, but rather a plane of consistency that goes beyond the traditional idea of nation and determines its new transcendental configuration. And it is in this sense that I use the term *experimental nations*. My nations are experimental in that they are above all nations that writers have had to imagine or explore as if they were territories to rediscover and stake out, step by step, countries to invent and to draw while creating one's language. It is in this sense that these nations may be called virtual, without for all that being imaginary or unreal. The virtual, as we know, "is opposed not to the *real*, but to the *actual*. The virtual *is fully real as it is actual*."[3] And so we can say that our writers invent what Proust called "states of resonance": the countries as well as the identities that they offer us to experiment with are, as Deleuze says, "real without being actual, ideal without being abstract, and symbolic without being fictional." (208)

Thus we ask the following questions in reference not only to memory (of places) and to thought (of difference), but also in reference to imagination (of the nation): Is there an *imaginandum* that is also a limit, what is impossible to imagine? And in reference to language: Is there a *loquendum* that is, at the same time, silence? (Deleuze, ibid.) It is experimental questions of this kind that our writers are asking and that I am attempting to reformulate here with them: Does the writer *belong* to a nation? What does this *belonging* mean for Francophone writers? How many different idioms are contained in their written language? How many countries, customs, crossed histories are to be found in their narratives? What are the relations between the actual nation and the virtual nation? And according to what plan? Each of the studies I propose here attempts somehow to reveal this plan. In the texts I consider in this book (mostly novels, but poems and essays as well), thought and imagination enter into a discordance and a violence, triggering a radical questioning of identity (in the concept of nation, for example) and of similarity in cultural artifacts. As Kateb so brilliantly put it: "Plans are overturned at every moment!" And this is what influenced both my choice of texts and my methodology.

Each text, exemplary in its own way, required the use of a particular critical protocol. But because of its attention to discord and to the disparateness of the texts, my investigation slowly uncovered what can paradoxically be called an empirical *transcendental* field where texts come together and intersect, while their differences remain intact and the uniqueness of their relationships remains undiminished. In any event, it is this kind of experimentation that I hope to have been able to reveal in this book.[4]

I

Nations of Writers

> What in great literature goes on down below, constituting a
> not indispensable cellar of the structure, here takes place in
> the full light of day, what is there a matter of passing interest
> for a few, here absorbs everyone no less than as a matter of
> life and death.

—Franz Kafka, *Diaries 1910–1913*, ed. Max Broad (New
York: Schocken Books, 1965), entry for December 25, 1911.

1. Cultural "Terrain"

In a speech at the first Algerian National Colloquium on Culture (Colloque National Algérien de la Culture), the Algerian historian and former Minister of Education Mostefa Lacheraf asked the following question in regard to the minimum conditions necessary for the development of an "authentic" culture in Algeria: "At what point—a point already attained or one that is yet to be attained—does a national culture cease to be mere entertainment, becoming instead as basic as the bread we eat or the air we breathe?" In the context of postcolonial Algeria, it is obvious that this kind of culture, as Lacheraf knew, was first and foremost a goal "yet to be attained." This is why in his speech he subordinated this question and the response it could elicit to a much more radical one. Indeed, he stated that "to look for an answer to this question is yet again to ask ourselves whether *a given terrain can profitably accommodate a given culture*; whether such an action does not require that this *terrain*—that is, the majority of men—must not first be in a position to meet both the cultural needs that drive this majority, and the demands made on it by a small group of their peers better equipped to meet these demands."

When one is aware of the havoc colonization wreaked on Algerian society and culture—or what this society and culture could have become—certain questions become inevitable. Who are these men to whom Lacheraf refers? What are their *sites* and their *means* (material, institutional, technical)? In what "state" are they to be found? Finally, what influence can a small group of writers and artists wield when most of them have created their work *in French*, that is, in a language the majority does not speak?

The aftermath of Algerian independence, as we all know, was fraught with consequences: in the countryside, men and women were completely uprooted from their culture; in the cities and towns, the "public" consisted "of mostly uneducated people." It is this last statement—more realistic than pessimistic—that led Lacheraf to ask the following: "Can a milieu (in particular the rural milieu) that has been seriously uprooted from its culture and neglected for so long manage to unite the conditions necessary to become a *public* in the active sense of the term, simply because it is being asked to do so?" (My emphasis)

This, then, is the catastrophic situation that Algeria inherited with independence: on the one hand, popular masses so uprooted from their culture that the very idea of a "public" seemed to be a luxury or, at best, a difficult goal to attain, and on the other, too few writers, artists (filmmakers, for example), and intellectuals to meet the existing needs and who for the most part were completely assimilated. Not only were "products" (or producers) lacking but so was the actual terrain where such products could come into being and take on meaning—the material and objective conditions for the existence of a public, a public sphere. And so at the time of independence, cultural problems were never posed in the abstract and universal terms of expression and production, but always, necessarily, in the regional and concrete terms of territorialization or reterritorialization using the fragmentary material, cultural, and spiritual elements the country had inherited so as to create a new geopolitics. There was, in other words, a concrete effort to build a new, collective subject—something like a national entity—from scratch but without improvising; to build upon the debris of a social and cultural community that had barely escaped disaster and total upheaval. Clearly, every decision, every commitment, was a matter of life and death here. For to create or re-create a terrain, to define something like a national trait, is an act of reterritorialization. But which elements were to be used to do this? The forgotten past? The ruins of popular memory? Folklore? Tradition? None of these carried within it enough force and cohesion to allow it to be a stable anchor for a national culture worthy of the name. Furthermore, believing in the possibility of a reterritorialization through folklore, the past, tradition, or religion would mean believing in the *sub specie aeternitatis* existence of a norm or an essence of an Algerian people on whom 135 years of colonialism had had absolutely no impact. It would also mean believing that one need only sweep away what is called, in cowardly fashion, the aftereffects of colonial rule to uncover an untouched, pristine spirit of the Algerian people. Obviously, neither this norm nor this essence existed at the time of independence. Lacheraf wrote: "To what normal situation can we return, if not to those fleeting aspects of an essentially defunct universe of which there remains only deceptive folkloric testimony that re-creates the past in its nonfunctional nostalgia?" According to Lacheraf, what had to be secured was "the continuity of a past linked to the present by new cultural and social facts, by tangible and reliable acts of resurrection more than of survival." If in fact something like a national trait did indeed exist, it was only as a goal yet to be attained, in constant dialectic with what remained alive and active in the past and not simply based *on* the past.

That said, the problems nonetheless remained abstract and unsolved, for whether it uses folklore, the past, tradition, or anything else, the re-creation or the *invention* of a specific, authentic culture must first have solved the problem of the *medium* through which all of this could come about. In what language should one write? In what language should one film? What language should people in schools, hospitals, government offices speak or write? Spoken Arabic? Kabyle? "Literary" Arabic? These are concrete, vital problems that explain the acuity of the tensions, contradictions, and difficulties that every artist and, more generally, every producer of culture faces in Algeria today. As I said, for these artists, each creative act is a matter of life and death, because each of their gestures, each of their choices, lays the foundation for things to come. In each instance a terrain must be constructed and a way out of the maze of languages must be found at all costs—a way of staking out one's territory, like an animal—of not leaving one's *Umwelt*. As Deleuze and Guattari so clearly phrased it in their book on Kafka: "Writing [and I would add: filming] like a dog digging a hole, a rat digging its burrow. And to do that, finding his own point of underdevelopment, his own *patois*, his own third world, his own desert."[1]

These are the concrete conditions that explain the complex mechanism by which it has historically been the theater—and not the novel, for example—that succeeded in reaching the goals one might have expected from a renaissance of Algerian popular culture. Theater is the living medium that allows a people to recognize its national character; it provides an identity within the diversity of local languages and cultures; it acts as a unifier for multiple ethnic groups and cultures; and finally, it demonstrates active solidarity within the disparity between urban and rural milieus and cultures.

2. A New Geolinguistics

In this chapter, I attempt to analyze certain theoretical and practical obstacles that Francophone Algerian literature has encountered in creating, against all odds, its own *language*, in elaborating a *terrain*, and meeting a *public* (three terms that are, as I have tried to show, absolutely indissociable in this context). I begin by examining the ideological and political problems raised by the question of language—that is, the medium of this literature—and then illustrate these problems using specific cases. In particular, I refer to Kateb Yacine's theater, as well as the work of other writers who have greatly influenced the rebirth and reinscription of an indigenous culture.

For the longest time, attempts to study Algerian literature written in French (bizarrely called literature "of French expression" in certain circles)[2] in its esthetic and ideological relation to "French French" literature were distorted by the illusion that there were two, and only two, antithetical possibilities for this literature at the time of independence. On the one hand, reterritorialization was to occur through the use of literary Arabic, and on the other, through bilingualism (French for the sciences and for technology, literary Arabic for the "soul," identity, and origins). In the meantime, the vernacular languages—especially spoken or dialectic Arabic and Kabyle, still very much alive at the time—found themselves shut out from the playing field. The result of such a narrow vision of linguistic phenomena was twofold: a misunderstanding of an essential part of national culture, on the one hand, and on the other, an inability to grasp the real practice of writers, artists, and the masses in general.

What was, for example, the situation of Algerian *writers* at the time? All of them—French and Arabic-speaking (*francisant* and *arabisant*)—found themselves face to face with a language that was itself deterritorialized, without any deep cultural or social roots. This was certainly the situation of Francophone writers who, writing in the language of the former colonial power, found themselves in an impossible position. In the aftermath of independence it was "impossible to not write," because, from their point of view as writers, "the national conscience, uncertain and long oppressed, must speak through literature." (Deleuze and Guattari, 30) It was also impossible to write in a language other than French, and this fact marked both a limit of and an irreducible distance from what they could only fantasize about, that is, a "primal Algerian territoriality," which they felt they were constantly betraying. For Algerians, the impossibility of writing in French was at the same time the impossibility of *translating* the idiosyncratic traits of the society in which they lived into a language of another culture. The problem for these writers was posed within strict bounds: *How can we live within several languages and write in only one?*

As we know, Maghrebi writers answered this question in a variety of ways, according to temperament, personal preoccupations, and political and ideological points of view. Some simply stopped writing.

Others tried to come to terms with their assimilation by continuing to write in French, even if it meant they had to mistreat the language to make it say what it was not always able to say; still others tried to write in literary Arabic and sometimes in spoken Arabic. It is important to stress here that none of them really managed to solve the problem I raised earlier, that is, none of them managed to create a relatively homogenous cultural terrain, and to actually find a public. Contrary to what writer and sociologist Albert Memmi believed,[3] the return to Arabic—including dialectal Arabic—did not suffice to resolve the many contradictions that arose, to fill the void that separated creators from their public. Whatever their medium, all writers wound up in the same impasse. Many reasons have been invoked to account for this phenomenon: the aftereffects of colonialism, the loss of a culture, the lack of human and material means, regional specificity, multiple ethnic groups, multiple conquests—but all of them are subordinate to one essential point, namely, that the dichotomy between high and low ("popular") languages, and specifically the false dilemma between Arabic on the one hand and bilingualism on the other, does not help us understand what is really going on in Algerian culture.[4] A rational, consistent sociolinguistics is lacking for the concrete understanding of the actual practices of the country.

Several Maghrebi writers did understand—although they were not always able to turn this understanding into *practice*—that within the given cultural arena in which they had to produce their works, they were not dealing with a single language, or even with two; nor was it a matter of high and low languages. Rather, *whatever language they used*, they were always in fact dealing with (at least) four very distinct *types* of language:[5]

1. A *vernacular* language, local, spoken spontaneously, disposed less to communicating than to communing. This language is composed essentially of the play of several languages: mother tongues from rural communities, such as spoken Arabic, Kabyle, and Touareg, for example, as well as a kind of deterritorialized, nomadic, and atypical language that is neither French, Arabic, nor Kabyle. It is a language composed haphazardly from various sources, living off stolen, mobilized words, words that have emigrated from one language to another: an incongruous medley of "proper" French and dialectal Arabic or Ka-

byle spoken in the cities and towns. For example: "Ouach rak bian?" ("How's it going?").[6] We will come back to this.

2. A *vehicular* language that, in a certain sense, can be qualified as national. This language—and for a long time it was French—is learned by necessity and used for communication in the cities and towns. In Algeria, French has been replaced progressively by Arabic, first on the regional and then on the national level, and in certain economic sectors (trade, industry, international relations) by English. The vehicular is thus the language of urban economic and political powers or, in Ferdinand Tönnies's terms, the language of the *Gesellschaft*. Here we are faced with a *new interplay of languages*: classical Arabic, French, and English.

One final very important remark on this point: Because they lay claim to being universal, these kinds of languages tend, as Henri Gobard has shown, "to destroy vernacular languages, whatever their sociolinguistic proximity or their genetic relationship." (Deleuze and Guattari, ibid.) Thus, whatever the language from which it originates, the vehicular is always a linguistic imperialist, a linguistic Attila, because wherever it travels, the "affect of [vernacular] communities" (Deleuze and Guattari, 43 4) (territory, way of life, food, nomenclature, etc.) withers and dies in the end. In this sense, any vehicular language is also a language of a *first deterritorialization*. Because it claims to be universal, it therefore claims to be neutral, objective, the language of each and every one. This is at least what the French administration and school system wanted its new subjects to believe. Yet as those writers whose works we explore in the following pages demonstrate, the politico-linguistic unrest that marked the first decades of independence arose in part from the confrontation, the clash, of these two types of languages.[7]

3. A *referential* language that "functions as *oral or written reference*, through proverbs, sayings, literature, rhetoric, etc." (Deleuze and Guattari, ibid.) and that is usually (that is, in societies that are not dislocated) destined to carry out a more directly cultural reterritorialization: songs, classical and popular music, poetry, and so on. All the vernacular languages carry within them pieces of the past, as do the three main vehicular languages: Arabic (in the poems and texts of Emir Abdelkader, for example), Kabyle (in the poems of Si Mohand in Kabylia), and French (the works of Francophone writers, historians, archivists, etc.).

4. Finally, a *mythic* language that "acts as a last resort, a verbal magic whose incomprehensibility is understood as irrefutable proof of the sacred." (Deleuze and Guattari, ibid.) In Algeria, this language is for the most part literary Arabic, the language of religious and spiritual reterritorialization.

Clearly, as Gobard has pointed out, none of these plays on and in languages share a spatiotemporal terrain. The vernacular is the *here and now* of the regional language or mother tongue; the vehicular is the *everywhere and later* of the language of the cities, both centralizing and prospective; the referential is the *over there and before* of national life; and finally, the mythical is the *beyond and forever* of the sacred.

Earlier I said that what is essential is the *medium*, the language itself, and not expression in general. But this is also too abstract. We must now ask: What kind of machine of expression can account for such a multiplicity of languages without bursting into pieces? In other words, what is the machine that can integrate all the functions (affective, psychological, ethical, poetic) performed by these different linguistic practices, without crushing them or reducing them to a single, abstract whole? Finally, what machine is capable of embracing simultaneously such diverse *terrains* and heterogeneous *temporalities*?

If we look at the works of scholars such as Edward Said, Homi K. Bhabha, and Mikhail Bakhtin, for example, the answer that immediately springs to mind is the novel. In the sociocultural conditions of dislocation that I described, however, the novel is incapable of carrying out this work. It is only in integrated countries, countries that have not suffered from colonial dismantling, that this kind of solution could be valid. Carlos Jose Mariategui wrote the following in his *Seven Interpretive Essays on Peruvian Reality*:

> In the history of the West, the flowering of National literatures coincided with the political affirmation of the Nation. It formed part of the movement which through the Reformation and the Renaissance, created the ideological and spiritual factors of the liberal revolution and the capitalist order.[8]

Now, if we take into account what I have tried to demonstrate thus far, it is obvious that only in the West can one claim "without a major risk of error that the novel, as a literary form, like journalism, has been one of the conductors of the essential force that preceded the emergence of Nations and Nationalism, and remains an important part of this phenomenon."[9]

In the Maghrebi context, however, it was not the novel that was used to form a national popular culture. It was, rather, the theater.[10] Writers and playwrights such as Kateb Yacine and men of the theater such as Abdelkader Alloula and Slimane Benaïssa clearly understood that while the "classical" poet and writer constantly stumbled over a word, an idiomatic expression, or a national (transindividual) psychological trait, popular theater could find its way around most of these basic obstacles. Because it is an oral art, the theater can muster everything it needs to play in a variety of keys: word, gesture, mime, music. Even if these elements are regional, they can still combine the various *accents* and *traditional stories* and *sayings* so as to contribute to the story (*dire*) of the nation. Obviously, this kind of mixture was carried off in the theater with varying success, depending on individual talent and genius. Still, playwrights have always been able to make use of a certain spoken language about which poets and novelists can only dream, limited as they are to one language. The Maghrebi theater community formed, in this sense, a group of the happy few who could express themselves in all the languages that nourished their artistic emotions, all the languages in which the national feeling could be expressed, however confusedly. It is quite different to have to *write* "Krrr! Krrr!" (as Kateb did in *Nedjma*)—which doesn't mean much to a Francophone reader (despite the footnote that informs us that the expression means "Confess!")—than to hear it *spoken* or *shouted* by an actor in a play.

By making use of the theater, by renewing ties with orality and discovering in it a way out of the impasse, Kateb Yacine and Abdelkader Alloula were seeking not so much a linguistic anchor in spoken Arabic as a movement of nomadic deterritorialization that allowed them to rework French *through* Arabic, to mobilize all the languages of everyday life and to provide the means to experience the moods and representations of the people. In this sense, we can find a trace of Kafka in Kateb, of the Kafka who was interested in Czech or Yiddish popular theater. And we can also find a reminder of Antonin Artaud's *Theater of Cruelty*:

As for French, it makes one sick
It is the great sick one
Sick with disease, a fatigue
That makes one believe that one is French
That is to say accomplished
Unaccomplished![11]

For Kateb, as for Artaud, it was necessary to "conquer French without abandoning it." For like Artaud, Kateb had been "holding French in his tongue" for fifty years while he had other languages "under the tree": French, Arabic, or Kabyle. Kateb did not hesitate to use all these languages in his theater in order to arrive at what Artaud hoped to achieve in his own antinationalist theater: "A scanned, secular, nonliturgical, non ritualistic, and non Greek humming, somewhere between Negro, Chinese, Indian, and French." (Artaud, ibid.)

If postcolonial Maghrebi writers in general and Algerian writers in particular had been content merely to produce works for the theater, then the question of the relation between writers and the languages in which they write would have been resolved, and we would have no need to pursue it further. As we know, however, and contrary to Memmi's prediction again, the three countries of the Maghreb did *not* limit themselves to writing plays in spoken or literary Arabic nor writing other literary works in classical Arabic. While some writers did devote much of their time and energy to writing and producing plays—like Kateb Yacine and Abdelkader Alloula—most of them have become known first and foremost as novelists. Paradoxically, it is precisely as novelists that Abdelkebir Khatibi, Nabile Farès, Assia Djebar, Abdelwahab Meddeb, Mohammed Dib, Mouloud Mammeri, Hélé Béji, and other postindependence Maghrebi writers have made themselves a name. Despite the cultural wrenching that recourse to the French language represented, despite the contradictions with which they were forced to deal in this deterritorialized context, each of these writers first commanded attention as the author of poems, novels, or essays.

Today we know that this situation of deterritorialization is intimately bound to a linguistic situation: the situation of Francophone intellectuals in a country that very quickly opted for Arabization; the situation of Arabophone writers in a country that was 85 percent illiterate at the time of independence and where French remained the dominant language in the administration, cities, and universities; the situation of the Kabyles, Moazabites, and Touaregs who had to abandon their language when they left the desert or the rural milieu; the situation of dialectal Arabic, which everyone speaks but which few people could read or write after independence, and with good reason. In Deleuze and Guattari's words, "How to become a nomad, an immigrant, and a gypsy in relation to one's own language?" (*Kafka*, 19) How can one account for what is specific to the Maghreb when the only language one has for writing and, often, for daily communication is French? And especially: What is the role of Francophone writers in a country that is increasingly Arabic speaking? Kafka wrote: "[S]teal the baby from its crib, walk the tight-rope." (Quoted in ibid., 19) And this is the heart of the matter: To write, to think in a foreign language "like thieves," to use the dominant language in the most outrageous ways, to make the most daring transformations: "L'enterr'ment di firiti i la cause di calamiti!" as Kateb said. The burial of truths is the cause of calamities. (*Le polygone étoilé*)

Like Kafka, Maghrebi writers had to "steal the baby from its crib": to loosen the hold of the French language in order to create their own situation from whole cloth. Here, too, it seemed at first that there were but two possible roads to follow. Either one could enhance this French language artificially, inflate it using all the resources of a delirious symbolism, onirism, and allegorism (and this is what we find in certain aspects of the work of Mohammed Dib, Rachid Boudjedra, and, somewhat differently, in Farès). But these efforts soon revealed themselves to be merely a "desperate attempt at symbolic reterritorialization, based in archetypes, Kabbala, and alchemy, that accentuates its break from the people." (*Kafka*, 19) Or one could move toward a maximum of "sobriety" and "poverty," toward a "blank, white writing," a "zero degree of writing," as in Boudjedra's *L'escargot entêté* [The stubborn snail], Dib's poems, or Assia Djebar's "The White of Algeria."

Still, to remain at such an abstract level would be to capitulate. What became increasingly obvious is that the forces that drove these writers could not be understood out of context. More specifically, their work had to be inscribed in the history of the Maghreb since independence. What can be seen more clearly today (in 2003) is that this kind of hand-to-hand combat with the language(s) of the country is inseparable from another combat—one that is more difficult and more distressing to define: the writer's struggle to become increasingly conscious of the status of his or her fabulation. At the time of independence, all means were valid to reach the desired ends, to produce a national entity or identity. Yet it soon became obvious that these ends would not be easily attained.

Simply put, as far as Algeria was concerned—but we can easily extend this reasoning to the two other countries of the Maghreb and to other postcolonial Francophone countries as well—we can outline at least three distinct stages in the process of the formation (or narration) of the nation.

The first stage or period can be situated in the years directly preceding the war of national liberation, with writers such as Mouloud Feraoun, Malek Haddad, and the first Mammeri, that is, with writers who still found themselves within the colonial sphere. Their writing already alluded to a form of Algerian or Maghrebi territorialization, but did not really succeed in bringing to light those characteristics that would wrest Algeria from the jaws of colonialism. This was, as Jean Déjeux remarked, the time of "acculturation and mimetism": there was talk of the Algerian "problem" or "malaise," of assimilation, equality, of new rights and freedoms, but there was no possibility of freeing the desired—or imagined—nation from what was beginning to be defined as its chains. The Maghreb and, more specifically, Algeria were still at the time the *French* Maghreb, *French* Algeria viewed from a "native" perspective.[12]

The second period emerged gradually in the 1950s, with works as varied as those of Kateb Yacine, Mouloud Feraoun, Jean Amrouche, Malek Haddad, and Assia Djebar.[13] This was a period of "self-affirmation and combat," again in Déjeux's terms. (71) "The writer," explained Malek Haddad, "is more the product of History than of Geography. . . . You don't become Algerian just because you want to. . . . Literary Nationality is not a juridical formality and does not come under the province of a legislator, but of History."[14] During this period (which one could call "Fanonian"), all compromise, all reconciliation with colonial France was rejected. What motivated the writer—mythical thinking or, to use Jean-Luc Nancy's term, "mything" thinking (*la pensée mythante*) is none other than "the elaboration of a foundational thought, or of a foundation through fiction." Writing was contemporary and synonymous with the *laying of the foundation of the nation to come.* For the authors mentioned above, the two aspects of mything thinking were not at odds with one another; rather, they converged to form a mythical thinking about myth: art, poetry, creative imagination were called upon to promote an Algeria in the making, an Algeria to come, that was to be created by the "new man" Fanon had envisioned. This period was thus characterized by the fact that the myth it engendered could only as yet be analyzed in terms of its own truth and, consequently, certainly not in terms of fiction. To write (the fiction of) Algeria was to write Algeria; it was to yield up an Algeria that, although mythical, was no less real, no less authentic, because it was "necessary"—and it was *necessary* because it was desired, desirable. Caught in the twisted logic of mythical self-fictioning, myth was no longer presented as the product of a *sui generis* truth, but tended to become truth itself. This, then, was the relatively fortuitous period in which decolonized writers had a real sense of participating in an effort of nation building. What they narrated about Algeria (through myth) was true, and the truth that mything fiction conferred upon the myth—of a single, unified Algeria—would continue to be reinforced during the first decade following independence.

Yet while this founding narrative was being established, another, dissonant voice was gradually making itself heard. And it is in the work of Nabile Farès that this voice found its first literary expression in the Maghreb. To my mind, Farès's work deserves a special place because it seems to contain, in Jean-Luc Nancy's words, a first "interruption of the myth," of the so-called founding myths of modern Algeria. Farès's writing pioneered a radical questioning of the transparency and the validity of the myth. Indeed for Farès, the "new myth" called "Algeria" (one that came on the heels of the myth of French Algeria) was not only dangerous but also vain and misleading. This was not only because it was fictional and could thus not truly account for the "real" Algeria, the "real" Maghreb, but also because it was essentially blind to what had made it a myth of origins to begin with. Farès's great realization was that the "forgetfulness" of the "nation"—any nation— owes something to myth and to the process (of fictioning) that corresponds to it. He was acutely aware that the appeal to the power of myth, whether "poetic" or "political," is always a double-edged sword: here, "founding narrative" (myth) and "fiction" are one and the same. Symptomatically, and somewhat prophetically, he wrote:

> The great explanatory forgetfulness *is what only a poetics can make people understand.* This poetics of Algeria was expressed by Kateb Yacine in NEDJMA, and this in spite of the fact that Kateb Yacine's NEDJMA is only a first step of poetic Algeria. In other words, Algeria fell into the trap of its own beauty and now, it is falling into the trap of *a realist viewpoint.* This is because any real approach to Algeria can only be—ARTISTICALLY SPEAKING, POETICALLY SPEAKING—a discovery of the allegorical reality of Algeria's beauty.[15]

Farès notes that Kateb's Algeria depended on a poetics that was only a "first step," and he proved, already in the early 1970s, that he was not fooled by the "allegorical"—that is, the mythical—nature of Algerian reality. At the same time, he denounced a certain mythological realism that he saw as a kind of naiveté regarding the fabulating power of myth and the dangers it held for an emerging nation. It is Farès's unique sensitivity to the power of allegory that gives his work its distinctive place in Maghrebi literature. His work marks a turning point and foreshadows the tragedy to come in Algeria. In 1971, however, he had no intention of playing the role of a Cassandra. His tone was still somewhat optimistic, for he believed, as did many of his compatriots at the time, that a country that had managed to wage such a difficult and in many ways exemplary war of liberation would be equally capable of fighting the right allegorical fight:

> This is why we (the inhabitants of the peninsula) will witness the transition from an allegorical reality to an allegory become reality. Hence our UNBRIDLED hope: to see artistic expression provide reality with a density it has not yet attained. (37)

As a true disciple of Fanon and of James Baldwin (his mentor in *Un passager de l'Occident* [A passenger from the West]), Farès still believed in the power of the myth of the artist within the framework of the nation. He still believed in the power of independent Algeria to carry out its second revolution, that is, a revolution in mentality. Referring to Baldwin, he wrote: "The artist is very important today. He is the one who can impose realities. He can up-end mentalities." At the same time, however, he understood that there was a risk that a certain kind of "realism" would win out in the end, and so he added the following: "I think it is even too late. They are too stupid . . . and they have killed all my friends."

With writers such as Farès (and Khatibi in Morocco, Béji or Meddeb in Tunisia, and Assia Djebar in Algeria could be used to illustrate the same problematic), we begin to see not simply the denunciation of national myth as a "transition from an allegorical reality to an allegory become reality" but as its interruption. And this is where the third and final period begins. With the writers of this period, the myth (of the nation) was interrupted, and its very interruption gives voice to and exposes an unfinished community, speaking *in a mythical mode without being a mythical speech (parlant comme le mythe sans être en rien une parole mythique)*. Nancy writes:

> There is then a voice of *interruption,* and its design is imprinted in the rustling of the community as it is exposed to its own dispersal. . . . There is a *voice of the community* that is uttered within the interruption and by the interruption itself. [Nancy, 156; my emphasis]

In Algeria, this voice (of interruption) was literature; it was writers who took charge of it. It was the voice of a literature that became increasingly irreconcilable, or, to use Blanchot's term, "improper" (*inconvenante*). Far from reinforcing any given myth of origins, any given fiction of the eternal nation or of the intact community, literature was transformed into a privileged instrument for the demystification or, rather, the demythification of a country that had been reduced to nothing more than the stooge of a State that would never rise to the task with which its people had entrusted it.[16]

Henceforth the part that would remain (*ce qui reste en partage*) would not be a single, unified nation, nor the communion, or even the completed, defined identity of all in one, "but the division *[partage]* itself and, consequently, the non-identity of all, of each one with himself and with the other, and the non-identity of the work with itself, and finally of literature with literature itself." (Nancy, 164)

Hélé Béji is no doubt the writer who best understood this in all its tragedy. In her book *Désenchantement national* [National disenchantment], she wrote:

> National consciousness and nationalist power are no longer on the same historical trajectory, even if a similar discourse is used for both. The freedom that had once united them (the dialectical movement of national consciousness toward the constitution of a State) today separates them. Placed back to back, national consciousness as movement, and the nationalism of the State as fixity, have functions that are radically opposed to one another in terms of freedom.[17]

As I will attempt to demonstrate in the following chapters, this freedom found its privileged terrain of experimentation in the increasingly radically refractory and exploratory practices of the Francophone writers from the Maghreb. They would, each in his or her own way, exploit the deceptive neutrality of literary space in order to make way for the multiple voices and languages of Maghrebi popular culture.

2

Cities of Writers

1. The Imaginary of the Medina in Francophone Literature from the Maghreb

> We are dreaming of another concept, another law, another politics of the city.
>
> —Jacques Derrida, *Cosmopolites de tous les pays, encore un effort!* (Paris: Galilée, 1997), 22.

> Our language can be seen as an ancient city: a maze of little streets and squares, of old and new houses, and of houses with additions from various periods; and this surrounded by a multitude of new boroughs with straight regular streets and uniform houses.
>
> —Ludwig Wittgenstein, *Philosophical Investigations*, 18.

The logic and rhetoric used to understand the European city as it has evolved from the Renaissance to the present are radically different from those needed to understand the origins of the Medina as urban fact or reality. Thus, in this chapter I begin with the problematic of the city as elaborated by Michel de Certeau in his *The Practice of Everyday Life*[1] in order to shed light on what I call the distinct poetical-rhetorical imaginary of the Medina.

In his chapter entitled "Walking in the City," de Certeau proposes three parameters for understanding the modern city and its role in people's practical lives. According to de Certeau, what is called a city today was founded upon an ideological, urbanist discourse defined by a symbolic "three-fold operation."

1. Historically, de Certeau states, the founding of a city consisted in establishing a "clean space" (*un espace propre*). To build a city implied the systematic and rational elimination of everything that could endanger the health of its inhabitants, in sum, the "repression" of "all physical, mental, and political pollutants" that risked compromising survival.

When Francophone writers, however—especially those from the Maghreb—refer to the "old city," to *their* Medina, they never fail to point out what is unique about it. When they bring up the delicate question of hygiene—of the cleanliness or dirtiness, the health or sickness of their city—they do not do so according to an *extrinsic* (that is, European) model or norm. Rather, they do so according to a principle that is inherent in and specific to their way of thinking, one that radically questions the criteria usually employed to speak about or to experience the city objectively. For these writers, this kind of objectivity is nothing other than the reverse mirror image of the extrinsic and overdetermined vision of a space they are attempting to free from norms and principles they deem totally inadequate for understanding the true nature of the Medina. As I will attempt to show, for these writers the Medina cannot be judged according to the abstract and extrinsic criteria of health and sickness, but rather, it must be interpreted through the perceptions and affects that emanate directly from their meandering through the Medina. And this meandering is more akin to a kind of initiation than to mere promenade.

2. According to de Certeau, the city also had to see to it that its inhabitants adopted shared "abstract" values that guaranteed the adherence to certain norms regarding the division of "social time." That is, it had to establish a "non-time, or a synchronic time" opposite the "stubborn resistance of traditions," which would destroy the "practices"

of those inhabitants who did not play the game of the "polis" and who, by means of crafty wiles and stratagems, undermined this same game. In this sense, the city was the "neutral" space in which each individual had to conform to the same norms: common measures, standardized prices, general standards, and so on. (175–6; 180 ff.; 190–191)

As we shall see as we follow our writers' footsteps, one of the characteristics of their encounter with the Medina is precisely the renewal of ties with practices that do not conform to these abstract norms. Elias Canetti is one writer who understood this about the Medina. In his *Voices of Marrakech*, as he relates events that seem quite ordinary on the surface, he leads us imperceptibly into a deep philosophical reflection on time, space, and the problems that arise from communication among peoples who belong to different cultures, with different customs. Each of his reflections is tightly linked to his encounter with the Medina—a Medina that is transformed from a simple tourist town into an almost magical site that subverts the order of things. The city is no longer considered as a surface of *projection* but rather as a "generator of thought" and an "operator of analysis." It has the privilege of initiating the passersby into what they are seeking, but does not necessarily show them what they had expected to find.[2] For Canetti, the Medina leads one to doubt all one's previous convictions: even the surest values—or should we say the surest value, that is, the price of things—is open to dispute. Coming upon what appeared to his Western eyes as disorder incarnate—the profusion of objects for sale displayed in the Souks of Marrakech—Canetti remarks: "You never know what things will cost; they are neither impaled with their prices, nor are the prices themselves fixed."[3] Later, faced with the apparent absence of (economic) rationality or norms in the Medina, Canetti notes that "part of the desolation of our modern life [and here no doubt he was referring to the norms of life in a modern European city in contrast to the Medina] is the fact that we get everything delivered to the door ready for consumption as if it came out of some horrid conjuring device." (Canetti, 19) Yet he is still referring (though silently) to the abstract norm that characterizes the modern, Western city when he writes that "in countries where the price ethic prevails, where fixed prices are the rule, there is nothing to going shopping. Any fool can go out and find what he needs.

Any fool who can read figures can contrive not to get swindled." (Ibid., 21) It seems that once writers come into contact with the Medina, they discover that they are (unbeknownst to them) really searching for another city, an underground or secret city that only the Medina can provide. This, in any case, is what Tunisian writer Hélé Béji experiences when she returns to the Medina in Tunis. She feels as if the veil of appearances has been lifted, allowing her to come into contact with "another city": not the city of her dreams, as the common expression would have it, but a city with a geometry that varies according to the variations of the "immense thought ["grande pensée"] she is seeking:

> The immensity I gave to *appearances that I thought I knew best*, rising beneath the fiercest sunlight, keeping me company with a slightly unreal reverberation, a kind of exuberance, struck—in the midst of the street-porters piling up their wares—against an empty caisson in the poor quarter where some dirty, sniffling kids were playing barefoot on the stones with a make-shift ball. The floating carcass of the real city was sinking into an abandoned work site, and *another city was overtaking me in an indistinguishable geography.*[4]

It is precisely this "indistinguishable geography" that our writers are trying to distinguish, or rather, to configure, to contour; it is this other city whose map they are trying to draw. To do so, however, they have none of the parameters of de Certeau's Concept-city at their disposal. It is this uncertain geography, the unfinished map of this open space that attracts and fascinates the writers of the Medina. It is a space they can come to know only by straddling it, and it will turn out to have hidden affinities with the space of thought. Viewed from a certain angle, the geography of the city merges with the equally indistinguishable geography of thought and its very (im)possibility. A *labyrinth* city, a *rhizome* city, the Medina is the perfect reflection of thoughts that are intertwined, step by step, as one follows its paths. And this is not mere metaphor. It is literally their feet that guide these writers on their walks. And sooner or later it becomes impossible to say if it is the desire to read and write, to decipher the signs that guide them, or if, on the contrary, it is the aleatory, fleeting nature of walking itself that stimulates their drive to write, serving as the operator of the inscription of signs on the page and conditioning the narrative impulse. The drive to write (*la pulsion scripturale*), the narrative impulse, and what we could also call the critical repulsion are in any event the three forces that are released by the confrontation with the rhizome Medina. Claude Ollier best articulated this peripatetic and rhetorical dimension of the Medina:

> A graphic short-circuit between the map's fading lines and the inked traces of the living word to narrate the everyday of the tribe, the family, the clan, the climate, the cruelties, inclemencies, and vengences, the rallyings, the compromises, the anger.
>
> A raw and brutal intricacy between these abridged texts noting the words of both ravished and rhetors, and the signs interspaced on the map when in contact with a blank zone where the colonizer's level falters, failing, from lack of curiosity or weariness, to point out the spot heights and shade the reliefs.[5]

To encounter the Medina is to find oneself facing savage, unimaginable practices. Intruders are forced to question themselves and to reconsider any value system that they had as city dwellers, citizens, modern men and women, prior to this encounter.

This last comment leads me to the third characteristic of de Certeau's Concept-city:

3. The city governed the creation of a "*universal* and *anonymous* subject" that became (the essence of) the city itself. (de Certeau, 94) Founded upon the banishment or eradication of anything that pollutes, soils, or corrupts it, on the one hand, and on the other, upon a network of norms and values that subjects its users to an efficient time in economic and commercial terms, the city became a sort of network of "a finite number of stable, isolatable properties that can be articulated on each other," forming a unicentered "subject," a highly individuated "person." Everything that was not "treatable"—in psychological terms of self-centering—was considered to be "refuse" by a functionalist and unified governing body. By favoring time that was "profitable" and oriented from progress toward cleanliness, centrality, unicity, and

so on, the functionalist organization of the classic (European) city caused it to forget the "condition of its own possibility": "space becomes the blind spot in a scientific and political technology." (Ibid., 95) This is how the modern Concept-city functions, as a place of "transformations and appropriations, the object of various kinds of interference but also a subject that is constantly enriched by new attributes, it is simultaneously machinery and the hero of modernity." (Ibid.)

The framework de Certeau uses to define the Concept-city as a social space homogenized by the panoptic eye of the modern *tout-état* allows us to see more clearly what will be at stake in every encounter with the Medina. What becomes evident on reading the texts I have selected is that, for their authors, "crossing the Medina" is always transformed into a "crossing of signs" that radically challenges the philosophical, esthetic, and moral categories characterizing the Concept-city.

Whenever they turn, or return, to the Medina,[6] it is not only (or perhaps, not at all) to go back to their so-called roots, to a pure and intact origin, but also to challenge the veritable notion of the city as a "totalizing and quasi-mythical point of reference" for socioeconomic and political strategies or ideological aims that have contributed to neutralizing or excluding as "deviant," "sickly," "dangerous"—or (worse yet) as "regressive" or "archaic"—certain urban practices: the "twisted, winding trajectory of cyclists" as they attempt to avoid the Medina's thousand obstacles, the "erratic gait" of groups of people passing "ugly ewers, bad copies of Berber jewelry, spangled ornaments on camels, sequins on Bedouin dolls, effluvia of *chansons de charme*, handcrafted water pitchers, raffia carpets, stellar domes and stucco imitations," the hordes of blind people crisscrossing the city, everything here begins to call to us:[7]

> Each thing here calls out to you, shifts the blank white between your words: a painted hand stenciled on a closed shutter, the crooked joint in two walls, the way someone carries his or her head, the piercing cries of children, the measured swinging of arms along an erect torso. And the letters, beautiful letters, sketched on the whitewash, cut out in the stucco, inlaid with gold on manuscripts: madly curving strokes, dia-

critic dots confronting the profane person's reading, white and round upon the infinite, invisible musical staff.[8]

To stroll through the old city, to lose oneself in it, is to find oneself constantly face to face with an undefined multitude of signs, the decipherment of which is imperceptibly transformed into a veritable crossing of writing. The Medinant—as the wanderer in the Medina is called—or the passerby (and these expressions occur spontaneously under the pens of writers as varied as Canetti, Ollier, Meddeb, or Béji) is the writer for whom the Arab city is experienced as an operator of analysis of what is at stake in the adventure of writing and, at the same time, as a generator of *topoi* that completely transform our relation to time and space and force us to experience a new kind of relation to writing and thought.

Because his or her experience is primarily that of a *writer*, the Medinant's movements through the Medina can no longer be considered as those of either a mere tourist or a common user of the city. While it may share many traits of and affinities with the experiences of other psychosocial types and users, the experience of the Medinant as a "*passant considérable*" (using Isaac Joseph's beautifully poetic expression)[9] is not the same as theirs. Whereas tourists, natives, or even those who return to their country have a tendency to reterritorialize themselves upon their experience, that is, to clear a space for themselves, Medinants have entirely different aims and ambitions. The space and the *dépaysement* they seek "are not only physical or mental, but also spiritual—not only relative, but absolute."[10] So it is not to the tourist or to the migrant that they must be compared, but rather to the *flâneur*, the land surveyor, and the philosopher. Like that of philosophers, the Medinants' stride is inseparable from the quest for a singular space—for what Deleuze and Guattari have called a Natal—to which each of their steps in the city-labyrinth bears witness. Whereas philosophers create conceptual characters to reach their goal, which is to think,[11] writers create that *passant considérable*, the Medinant, in order to "manifest the absolute territories, deterritorializations and reterritorializations of thought." (Deleuze and Guattari, 67) That is, the Medinant is not so much a storyteller as a thinker or even a character whom the writer creates (for himself or herself) in order to be able to think (himself or herself); in order to conceive the exile that is his or her language, to conceive what Chris Marker has called the *dépays*.[12] His or her birthplace. His or her land. His or her city, or *Umwelt*. Nothing about this experience, however, can be taken for granted; nothing is already acquired or conceded—everything remains to be done, discovered anew.

It is only because of and thanks to this scriptural crossing of the Medina that a conceptual character of whom we were previously unaware begins to think within us. And at that point, "it is no longer empirical, psychological, or social determinants" that characterize the impenitent walker in the Medina, but rather "intercessors, crystals or seeds of thought" (Deleuze and Guattari, 68) that transform strolling into writing and meditation into "medination":

> Descending the stairway facing the slope that leads to the cul de sac where the school is located, I found myself on equal footing with the Medinant: narrow passageways where footsteps echo strangely in the shade. The covered parts of alleyways: canopies of cymbals and echoes. . . . I smile at the woman. She invites me to follow her. I pursue her. Where will she lead me?
>
> Following her, mazes of discoveries, recognition, being careful to lose all convergence, the faceless predella of doors, altar pieces to meditate prayer, among the entranceways that attract me [is] one that belongs to a lord married to a lady from the time when . . . protective endogamy ruled. [Meddeb, *Talismano*, 25–6]

So goes the Medinant in his medination: walking, leaving, staying, avoiding, quibbling (these words are chosen at random!), conjugating all the verbs that describe this meandering in the present participle, so that "no [snapshot] can provide the correspondence" (Béji, 127) that is so obstinately being sought. You cannot, even if you try, trace a line of demarcation between a correspondence and the meandering of the city's alleyways, for "its sentence will be the city, and its meaning will be the map," as Ollier wrote. "To walk" has become synonymous with "to write," and "to write" (and to read) is what feeds the desire to lose oneself in the city-labyrinth to the point where meaning and/or meanings dizzily collide. This is the law of that stubborn walker, the Medinant:

> The stubborn walker follows his path, happy to persevere in his wandering, anticipating a landmark, advancing steadily like a denizen of the neighborhood, knowing full well that few Christians live there and that everyone knows them, that he can only appear to be what he is, advancing nonetheless, dreading somewhat, slight intoxication, exhilaration, for everything and anything can happen here he says to himself, avoiding taking out the map that would betray him, rereading it in his mind's eye, but things move so fast, is this the second or third turn, and this intersection, this long white wall, headlong pursuit, slight dizziness . . . uniting by the sequence of footsteps the flow of the journey and the flow of the idea that is germinating, sketching the model, shared time of strolling and reflection, twin circuits nourished by corrective shifts and returns where representations take on a rough shape in the tight weft drawn by his strides. [Ollier, *Marrakch Médine*, 100–101]

And soon what will both delight and disconcert the Medinant is the fact that "anything and everything can happen, at any time and at any point of the circle, much more assuredly than where you come from, this point of departure that you still know how to say—not, of course, the one from where you come." (Ibid., 20)

As they are confronted with the language of power that has become urbanized and policed, travelers searching for novelty or natives searching for their heritage will be led by the Medina to "contradictory movements that are counterbalanced and combine themselves outside the reach of the panoptic power." (de Certeau, 95) As it is reexperienced, relived via the interposed Medina, the city "becomes the dominant theme in political legends, but it is no longer a field of programmed and regulated operations. Beneath the discourses that ideologize the city, the ruses and combinations of powers that have no readable identity proliferate; without points where one can take hold of them, without rational transparency—they are impossible to administer." (Ibid.) It is this "impossibility" to administer the multiplicity of contradictory signs that come (to me) from the city that lies at the heart of the originality of the imaginary proper to the Medina, in opposition or contrast to the modern city or megalopolis that Edgar Allan Poe, Victor Hugo, and of course Baudelaire have bequeathed to literary posterity. The Medina has absolutely nothing in common with Baudelaire's melancholy Paris or Shelley's cynical London; it has become the site (in both the physical and rhetorical sense), the *topos par excellence* of the meandering of a new kind of *flâneur*. As Meddeb writes about Tunis:

> Here I am once again in the city-maze, moved to amuse myself with childhood: to find yet again the ancient aromas . . . to pierce the secret of streets and dead ends that were never trodden, weren't these the ancient itineraries of a paradisiacal childhood that I did not invent?[13]

And Béji, using the same tones, writes the following, also about Tunis:

> That the reality of the sites corresponded to an archaic life perhaps added to the charm of nostalgia and memory. But most important for me here is that the past is overthrown in favor of the moment! . . . And even though I had prepared and dressed my memories, and placed them like still silent and immobile actors behind the lowered curtain, as soon as I entered, as soon as they came out of the past into the present, resplendent in their pourpoints of living time, they *threw nature and the order in which I had placed them into confusion, and reopened a vastness that had faded in my memory.*[14]

From street to house, an entire order of things is challenged so as to return to the vastness of a memory that one had thought was lost and that is then reborn as one moves through the city of childhood.

I have chosen texts as different from one another as those of Canetti, Ollier, Meddeb, Béji, Marker, and Deleuze to try to demonstrate that the Medina, understood as a traditional Arab city, Casbah, or oriental city, is always a place and time of a veritable questioning of established values and of the self. By speaking of a poetic imaginary and referring to texts about the Medina, I wanted to show that this encounter was above all the opportunity for the writer to challenge radically the unifying and rational vision of the panoptic power that presided over the establishment and development of the modern city. Again to quote Béji:

> The architecture of our ancient dwellings is the formal out-pouring of their moral life, which is otherwise contained and chaste, and by its sober and rigorous visibility beneath the naked brilliance of the sun, the soul of our houses seemed to rid itself of its secrets and private vicissitudes, in the conciliating and worthy form of urban harmony in which its imperfections and sufferings were removed. [Ibid., 101–2]

In this sense, to write/to live the Medina is to travel through time, to reinscribe the time of (hi)story and of the duration of footsteps and walking in the abstract nontime of the modern Concept-city. Gradually we become aware that, by means of this walking, the writer will present "a series of turns [*tours*] and detours that can be compared to 'turns of phrases' and 'figures of style' that constitute a veritable 'rhetoric of walking.' " (de Certeau, 100)

From this point on, reference to the city becomes inseparable from style as a "fundamental way of being in the world of an individual man [or woman]." This is the idea that A. Médam called a "residing rhetoric" (*rhétorique habitante*), that is, a rhetoric that unites verbal figures and "winding figures" (*figures cheminantes*). (Ibid.) Each of them in effect opens a path or paths that allow the Medina to reappear each time anew as a space constituted against the basic assumptions and expectations of the modern or classical Western city. The wending of the authors I quoted refers us to the city as communal space where various social practices are distinguished and gradually break from the leveling logic of the so-called rational panoptic city. A city that "disorients [*dépayse*] [us] to the point where we are no longer [ourselves] except within this *dépaysement,* our *dépays.*"[15]

2. Algiers/Paris, or the City as a "Site of Memory": Merzak Allouache's *Salut Cousin*

Under what historical conditions is a city, and a postcolonial city at that, transformed into a "site of memory"?

In the introduction to the book in which she analyzes the different faces of categories such as race, gender, generation, and sites in an age of globalization,[16] Emily Apter points to the importance of certain sites—cities in particular—in the creation of the imaginary of a people or a nation. This in fact is what had led her to give a place of prominence to Pierre Nora's work on French sites of memory. But in fact, reminding us that London, Montreal, and Algiers have been excluded from the list of sites likely to appeal to the historical and affective memory of the French today, Apter remarks: "Even the most recent volumes of Pierre Nora's richly textured *Les Lieux de mémoire*, with their new historical attention to the mystificatory components of national identity, clumsily justify their choice *not to include Algiers or Montreal as hauts-lieux, or psychotopographies worthy of revisionist nostalgia.*" (Apter, 2)

Indeed, if we refer to the volume in which Nora attempts to account for the rationale behind the choices of these French sites of memory, we see that his reasons for including certain sites and excluding others—Montreal, London, or Algiers, for example—are impossible to fathom. No matter how the arguments set forth to justify these choices are viewed, they remain, to say the least, problematic. Nora believed he would have been giving in to a kind of "individual and arbitrary vagabondage" had he considered Algiers, Montreal, or London as "authentic" sites of historic memory or as cultural centers likely to make "the heart of France beat most intensely":

> The series on privileged sites poses an entirely different kind
> of problem. *Where outside its heart could one admit that the
> heart of France beats most intensely?* The temptation was
> strong here to allow for the choice of entirely personal places
> and moments, in order to endow them with a historical prob-

lematic, as Michelet endowed Ouessant and the circus of Ga-
varnie, with a geopolitical problematic. Or again, to *profit*
from the occasion *to introduce places outside the hexagon such
as Algiers, London, Fort-de-France, or even Montreal*, which
precisely this year celebrates the 350th anniversary of its foundation. But against this *individual and arbitrary vagabondage*
we have preferred *three less controversial criteria*: the aura of
large temporal strata, the homogeneity of examples—reso-
nant sites, important places and monuments of demonstra-
tive power—and finally, the authorization of the collective or
foreign gaze. The intersection of these criteria has dictated
the list.[17]

Even if it is entirely possible to locate what could be called gaps in
memory similar to those we find in the history of the United States
when it comes to its imperial past—Vietnam and Latin America, for
example (sites of memory still waiting to be integrated in American
history)—it is quite surprising to see just how many taboos still exist
when it comes to France's history of colonization in Africa, the Middle
East, and especially the veritable scotoma that exists in relation to the
history of the Algerian War. And this is what leads me to Merzak Allouache's film.

My hypothesis for reading this film is that it exists to fill a gap
in the repertory of French (and Algerian) sites of memory with the
work of anamnesis it offers its viewers. In this sense, the film disputes
the validity of Nora's monumental work as well as the validity of the
tradition of colonial historians who had tried to foist off their own
version of history on the colonized. This tradition in fact goes back to
Ernest Renan, who made forgetting, and later omission and denial, the
"unavowed"[18] (unavowable?) essence of the nation.

The perspective of postcolonial intellectuals on the question of
forgetting and on the history of the Algerian war in general is not entirely in accord with the theses that Nora seems to have inherited directly from Renan. I am thinking, for example, of the position taken on
the Algerian War by *Beur* writers such as Azouz Beggag and Abdellatif
Chaouite in their *Écarts d'identité*. I am also thinking of the *pied-noir*

historian Benjamin Stora and the Francophone Moroccan Tahar Ben Jelloun, both of whom took a stance on the question early on.

In *La France en guerre d'Algérie*, a book he wrote with Laurent Gervereau et Jean-Pierre Rioux, Stora makes the following comment:

> [T]his unclassifiable war, *which was refused national recognition*, can only be brought back doubly, incessantly relived in the memories of those who suffered because of it in different ways. . . . What is at stake for the French, thirty years after the blood and tears of Algeria, is thus, undoubtedly, having to *forgive themselves for having turned a page that they knew all to well was not blank.*[19]

In another work, *La guerre d'Algérie et les Français*, Rioux went even further:

> Since 1962 there has been no French national memory of the Algerian conflict; *this war without a name* has never received the honors of memory. Please forgive the violence of these statements, which may shock some members of some groups that fervently maintain their own recollection of the tragedy. But the evidence is overwhelming, endless, and undeniable: in the memory of metropolitan France, this war has been both a "phantom" and a "taboo."[20]

Ben Jelloun echoes this response in his *Hospitalité française*:

> For some people, the Algerian war is not yet over. The presence of some one million Algerian immigrants on French soil arouses in the French a nostalgic hatred, and when they attack an Arab, that act *is directly inscribed in the impossible and intolerable mourning that history demands regarding "French Algeria."*[21]

Phantom, taboo, forgetfulness: the metaphors change, but they all point in the same direction. They speak of what is forbidden, of the taboo that strikes at the heart of the history of this unclassifiable war. They emphasize the unconscious desire to erase what has been called the war without a name and the impossibility of either speaking about it or of giving it up as lost for good. Perhaps, though, the kind of forgetting Renan recommended was not the best solution. On this level we could say that there is a kind of melancholy that strikes the French psyche every time those sites that France has deserted are mentioned. This melancholy is related not so much to the impossibility of mourning a lost object (according to the classic thesis) as to the impossibility of giving up for good an object that *one has not lost* or that one is having trouble "forgetting" (according to Lacan's inverted, paradoxical interpretation in *The Ethics of Psychoanalysis*). It seems to me that it is rather this kind of "paradoxical mourning" that Merzak Allouache invites us almost casually to experience, using the story of a young Algerian in Paris as a pretext to lead us on a journey through the paradoxical melancholy of France today.

To get a better grasp on this situation, it seems worthwhile to me to make a slight detour through historian Henri Rousso's *The Vichy Syndrome*. In this book, Rousso writes that World War II was, along with the Dreyfus Affair and the Algerian war, one of the "most profound crises in French unity and identity." He analyzes the post–World War II phenomenon that he calls "the Vichy syndrome" as it has affected the memory and psyche of the French in four specific phases, which have led them from *amnesia* to *obsession.*

The first phase (1944–54) was one of "interrupted mourning"; the second (1954–71) was that of "Repression" ("forgetting" and "amnesia") and was repeated during the Algerian War; the third, shorter phase (1971–74) was characterized by a "return of the repressed" and the start of a questioning of the myths surrounding the war; the fourth phase—which is the one we are going through today—is on the order of an obsession (think of all those recent debates in France on the responsibility of the French state in the deportation of French Jews; think of Drancy, of the "Vélodrome d'Hiver," and also of the Papon trial, to take just a few examples).

Several clear conclusions can be drawn by transposing this syndrome from Vichy France to the Algerian situation, as Anne Donadey has done in her admirable recent book, *Recasting Postcolonialism: Women Writing Between Worlds.*[22] Here Donadey describes how France, once it had passed through the phase of "interrupted mourning," soon found itself caught up in the second phase of the syndrome, that is, repression (of memory). This phase was marked by a bizarre amnesia, or denial, of what had happened during the Algerian War. Such amnesiac repression lasted until the late 1990s. The effort that France and the French put into repressing the memory of the Algerian War created—just as in the case of the return of the memory of Vichy—what Rousso has called "a replay of the rift."[23] As a result, the trauma and the unresolved problems of World War II were talked about all the more obsessively because it was so difficult to talk about what had happened in Algeria.

According to Donadey (who bases her analyses on those of Rousso and Stora), it would not be until 1992, on the thirtieth anniversary of the end of the Algerian War, that the third phase of the "Algerian syndrome"—what in the end was called "Nostalgeria"—would begin tangibly to manifest itself. This was when we began to see works that started to deal with what had been literally repressed. As a 1992 poll in the popular magazine *Paris-Match* revealed, although the French thought that the Algerian War was the second most important event for France since World War II, 44 percent of the people who responded were against celebrating the anniversary of the war's end because it "brought back painful memories." Equally surprising is that, whereas reference was made to *pieds-noirs* and *harkis* in these pages, *Algerians* and *immigrants* were hardly mentioned. The general attitude revealed by the survey was one of *denial* or *refusal* of, if not simply a total lack of interest in, anything that had to do with Algeria, Beurs, and immigrants. Yet there was no hesitation whatsoever to reproduce photographs of that happy time—"tender and marvelous memories"—of Algeria before the war. However, the war itself is never mentioned. Nor is the racism that cost so many young Algerian immigrants to France their lives in the previous fifteen years mentioned, despite the fact that the link between ignoring the Algerian War and the numerous crimes committed since independence has become increasingly obvious.

Merzak Allouache's work of unveiling and *anamnesis*, the struggle of active memory against forgetting, goes counter to Renan's injunction that national identity can only be created at the cost of forgetting. For Allouache, as for many other filmmakers (I'm thinking of Bourlem Gerdjou's *Vivre au Paradis*, Yamina Benguigui's *Mémoires d'immigrés*, Dominique Cabréra's *De l'autre côté de la mer*, among others), to re-remember oneself is the only way to break the unconscious cycle of the repetition of figures imposed by the Algerian syndrome and the stream of violence that came in its wake. For Allouache, as for Tahar Ben Jelloun, Azouz Beggag, Rachid Mimouni, Benjamin Stora, and many other historians and writers today, "forgetting offers bad advice," for whenever it "settles in history, it mutilates and misappropriates it."

What I find most interesting in Allouache's film, however, is the fact that he carries out this work of anamnesis and recollection indirectly, in an almost roundabout way. By inventing this story (so real!) of Alilo—the young Algerian *trabendiste* who finds himself caught between his business partner in Algiers and his cousin and Fatoumata in Paris—Allouache shows us some of what is at stake politically, socially, and culturally in contemporary "real" France, without resorting to militant didacticism or bitter recriminations. The mere presence of these young Algerians adrift in the city functions as a veritable return of the cultural and political repressed of France and Algeria's twinned histories.

Once freed from the stereotypes that had made them the bogeymen for propagandists of the National Front, all the main characters—Mok (the extremely Frenchified mythomaniac), Allio (the uprooted Algerian), Fatoumata (the defiant Guinean woman at odds with society), Monsieur Maurice (the deterritorialized and nostalgic Jewish *pied-noir*)—are transformed into signifiers that allow the fixed perspectives that were previously dominant in cinema to be overturned and the screen that masked the reality of the war to be removed, making them intelligible (and even sympathetic) to the French and to themselves. But the film's greatest accomplishment—its astuteness, if you will—is to have shown them to us as figures—"sites" of speech and of memory—that are inseparable from the *current* history of the two peoples.

By creating sympathetic characters like Alilo, Mok, Fatoumata, and Monsieur Maurice—that is, individuals who previously had no right to speak—by giving them a voice and even, one could say, a soul, Allouache uncovers for us a world that had been "spectralized,"[24] a world in which Beurs, immigrants, and foreigners in general had been transformed into the other, and in which they had nothing to do with "us." The film's artistry lies in its providing, through its characters and the situations in which they are placed, floated signifieds in place of floating signifiers, not in order to arrest the process of signification but, on the contrary, to make it proliferate, to bring new signifiers to the surface, which will in turn bring yet other signifiers to light. From a "de Manian" perspective, we could say that, in his film, Allouache has produced a history of the people of contemporary France, and particularly of what has been called the "Beur nation" as PROSOPOPEIA, that is, as "the fiction of an apostrophe [or an address] to an absent, deceased, or voiceless entity, which posits the possibility of the latter's reply and confers upon it the power of speech."[25] As PROSOPOPEIA, the film becomes a "voice-from-beyond the grave" (of history) in which the "dead" or, if one prefers, the "laissés-pour-compte" or the forgotten of history are finally able to tell their own story. One also remembers that in the same text, de Man suggested that prosopopeia has an essential relation to DEFACEMENT: as PROSOPOPEIA, Allouache's film also deals "with the giving and taking away of faces, with face and deface, FIGURE, figuration and disfiguration." (de Man, 76) As a rewriting of history and revisiting of memory, Allouache's film "defaces the face it confers, at the same time it disfigures the MASKS it restores."[26]

On the one hand, by means of the film's varying viewpoints, the cities of Algiers, Constantine, and Oran are almost *magically* transformed into sites of memory *for the French*, who now must acknowledge that these cities have become—or perhaps always were—emblems of their memory and inevitable signifiers of their identity. In effect, because our guides are Beurs or Algerian immigrants, Africans or *pieds-noirs*, we move across Paris by means of *their* experience, desires, fears, and fantasies, and this Paris bizarrely resembles Algiers, Constantine, Oran, and Annaba. In a way, we ourselves experience a becoming Algerian or African of Paris through these young people's worries, fears, and desires *in the short time that Alilo visits his cousin Mok.* This becoming Algerian is very clearly portrayed, for example, in the sequences leading the young *trabendiste* to Monsieur Maurice (the luxury clothing salesman), a Jewish *pied-noir* still haunted by "Nostalgeria."

On the other hand, Paris, Barbès, La Goutte d'Or, and other working-class neighborhoods in Paris are revealed to be the centers of *Algerians'* (and Africans' in general) memory. Little by little these neighborhoods become an integral part of their identity, their history, and their memory. In this sense, we find here a becoming French of Algeria, or rather, a becoming Parisian of Algiers. In the scene in Monsieur Maurice's clothing store, we witness the Algerianization of Paris: a Paris that is Algerized or Algerified according to a play of anamorphosis that gradually transforms Monsieur Maurice's impersonal boutique into a space where all of Algiers—its scents, its alleyways—materializes within us, thanks to the music coming from a record player. Paris is revealed to be slightly Algerian, belonging to a complex network of exchanges that seals the fate of both cities. It is this chiasmus-like exchange—this space of the deterritorialization of the cultural signifieds of both cultures, this *chassé-croisé* or flip-flop—that seems to me to make Allouache's film stand out in relation to so many fictional or documentary films that treat France and Algeria as if they were two entities forever separated, no longer owing each other anything.

From this point on we can say that for many minor writers and artists, identity no longer passes through traditional categories such as nationality, race, or even language or religion. These writers approach questions of identity and belonging with a total awareness of the transformations that have affected French society. The young people portrayed do not confuse their multiple and at times contradictory senses of belonging with any dimension of their (ethnic or religious) identity. This identity is no longer *singular* because it is itself in the process of becoming.[27] And this becoming (*devenir*) implies an experience of an outside of (the) self, of a self or an origin *toward which* one could return (*re-venir*). It is thus presented as a paradoxical experience of a going outside of oneself that does *not presuppose* an inside of a subject limited by any one given self or identity (psychological, national, or even linguistic). Allouache's film clearly shows that an authentic experience of becoming obliges the subject who is experiencing it to rethink his or her (social, political, ethical) position vis-à-vis the majority. I used to be an Algerian or French subject—an essentialist move—and suddenly I am transformed into a larval subject in search of identity, of becoming. "Why are there so many becomings of man," wrote Deleuze and Guattari, "but no becoming-man? Because man is the majoritarian par excellence, whereas becomings are minoritarian, all becoming is a minoritarian becoming." People know themselves to be "hybrids" and always a little "mestiza." They know they no longer belong to a (single) nation and, moreover, that the nation to which they all belong and where they live *is itself a becoming.*

So is anything solved or resolved for all that? The mocking and at times frankly comic tone that Allouache adopts in this film (as in others) can be misleading, and this is how I understand the reversal of the situation that occurs at the end of the film. It is yet another chiasmus in a way, another turnaround, another kind of inverted world that immediately refers us to the crudest reality. While Alilo and Fatoumata are confessing their love for each other on the platform at the Gare de Lyon, Mok is being expelled from France by the police for having participated in a phony marriage. Is this merely a return to the starting point, the repressing of the Algerian War? This final figure may be read as a political allegory that describes better than words ever could the fate that still awaits the sons and daughters of immigrants when, like their children born in France, they *are* entirely French. Yet perhaps this figure is also the sign of the work of anamnesis that has indeed begun.

What is certain is that, as I said at the outset, even if he does so in a roundabout way, Allouache has succeeded in setting the record straight: the chapter that was missing from the French sites of memory nevertheless has made its way into the memory of the French and Algerians today. The repressed of the text of official Algerian history, the blind spot of Franco-French history that took almost half a century to contend with the Vichy episode, the sanctioning of the gaze by the collective or by the other, has at long last been inscribed in French history by means of this film. Algiers and Paris have indeed turned out to be centers of French memory in this early part of the new millennium. Thanks to Allouache's film, these two cities will perhaps come to occupy the rightful place that should have been accorded them—at least symbolically at first—in the imaginary of both peoples.

3

Nabile Farès, or How to Become "Minoritarian"

All exile presupposes a center, a point of origin from which one stands out or moves away. As "eccentric/ex-centric" as Nabile Farès's work may seem, rather than moving away from a specific point, it actually draws nearer to new points, new ideas, and assembles around them multiple centers. In any event, Farès's main idea seems to be that all genuine becoming presupposes an exile of some kind, the experience of either something outside of (one)self or outside of one's origin to which one could *return*. Both becoming and exile in Farès's work are thus presented as *para*doxical experiences of going out(side) of the self; yet this *in no way assumes* that there exists an inside of a subject curled up around a given self or (national, psychological) identity.

Here is one example among many from *L'état perdu* [Lost state]:

> Car "Tu" ne peux dire "je"
> dans la parole la plus simple, le discours
> le plus naif, la langue la plus neutre.
> "Tu" ne peux dire "je"
> Au fond du gouffre (le Gouffre)
> Et non la différence.
> "Tu" ne peux dire "Je":
> et d'autres parlent pour mieux dire ce que
> "Je" (où?) suis . . . [18]

For "you" cannot say "I"
in the simplest word, the most
naïve discourse, the most neutral language
"You" cannot say "I"
At the bottom of the abyss (the Abyss)
And not difference
"You" cannot say "I":
And others speak in order to better express what
"I" (where?) am . . .

To understand Farès's reasoning, however, we must recognize that becoming and exile are themselves impossible to dissociate from the subject's belonging (and we shall see why this expression is problematic) when that subject belongs to a minority that is *itself in the process of becoming*. Once we realize this, we get the following equation, which can be approached from either term: Any experience of an authentic becoming forces the subject experiencing it to rethink his or her (cultural, ethnic, linguistic, social, political, ethical) position vis-à-vis the majority. Take even the very recent example of women in Algeria: they were Algerian women, and because of the danger that the revision of their status in the Algerian constitution by the FIS (Front Islamique du Salut) represented, they have been forced into a *becoming-woman* that goes well beyond simply belonging to a nation, gender, or social group. This is because they quickly grasped that the becoming of women that was in store for them was completely different from the *becoming-woman* that they themselves had been promoting since Algerian independence. For Algerian women today, it is not enough simply to claim their Algerianness and, at the heart of this (substantivized) Algerianness, to demand a place, rights, and freedoms. They understood that what was at stake in the political struggle for Algerian women's rights or the family code was not something that had already been granted, but movements, flows. They understood that what others wanted to deprive them of was not their *being*-woman (this could easily be granted to them), but their *becoming*-woman; in other words, that which is *uncompromising* in them, the uncompromising itself.[1]

"Why are there so many becomings of man, but no becoming-man," write Deleuze and Guattari. "First because man is majoritarian par excellence, whereas becomings are minoritarian; all becoming is a becoming minoritarian."[2]

If I compare the works of Deleuze and Guattari to those of Farès and the questions raised by Algerian women,[3] it is because they tackle the same problems—even if in radically different ways—of minority, marginality, and ethnic, religious, and sexual difference, yet they avoid getting trapped by the deceptive simplicity and transparency of the responses to the political and ideological difficulties these notions raise.

Indeed at first glance the problem of minorities seems remarkably simple to define: There would be on the one hand a majority or majorities made up of the greatest number of people in a given community who would represent dominant values, standards, and so on, and on the other, a minority or minorities that could be distinguished by number (in this case, a smaller number), race, language, culture, or all these elements at once.

What strikes me in Farès's work—and this too leads to the comparison between his work and Deleuze's—is that neither he nor Deleuze rehashes any elements of the *doxa* regarding minorities. Let us consider, for example, the question of number, or rather of numerical quantity:

> When we say majority, we are referring not to a greater relative quantity but to the determination of a state or standard in relation to which larger quantities, as well as the smallest, can be said to be minoritarian: white-man, adult-male, etc.
> [*A Thousand Plateaus*, 291]

Thus, to be able to speak of both the majority and the minority, we need a state or a standard that goes beyond both of them and to which we can compare them both.[4]

There are additional important characteristics related to the question of minority/majority: first, the majority takes for granted a state of (political or cultural) dominance, and not the opposite; second, the majority also takes "as pregiven the right and the power of man" (*A Thousand Plateaus*, 291), that is, what I shall call a kind of *hypostasis*. Farès sees this hypostasis as reaching its apogee in the supremacy of the Algerian patriarchy and bureaucracy.[5] And third, another meeting point between Deleuze and Guattari and Farès is the distinction they make between the minoritarian as becoming or process, and the minority as an already constituted aggregate or state.

> It is important not to confuse "minoritarian," as a becoming or a process, with a "minority," as an aggregate or a state. Jews, Gypsies, etc. [and we could add Algerians, and all Maghrebis in general] may constitute minorities under certain conditions, *but that in itself does not make them becomings.* One reterritorializes, or allows oneself to become reterritorialized, on a minority or a state; *but in a becoming, one is deterritorialized.* [291; my emphasis]

From this point of view, *Un passager de l'occident* may be considered as the perfect instrument for this becoming-minoritarian and for this deterritorialization as becoming, since it results from the double movement of deterritorialization that characterizes its mechanism as

> one by which a term (the subject) is withdrawn from the majority, and another by which a term (the medium or agent) rises up from the minority. There is an asymmetrical and indissociable block of becoming, a block of alliance. [291]

Both Farès'—the Algerian and the non-Algerian—enter into a becoming-Kabyle. And in reality, things are even more complex with Farès, since there are always at the same time other becomings that destabilize the national majoritarian good conscience and all majoritarian good conscience in general.

As Deleuze and Guattari write: "There is no subject of the becoming except as a deterritorialized variable of the majority; there is no medium of becoming except as a deterritorialized variable of a minority." (292) In *Un passager de l'occident*, Farès makes himself into this medium and becomes this deterritorialized and deterritorializing subject. He is *deterritorializing subject* in relation to his own *Algerian majority*, whose transparency and historical grounding he questions when he reinvents himself as Brandy-Fax or Ali-Said; he is *deterritorialized subject* in relation to the *Kabyle minority* when he appeals to James Baldwin in order to deterritorialize his own belonging to the Kabyle minority, linking it to a becoming-black that destabilizes and renews it. In so doing, however, he clearly shows that becoming minoritarian is not merely an individual or psychological question but essentially a political one as well: "Becoming-minoritarian is a political affair and necessitates a labor of power (*puissance*), an active micropolitics." (292) Thus, to this *molar-becoming* we must now oppose an active micropolitics of a *molecular* becoming that involves a line of becoming that passes through points—stases, states—and comes up through the middle.[6] In other words, in Farès's work the boundary no longer falls between history and individual memory but rather between punctual systems (history/memory) and multilinear or diagonal organizations that no longer refer to the eternal, or even to the historical—to a "cathartic" history, as Farès calls it[7]—but to a becoming of both history and memory. This is what Farès calls a "total history" of Algeria, an "authentic" history of Algeria. After all, Algeria was not always colonized or Muslim, it *became* colonized, became Muslim. So Farès prefers "Paganism"—"the very old belief, despite all opposition" (*Un passager*, 73)—to the *basso continuo* of Man or Islam: "This belief is pagan, for it would never occur to anyone to deny that Algeria was an important center of paganism before becoming the stomping grounds for the edifying discourses of Christianity or Islam." (73) This, in any case, is the mission he assigns to poetry and to artistic work in general, work that should continue to explore this theme: "Today, paganism is definitively, incontestably buried in Algeria. And in relation to the political discipline that is dominant here, only an artistic discovery, or a life that is LIVED ARTISTICALLY can make sense of, or bear witness to a meaning other than political servitude." (74–5)

Farès catches *contemporary* Algerian history in another *double movement*: a movement of deterritorialization that wrests it from its present history by bringing it back to its *prehistory* (paganism), and a movement of reterritorialization that, by confronting Algeria's present history with a cosmic history—"Dialogues Between Earth and Twilight"—summons us to quickly find a way to get our feet back on the ground and rediscover the country:

> A country where you can simply live, go to the cafés, have a drink, flirt with girls, study, go out dancing at night, and work 15 hours a day, a cigarette in your mouth. In short, a country where the citizens could build bonfires, find shelter from the oil wells, and eat their couscous and meat flavored with orange flower or olive oil whenever they wanted. A country, in short, on a par with its political reality. A country, in short, really political. [77]

Thus, as I intimated, the "Dialogues Between Earth and Twilight" that close the book were not concocted to relativize things, or to show their arbitrary nature. For Farès, neither colonization nor Islam are "arbitrary."[8] Rather, it seems to me that, above all, he wants to make things undergo an eternal return that would reveal their fundamental *contingency*. And in this sense, Farès echoes Mallarmé's wonderful phrase, "Un coup de dés jamais n'abolira le hasard!" That which brought Islam can once again bring paganism! Islam was imposed by the repression of ancestral paganism. But this paganism is perhaps the only true *basso continuo*, the only fundamental movement that will resist historically and perhaps return. Everything became on a foundation of paganism. Once again, it hardly matters whether its return is possible or not, utopian or realist. The task of the writer lies elsewhere. The only thing that matters is the minor variable, the minor mode. Yet we need to understand that for Farès, this minor mode must also be made to move, made dynamic by the fact that in all becoming the terms are not interchangeable: never, in this sense, will the authentic minoritarian become majoritarian. Both are caught in an asymmetrical block where the one must not change any less than the other. Thus the Kabyle's becoming-black American (or Sahraoui) must correspond to the Algerian's becoming-Kabyle. This does not mean that concessions to either block must be made. On the contrary, both blocks must undergo a movement of translation or deportation through which the majoritarian block will see the movement of deterritorialization that carries it toward a becoming-minority accelerate, and the minoritarian island will transcend its marginality, its regional localization through the acceleration or intensification of the movement of deterritorialization that carries it along and that will result in "changes of all *states*."

> (Words of dusk): "Beautiful woman of the Earth, are you
> unaware of the change; the change? not the change from
> one state to another; but *the change of all states*. This long
> wound that you know, and that goes through me through
> you, what else is it? a change of state? or a change of place?
> of all places?"⁹

Such were Farès's ideas on the *states* (of the Maghreb) and of their *becoming* in *Un passager de l'occident*. In *L'état perdu: Discours pratique de l'émigré*,¹⁰ it seems to me that Farès has moved to a more advanced and at the same time more complex phase. It is as if it were no longer a question of elaborating a theory of becoming—and of staging it or making it visible—but rather of resolutely moving on to *practice*. He no longer seems to be dealing with an economy of *ideas* about a state or a stasis but rather with the *book* that corresponds to them. With *L'état perdu*, Farès seems to put forward the idea that one cannot change attitudes or habits regarding things or the world without changing the nature of the (static/statist?) relations that exist between the book and the world, the book and ideas, and, finally, the book and subject. For Farès, there were too many books in the Maghreb that were still merely the palest reproductions of social, political, and esthetic reality that we view as already given, that is, as carbon copies or tracings (*calques*). Even when they dealt with realities that were always already destructured and/or in formation, too many Maghrebi writers continued to write as if the eternal task of the book were to represent an organic beautiful totality as a signifying and subjective interiority, or as an imitation and reproduction of the world. What Farès seems to be suggesting, rather, is that this epoch of the book as the reflection of the

One and the transparency of the world has come to an end. From now on, what must guide us is not what a book (or an author) wants to say or means, but how the book functions, or, better yet, how it is connected to the world, how it adjusts to the world in order to be in direct contact with it. In such a context, "[W]e will never ask what a book means, as signifier or signified; we will not look for anything to understand in it. We will ask what it functions with, in connection with what other things it does or does not transmit intensities, in which other multiplicities its own are inserted and metamorphosed, and with what bodies without organs it makes its own converge."[11] This is the kind of rhizomatic book that Farès wanted to promote by writing *L'état perdu*. It is a rhizome-book because, unlike books that draw their inspiration from models of the tree or of the root, it does not hesitate to connect "any point to any other" and to bring into play "very different regimes of signs, and even nonsign states." (*A Thousand Plateaus*, 21) Like the rhizome-book according to Deleuze and Guattari, it

> is reducible neither to the One nor to the multiple. It is not the One that becomes Two or even directly three, four, five, etc. . . . It is composed not of units but of dimensions, or rather directions in motion. It has neither beginning nor end, but always a middle course [*milieu*] from which it grows and which it overspills. [Ibid., 21]

Unlike the narrative-representative book that proceeds by mimesis and reproduction, *L'état perdu* is made up of only lines (and sometimes literally even lines): "[L]ines of segmentarity and stratification as its dimensions, and the line of flight or deterritorialization as the maximum dimension after which the multiplicity undergoes metamorphosis, changes in nature." (Ibid., 21) What strikes us here is that each *trait* no longer necessarily nor always refers to a linguistic sign: semiotic links of all kinds are connected to very different modes of encoding: biological, political, economic, and so on, that bring into play not only different regimes of signs but also the *statuses of the state of things*. The book is no longer content merely to re-present the world or reality, it is no longer a copy or a photograph or even a simple drawing, but a map "that must be produced, constructed, a map that is always detachable, connectable, reversible, modifiable, and has multiple entryways and exits and its own lines of flight." (Ibid.)

In fact, how does *L'état perdu* begin?

"The cover illustration is an Attic borrowing in which the various elements of Berber and Mediterranean symbolics still in use today are combined." (*État perdu*, note, first unnumbered page)

Thus, from the outset, a drawing or design short-circuits or emphasizes the hegemonic nature of the linguistic sign. Indeed there is an emphasis, but more in the sense of the Hegelian *Aufhebung*: for if there is in fact both a going beyond and a retaining of the sign, this retaining (of the Berber sign) is also a going beyond, a subversion, a transformation. If in *L'état perdu* the drawing intervenes in the work, it is no longer to illustrate or decorate it, no longer to create a kind of local color, but rather the drawing is there to mobilize those signs that, because they are emotionally charged, allow the text to be transformed into a veritable accelerator of signs. Farès does not transfer the text onto signs (Berber or otherwise); he does not transfer the copies onto the map of the text. Rather, he transfers the copies onto the map, the signs onto the text, the text as a cartography of desire. In Farèsian semiotics, then, the sign—whether drawing, pictogram, and so on—no longer signifies only as a signifier that refers to a signified, but above all as it is emotionally charged, as it is itself a particular emotional charge. In this sense, the sign is transformed into a scarification, becoming like a gash on the text, or better yet, like a *stigmata*. The sign is like the *symptom* of the repression of a language or a more ancient, more archaic system of signs, rather than like the signifier of a signified. In fact, from the moment it is inscribed in an arrangement where it is no longer emphasized or co-opted like in a book of images, stories, or linguistics, the sign undoubtedly contaminates the entire field of thought with its emotional (symptomatological) and historical charge, finding itself directly connected to an unprecedented reality. By integrating as he does the Lybic, Berber, or Tiffinagh signs in a text where they no longer figure as illustrations of a theory, Farès transforms them into the practical inscription of cultural difference. Because they are inscribed in a system that is "a-centered, non-hierarchical, and non-signifying, without a General, without an organizing memory or a central automaton ... *defined only by a circulation of states*,"[12] these signs from now on refer to a (potential or virtual) reality that until then had no right to exist. The sign no longer (only) presents itself as a linguistic-representative sign, but as a numeral, a kind of registration number profoundly marked both emotionally and historically:[13]

> The registration numbers found throughout this book (numbers that are ciphers in the sense of codes and decipherings) are numbers of chapters as well as numbers imposed by the registration or inscription of a name and a language that, always according to the same history, were *borrowed*. Journeys to the heart of the signs-therefore-where the serpent represented xxxxxxxxx manifests the meaning of a *reality*.[14]

One appropriation leads to another: First we are told that the borrowings are from Berber, and now we discover that French itself is a "borrowed" language. What, then, is the true language? Or could it be that all languages are *borrowed*? In fact, once it is assimilated to a politics of numbers and numbering—and thus to a politics of identification—language, and here French in particular, becomes the object of a coded trajectory (*parcours*) that allows it to be assigned a status it did not have prior to the *deciphering* it undergoes in this book. Because it has been subjected to operations of grafting and cutting, the borrowed language—French—is made to reveal a number of things. First, it reveals a dimension that had gone unnoticed by Maghrebi and Francophone authors who used it without questioning it: it reveals itself to be a language that constantly overcoded other languages. By *deciphering* myself in a borrowed language, I can only find myself in a *registered* identity: a state, a (sociological) fact, a condition—that has been reified, or in a "state" (of mind) that has been substantivized, monadized. Finding itself thus attached to a regime of signs that is profoundly heterogeneous to it, French reveals itself to be *one code among others*—and, for the Maghrebi, an *arbitrary* code at that. Or, in Farès words, "the sequestered form of the word that cannot pronounce the tune of its nomination." (20)

Thus, far from finding himself alienated from the French language—that is, acculturated, Farès inscribes this language—the signs of the French language—in a *process* where it can finally appear in its historical function, that is, as a language that has covered over and even debarred another.[15] Practically speaking, Farès could only make this aspect of things apparent in an active—practical!—way by an assemblage of heterogeneous signs and semiotic links that go on to connect yet other regimes of signs, organizations of power, and occurrences that refer to the arts, history, the sciences, and to social struggles as well.

It is in this sense that the title of the book—*Lost State*—is important. What is lost is any state that does not take into consideration the multiplicity of languages, races, cultures, and mores that exist in a given country. What is also lost is the state of a language that has become monologized, or monolingualized. To the degree that identity— a certain type of psychological and national identity—is linked to a state (stasis) of language, by questioning the stability of language, Farès simultaneously questions the identity of the subject that it registers and the reasoning behind the different modalities of registration. In this sense, Farès seems almost to repeat, word for word, something that Roland Barthes said during his inaugural lecture at the Collège de France: "Language is fascist." For Farès also, each time language is considered—used—as a code that *preexists* the forces, emotions, and ideas it is supposed to trans-scribe, it becomes an instrument of the reduction of the multiplicities at work in the slightest little thought, the least reality. It transforms itself into an instrument of the state. Shall I quote him? Provide passages from his book that corroborate what I'm saying? In this book, as in many others by Farès, there are numerous passages that could be quoted, summoned to support this thesis. Here is one for the "amateur," taken almost at random:

> The compass card [*rose des vents*] indicates that the movements of stars and countries are mixed in a diverse, corporeal work, even if—once again—*there exists the fear of touching a*

word, of taking it exploded, as a personal Rose of sand or Blood: fear of being, in the closed book. "But where on earth did you find this illusion of signs?" The permanence of the important gaze that exile from the earth fixes in the days. [25]

We could easily find a number of other passages to attest to the reasonableness of this reading. If we accept it too readily, however, we would no doubt miss what seems to me an absolutely crucial dimension of Farès's approach in this book as he transfers the movement of the deterritorialization of signs mentioned earlier to *the entire text*. Once again for Farès it is not sweeping declarations of principle or significant (ideological or political) ruptures that allow change to occur; rather, it is contamination, cutting, grafting, an asymmetrical assemblage of heterogeneous signs that can accomplish this. These are what it takes to see, to provoke an event. It is not significant or rational ruptures or breaks that must be carried out, but irrational ones.[16] To write? Yes. But writing as wandering, strolling, migrating. To write like a nomad and produce books that will be like war machines against the ideological apparatuses of the totalitarian state and their registration cards. To write a book with neither beginning nor end, but one that would also be "in the middle, between things, interbeing, *intermezzo*." (*A Thousand Plateaus*, 25)

And it is on this level that we can legitimately establish a relation between Farès's writing and Ezra Pound's. It is neither the general configuration nor the external appearance of their texts that allows us to compare them,[17] but rather the method they implement and the nature of the relations among elements that this method conditions. When Pound wanted to convey an idea of his "creative method"[18] (Francis Ponge), he did not attempt to define concepts, but instead proceeded to enumerate a series of cases. To provide an idea of what might be considered good method—scientific method—in poetry, Pound began by evoking the work of the sculptor and art historian Gaudier Brezska. In his book entitled *L'histoire de la sculpture de l'âge de pierre à 1915* [The history of sculpture from the stone-age to 1915], Brezska was one of the first to formulate the idea that the history of art should not be a history of *contents*; rather, it should be primarily a history of *forms*, or more precisely, of the *change of forms* and of their *montage*.[19]

Far from being anarchic, the history of sculptural forms obeys a rhythm and a perpetual change whose basic form of plastic expression is the *sphere*. The Egyptians developed this sphere *vertically* because of their metaphysical aspirations, whereas the Semites of Mesopotamia raised it in order to create the *horizontal*. Gothic sculpture, on the other hand, according to Gaudier and Pound, was derived from "Hamito-Semitic energies" and thus was a kind of synthesis between the Egyptian aspiration toward the heights and the Semitic tendency toward horizontal translation. The "primitives" of Africa and Oceania, for their part, were said to have mobilized their mental energies in order to push the sphere in a convex direction, which in turn promoted the *cone* as a model for their sculptures. Finally, the "moderns" (Gaudier himself, as well as Epstein, Brancusi, Archipenko, and Modigliani, for example) "crystallized the sphere into a cube," thereby creating a combination of "all the possible shapes of mass."[20] Later Pound would use his theory of the "great bass in music" to elaborate the notion of the permanence and secret persistence of *the same form* throughout the ages.

According to this theory, says Pound, "down below the lowest note synthesized by the ear and 'heard' there are slower vibrations. The ratio between these frequencies and those written to be executed by instruments is OBVIOUS in mathematics. The whole question of tempo, and of a main base in all musical structure resides in use of these frequencies."[21] Thus, in music, too, a kind of bass moves silently throughout the various individual works.

But Pound goes further still. After referring to the great bass in music, he moves on to Leibniz, or more precisely to the case of Leibniz and his "insquashable monad." This, says Pound, is a monad that may seem outdated by the new nuclear physics, yet it continues to hold up over time, not as a scientific model for physics but as a philosophical concept. It holds up not as a point itself, but because it was the "philosophic complement of the emerging empirical sciences based on observation."[22] When he arrives at this point in his exposé of cases, Pound pauses, and summons his readers in these terms: "*These disjunct para-*

graphs belong together, Gaudier, Great Bass, Leibniz, Erigena, are parts of one ideogram, they are not merely separate subjects."[23]

The question then becomes one of the logic behind this correspondence: In what way do these heterogeneous cases correspond to each other? How does this correspondence become the image of poetic creation? What links it to the ideogram?

One of the answers we are tempted to propose, at least in reference to Pound's work, is that these heterogeneous cases communicate and may be reduced to a common denominator if we compare them to the various elements that make up a single ideogram. Hadn't he already shown elsewhere that, in order to denote the abstract entity "red," the Chinese poet (or his ancestor) "put together the abbreviated pictures of

ROSE	CHERRY
IRON RUST	FLAMINGO

and that the "Chinese 'word' or ideogram for red is based on something everyone KNOWS,"[24] meaning that the production of even a general idea passes through the most concrete experience of things, through sensation even. For Pound, poetry proceeds from a "logic of sensation" (in Deleuze's sense) and aims at emotionally charged psychic experiences and not at general, unembodied (desingularized) concepts. Even the scholar can only know his or her most abstract object by means of this practical experience. Without affect, without perceptible, sensate intuition, a concept or a representation is empty, as is—even more so— a poetic word.[25]

But as Géfin has shown in his excellent work on the esthetic of the ideogram in Pound's work,[26] the difference here is that when Pound evokes the "ideogrammatic method," he is not referring to the simple *overt* qualities of things but rather to the complexity of the essential relationships that exist within and between each subject. When we are no longer dealing with the various overt qualities of particular objects but rather with abstract concepts such as *usury*, for example, we must move on to an *expanded* equation of the economy of the ideogram. Referring to the cases of interest to us, Géfin remarks that "each unit [of the poem] has two components in common with the rest: an attempt to establish a *basis* and a desire for unification." And he continues:

> In Gaudier, the basis of sculpture and the form from which all other plastic expression stems is the sphere; all sculptural modes—vertical, horizontal, conic, cubic—are unified through this one basic principle. The "great bass" (or "base") is an unheard vibration below the heard; it is a foundation which, according to Pound, the great composers never neglected in composing their "heard" compositions.[27]

For Pound, only cumulative ideogrammatic writing is able adequately to render the nature of the conjunctive-disjunctive syntheses that come into play in apprehending the slightest poetic object. This, in any case, is the method Pound uses in the *Cantos* to deal, for example, with history, usury, or the beauty of a face that enchanted him in the subway:

> Here the material juxtaposed (as in the rose-flamingo or Malatesta ideograms) is based on fragmentary sub-wholes pertaining to a historical event or an individual, and their identity of structure is not immediately apparent.[28]

Pound leaves a margin of indeterminacy or underdeterminacy—blanks, gaps, pauses—that is absolutely essential to the functioning of the text as a machine of effects or delays. And this is why one must no longer trust in a *grammar* of natural language, but rather in an ideogrammatic juxtaposition of apparently heterotopic or heterogeneous elements, which this *particular organization* will know how to transform into a veritable particle accelerator. No longer should the story be left to a *grammar of narrative*, but it must instead rely on a new logic, a new way of selecting and organizing the elements of the narrative. For new thought there must be a new logic and a new rhetoric. As Francis Ponge said, "[T]o each poem, its own rhetoric!"

I believe we are dealing with the same sort of approach in Farès's *L'état perdu*. In this text, every classic formal and grammatical connection is effaced to the benefit of a new logic in which the juxtaposition of apparently completely foreign elements allows the new "idea" to arise, that is, allows for a new understanding of the reality of the emigrant's or the exile's condition. This task is not left to concepts or to simple narrative, for no concept or narrative can subsume the multitude of traces and the incessant back-and-forth of the emigrant's or exile's wandering. Here, each theme, each narrative—and there are as many as there are emigrants, as many as there are kinds of exile—affects the theme that precedes and conditions it by constantly transforming the totality in formation to which they all belong. It is for these reasons, it seems to me, that from the outset Farès writes the following:

> O. This book is *neither poem, nor novel, nor narrative.* Simple word that, beneath the vault of the police and arrests, deepens the privilege of being beyond insignificance. [*L'état perdu*, 11]

But the logic that is implemented here does not follow causal or predetermined lines. It moves in the opposite direction, according to an almost stochastic logic that mimics the "de-order [sic] of the identity" of the emigrant.[29] As opposed to syllogistic knowledge, this new logic proceeds more from the particular to the general, in accordance with the most direct, lived experience of emigration.[30] As in one of Jean-Luc Godard's films or Max Ernst's collages, the elements that seem the most heterogeneous and the ones that respect their origins the least gradually begin to make us hear the *basso continuo* of emigration, the story of the emigrant:

> Neither a state   nor a fact   nor a moral   nor
> a condition   to be an immigrant
> is to be
> history & You know something about that. (19)

The new "All" is no longer made up of general comments, general ideas about emigration, or of deductions, but like in Pound when he speaks of *Usura*, of a "sufficient phalanx of particulars."[31]

In *L'état perdu*, Farès mobilizes the power and the dynamics of the logic of the Poundian ideogram in order to reevaluate the status and the reality of the emigrant and, while he's at it, of anyone who has known exile—any exile. Obviously, for Farès, the nature of the components juxtaposed to form the ideogram is radically different. But the method, or, if one prefers, the intuition and the basic sensibility—the quest for silent and transversal resonances, the passion for montage and juxtaposition, and so on—remain the same as for Pound. This method will always prefer relations to terms, producing a multitude of "relations-in-process" (Géfin, 39) in a language and writing that go beyond metaphors. And thus, in Farès, a privileged position is granted to the coordinating conjunction *and*:

> Stomach open facing up, after the explosion, he said to him: I did not invent your name & I did not invent your body & I did not invent your claws & I did not invent your skin & I did not invent your world & I did not invent your death & I did not invent your wars & etc. [12]

The book-tree and the book-root imposed the verb *to be* and the registrations that go with it:

> Cries
> Check/Customs/identity
> Everything that *the state*
> could not understand
> such as *me* or *I*? [46]

But the driving force behind the book-ideogram or the rhizomatic book that Farès offers us is the conjunction *and*: a weak conjunction, weaker, it would seem, than the verb t*o be*, but which, in the hands of the *ideogram*, will find enough strength to "shake and uproot the verb 'to be.' "[32] This is because the emigrants no longer claim (themselves) a *being*, but a *passageway*. It is not *to be* that interests them; *to be* never interested them; what interests them is passing, crossing between two languages, two borders, two identities, and moving among registrations. Farès is not concerned with filiation, origins, or, as a result, with returning. There is no returning, and the departure was already there. With this book, Farès shows that he is done with filiations, with the tree and its dichotomies, the tree and its filiations. His particular tree is rhizomatic. It takes root through its branches. It is a tree made up of multiple graftings, and these graftings produce new fruits, new plants: new words, new encounters, new networks, and ever new alliances. What we need is not new ancestors—no more Keblout! No more myths!—but new *blocks of alliances*. What is needed is to create a rhizome, to constitute new blocks of alliance and, in so doing, to find one's own point of underdevelopment, to create one's own *basso continuo*, to find one's own point of silence, the point where "the body becomes an opera where the simplest joy of life is playing; a poetry" (99) that will, finally, "lift the tree from its fall, the day from its eclipse, the earth from its decline; a poetry that will open the world like a beloved gaze spread beautifully upon the visible gaze of land and plants; a poetry that will reconcile presence, liberty, being, and life; that will divert death, the void, slavery; a poetry that the hand draws." (99)

Is this an invitation to make a clean slate of things, to begin again from the beginning? Are we dealing with a call for a new, pure foundation or beginning here? Has Farès regressed all of a sudden? When we see the importance he attributes to the zero point and to the zero,[33] we could naively assume that this is indeed the case and that we are dealing with a desperate quest for an absolute rebeginning, the desire for a new departure. A fresh start! But that would be to read Farès backwards, from back to front, that is, to read him syntactically and not, as we have tried to suggest in this reading, *paratactically*,[34] tactically. Fold by fold.

To read the last paragraph of the book as a conclusion would be wholly to lose sight of the logic that holds no element of the poem to be final, anterior, or posterior to any other. *L'état perdu* is a *palindrome* text that can be read starting from any point, but it is also an ideogrammatic text whose fragments can only be read in relation to the silence—the "great bass," if one prefers—that makes them correspond asymmetrically and nonhierarchically. Then and only then can we understand that it is neither a matter of an initiatory concept here, nor of a symbolics of the voyage and migration. Rather—just as we find in Pound, Kleist, Buchner, and Baldwin—it is a way of journeying by and through *the middle*.[35] Or as Farès writes, it is "like clouds of vibrating insects." (85) To write paratactically, to institute a logic of the *and*, is to reverse ontology, subvert hierarchies, dismiss foundations, abolish ends and beginnings. This is, at least, one of the great—successful—ambitions of this beautiful text. The rest is a matter of reading, writing, and traveling. But for this particular journey, no one can summon us.

4

Postcolonial Nations

Political or Poetic Allegories? (On Tahar Djaout's
L'invention du désert)

> Elsewhere, history crumbled in its course; it comes down to
> us in ruins.
>
> —Tahar Djaout, *L'invention du désert*, 82
>
> Time here is enclosed, a trajectory without crossroads.
>
> —Ibid., 115–6
>
> There's nothing left to salvage, the signs of the world have
> come undone.
>
> —Ibid., 27

At a time when studies termed *postcolonial* were still in the first stages of
theoretical elaboration, Fredric Jameson's article in *Social Text* entitled
"Third World Literature in the Era of Multinational Capitalism"[1] immediately sparked an outcry perfectly indicative of what the future
would hold for the project of postcolonial theory.[2] Jameson's thesis
formulated the relationship of the literary text to political and historical
reality in what could not have been more pointed terms:

> *All third-world texts* are *necessarily*, I want to argue, allegori-
> cal, and in a very specific way: they are to be read as what I

will call national allegories, even when, or perhaps I should say, particularly when their forms develop out of predominantly western machineries of representation, such as the novel. [69; my emphasis]

A few lines later, Jameson refines his thesis, writing:

Third-World texts, even those which are seemingly private and invested with a properly libidinal dynamic—necessarily project a political dimension in the form of national allegory: the story of the private individual destiny is *always* an allegory of the embattled situation of the public third-world culture and society. [Ibid.]

As Ahmad Aijaz pointed out in "Jameson's Rhetoric of 'Otherness' and the 'National Allegory,' " Jameson's generalizations in formulating his thesis could easily lead to confusion, and they imply a process of essentialization and/or reductionism that could only lead readers who had a specific cultural and historical register in mind to answer back. From my point of view, for example, which is to say that of a postcolonial Algerian, the attempt to inscribe "all third-world texts" under the same regime or genre of signification leads to doubt and suspicion: doubt about the meaning of the totality in question ("all texts"), and suspicion about their nature and place of origin or transmission. Are we mainly talking about works of fiction, that is, novels, or should poems, plays, critical essays, and, more generally, all texts understood as "literary" be included in this undetermined totality? And in that case, how would we decide where to place the boundaries of what is considered literary? Given the importance in the Maghreb of writing called poetic, and given the diversity of literary genres mobilized in the production of literary works in Algeria, Morocco, and Tunisia, Jameson's assertion leads to even greater reservations and perplexity.[3] If it is indeed true that an allegorical dimension[4] persists in most so-called postcolonial texts, allegory is clearly almost never the primary or sole ambition of the authors in question. When it is, however, experience has shown that we often find ourselves faced with texts that could be called didactic, the artistic or literary value of which is slight or nil. This is true for literature proper—as in novels and poetry—but also for films. Legion are the novels and films produced by postcolonial writers and filmmakers that can be read as allegories, though not so much as allegories "of the embattled situation of the public third-world culture and society" as right-thinking and familiar discourses on good and evil, on the pure and the impure, on true and false identity, on the glorious past scorned by colonialism, and so on. In short, as Roland Barthes would say of the *pensum*: The message can be made out from the first sentences, stanzas, and sequences.

With this in mind, it becomes clear that when dealing with so-called postcolonial literatures, Jameson's thesis is rendered problematic not so much by the idea that the allegorical exists in postcolonial texts[5] as by the absence of any reference to or problematizing of the matter of the languages concerned. Indeed, one of the conditions that allows the critic to inscribe a given body of texts under the heading "all texts" or worse, "all third-world" or "all Chinese" texts, is a patent disregard of the medium used to produce these works. In fact, had he thought to take into account the delicate question of language choice in the production of these works, Jameson could never have put forth such an all-encompassing thesis. For if there is a single important political, cultural, theoretical, and even moral question faced by postcolonial writers, it is that of the language in which they will give form to what they wish to express to their readers. As the critic and theorist Albert Memmi has shown, for example, the predicament of postcolonial Maghrebi writers was never mainly that of knowing what to say— they were never truly lacking in subject matter—but that otherwise more sensitive question of knowing in what language to write.[6] As I have attempted to show elsewhere, this is also a question of *audience*: indeed, whether they write in Arabic, in Berber, or in French, these writers continually face a situation in which the majority of the population either does not read the language used by the writers or does not know how to read at all.[7]

In order to shed light on the various angles of this problematic, we could consider the interesting example of a novel appearing to satisfy all the criteria Jameson used to characterize third-world texts, *L'in-*

vention du désert by the Algerian writer Tahar Djaout.[8] If we bear in mind the fact that this novel was published by a first-world publisher, it seems to conform to the characteristics Jameson enumerated in his article: It is a text written by a third-world writer, and it is presented from the start as an allegory of the nation. Devilishly allegorical, the title already invites metaphorical speculation. What is it to invent the desert? Which desert is at stake? The real Algerian-Maghrebi desert or, as is suggested throughout the text, the poetic desert celebrated by the Emir Abdel-Kader and by the mythical Rimbaud, who accompanies the narrator as he travels throughout the various Arab countries in the course of the novel? In addition, the narrator's quest or query invites us at the same time to read the novel as a parable with a greater world historical scope. The project of writing the story of Ibn Toumert—the founder of the dreadful Almohades Dynasty and chief of the hordes that were to sweep away the Almoravides and attempt to establish the order of Islamic faith and purity—automatically invites the reader to set up a parallel between what happened in Algeria in the twelfth century and what is happening in our own time. In any case, it forces the reader to ask questions—entirely allegorical ones, to be sure—of the type: Why is there Islam in Algeria and not, rather, nothing? Was Islam simply a fold in the history of Algeria, or does it represent an insurmountable dimension of the Algerian ethos? Can we analyze Islam from our present perspective when it turns out that its mark was already inscribed on Algeria more than thirteen centuries ago? What links, what relations, might be established between the partisans of the *Mahdi* Ibn Toumert and the founders of contemporary Algeria's Brothers of the Purity of Faith and Salvation? Is Algeria doomed to experience fundamentalism, Puritanism, and intolerance to women? Is this its destiny? By trying to reconstruct Ibn Toumert's relationship to Algeria and the story of his victory over the Almoravides, Tahar Djaout was, in any case, deliberate in wanting to bring the contemporary situation in Algeria to the forefront, inviting his readers to reread, at least analogically, Algeria's relationship to its past, to Islam, to fundamentalism, and so on. No less importantly, *L'invention du désert* is also presented on some level as "the story of the private individual destiny," which is to say, as "an allegory of the embattled situation of the [Algerian] public in third-world culture and society." (Jameson, 69) Even though he speaks of himself in the third-person singular—"He sees himself multiple, he fights . . ." (Djaout, 9)—and has frequent recourse to interior monologue, the novel's narrator does not hesitate to reveal the thoughts as well as the most intimate feelings—or even the most "libidinal" in Jameson's sense—of a hero who is none other than himself. Consider a random example: "I am walking beneath the tyrannical sun. It is difficult to think. The most furtive rumination puts my head to a harsh test. I walk, sometimes catching the clandestine scent of algae stirred up by the recrudescent sun. Desires of burying rise up, of falling toward the abysses." (Ibid., 101) Indeed, we could use Jameson's analyses here as well to affirm that, as with another third-world writer, Lu Xun, "[T]he relationship between the libidinal and the political components and social experience is radically different from what obtains in the West and what shapes our own experience." (Jameson, 71) In fact, the least we can say is that *L'invention du désert*'s narrator's slightest action or thought is ideologically and politically overdetermined: Djaout is obviously not writing to amuse his readers, nor simply for his own pleasure. Everything he writes can be read as belonging to at least two scenes: one in which the narrator recounts his peregrinations in the Middle Eastern countries he visits, describing his impressions, translating his thoughts, and sharing his reflections on the return of Islam or even of religious fundamentalism in Algeria; and another scene, often the same one for all that, in which the narrator seems to write with the sole purpose of leading the reader to reflect on what the return and repetition of the history he discloses might mean for the readers of today. So in this sense, everything seems to confirm the difference Jameson sees between first-world and third-world writers, which is to say, the fact that in the case of the latter, the libidinal investment "is to be read in primarily political and social terms." (Ibid., 72) This assemblage of similarities also "brings us to the question of the writer himself [*sic*] in the third world, and to what must be called the function of the intellectual, it being understood that in the third-world situation the intellectual is *always* in one way or another a *political* intellectual." (Ibid., 74; my emphasis)

Knowing Djaout's tragic fate, we obviously cannot but agree with such an assertion: It is because he was a politically engaged intellectual that Djaout was the target of fundamentalists. It is because his work was read as politically and ideologically dangerous that Djaout was pursued, persecuted, and in the end, assassinated.[9] The portrait he gives in the novel, for example, of the Imam Ibn Toumert—"that grouchy little village prophet [who] was to become the supreme imam of an entire nation" (17)—is enough to explain the ire of so many aspiring imams and what followed. Even if *L'invention du désert* appears to be a novel the subject of which is twelfth-century Algeria, it was read as an allegory of the nation, the current Algerian nation—and this is what, among other things,[10] led to its author's being treated as an apostate, and assassinated.

Even if we know all of this, is it possible for Djaout's novel to be reduced to the allegorical dimension I have described based on Jameson's definition? What happens when only this dimension is brought to light? And what, then, is left in the dark? Finally, are we done with *L'invention du désert* once we have exposed the framework that, using Jameson as our guide, we described as allegorical? It seems obvious that only by reducing the notion of allegory to one politico-ideological overcoding or another can *L'invention du désert* be made to fit the mold we applied to it. In other words, if and only if Djaout's ambition had been to put forward some "thesis" on present-day Algeria based on his personal experience and on Algeria's contemporary history, would the allegorical reading of his text be satisfying. And so we are left with the following questions: Can a simple allegorical explanation of this novel suffice? Did we do justice to *L'invention du désert* when we emphasized this line of interpretation?

To respond even tentatively, it seems crucial to effect a displacement or, more precisely, a recentering of the questions, and to inscribe them in a critical and theoretical context in which the notion of allegory no longer introduces the same characteristics of interpretive stability and transparency we have granted it until now with Jameson. In this case, the men, women, and events described in the novel, "are not simply historical events or parts of a patriotic body politic," but rather, "a complex rhetorical strategy of social reference where the claim to be representative provokes a crisis within the process of signification and discursive address." (Bhabha, 267) And in fact, as soon as the reference to the allegorical dimension of a text is no longer susceptible to a purely historical or even political explanation; as soon as the ideological or political analysis of a text is no longer grounded in a confusion "of reference with phenomenality," of the linguistic with natural or historical reality, "it follows that, more than any other mode of inquiry, including economics, the linguistics of literariness [become] a powerful and indispensable tool in the unmasking of ideological aberrations, as well as a determining factor in accounting for their occurrence." (de Man, *Resistance*, 11)

What does this mean for us? It means, as Bhabha has astutely shown, that when it is a matter of the production of the nation as narration, and as text, "there is [always] a split between the continuist, accumulative temporality of the *pedagogical*, and the repetitious, recursive strategy of the *performative*." (Bhabha, 297; my emphasis) Indeed, one line of force that moves through Djaout's text is not so much the transparency of one historical layer in relation to another or the congruence of events in one scene (that of the history of the twelfth century) with those of another scene (that of the narrator's present), but the tension between two radically heterogeneous or even opposite modes of exposition and translation of Algeria's real present. There is a tension between the pedagogical and the performative, according to the paradigm proposed by Bhabha, but there is also a tension between the syntactic in this text—an account, a narrative, even a straightforward story—and the rhetorical: the invention, that is, the mapping out (*balisage*), as the narrator repeatedly expresses it, of the desert, or in other words, the experience of the impossibility of giving form to or narrating the nation (and himself as well). The unnarratable itself! At this level of analysis, we can no longer refer (only) to Marx's *German Ideology* to realize what is happening in Djaout's novel; we must also refer to de Man's *Allegories of Reading*. In other words, it is no longer a simple historical or narrative logic that must be brought to bear, but a theory of rhetoric that takes into account all the effects of tension mentioned above: the multiple significations of the desert; the shifting overlaps of meaning between ancient Algeria's history and what, in contemporary Algeria, seems to repeat the same framework. Yet here, like in the anecdote de Man relates about Archie Bunker's shoelaces, "[T]he logical and grammatical model of the narrative also has become 'rhetorical' not because we have, on the one hand, a literal meaning and on the other hand a figural meaning, but because it has become impossible to decide by grammatical or other linguistic devices which of the two meanings (that can be entirely incompatible) prevails."[11] As soon as we begin to explore the significance of desert, of text, and of Ibn Toumert himself, of Djedda, of Sanaa, of Aden, the whole text begins to crisscross, rendering completely impossible—ridiculous even—the slightest temptation to summon the latent dissemination of one transcendental signifier or signified or another, whether origin, ancestor, tribe, clan, or dynasty. When he speaks of the desert, is Djaout speaking of the Algerian Sahara or might he, rather, be proposing an allegory of the (impossible) text about Algeria that he is trying to write? Conversely, when he evokes the text, is he referring to the text we are reading or to the Koran? The margin separating one entity from another is practically impossible to determine. The borders between one city and another, one Arab country and another, one story and another, and, before long, one word and another, tend to blur. Confronted with the text, even the Prophet tends to "efface" himself so as to leave a space for . . . "America"!

"The desert: the margin without limits that hunts the Text beyond its bounds," we read on page 81.

"The Prophet, good strategist, effaces himself to let America speak, the sole runner capable of getting him past the rapids of the twentieth century"! (Ibid.)

Later the wording becomes still more explicit, connecting the process of writing to an aimless drifting and to uncertain trajectories, doomed to wander.

> Are you strong enough to begin again? To mark out in writing the trajectories doomed to be blank? Only then would you begin to understand the enigma of Almoravide history—and that of the whole Maghreb, no doubt: to mark out a moving surface that swallows boundaries in its restless wandering. [Djaout, 103–4]

Above all, we must be aware of the tenuousness of landmarks and of giving ourselves the means to map out a world that the text—"which muzzles the world with its intransigence" and "tolerates only acquiescence" (Ibid., 115)[12]—did not manage to *keep in check*. From this, the tragedy that permeates this text, which manages to find neither its subject, its object, its direction, nor its place of inscription, reveals its link to the insurmountable conflict existing between the pedagogical enterprise of telling the story of the nation as if it were able to be narrated—by recounting itself, identifying itself, or giving itself an identity through the story told!—and the performative endeavor, which is that of writing (the nation) and which turns out to be, above all, the bearer of a compulsion to repeat (history) that at every moment risks losing the whole project in cacophony or perhaps even madness. "Plans are thwarted every time!" as Kateb would say.[13] But whereas for Kateb chaos was still the bearer of hope—guided as he was by the beacon that was the country's liberation—for Djaout, it is chaos that crops up at each step, reinscribing itself in the (little) text (of poetic writing)[14] with each descent into the history of those who can henceforth be called the Almohalgerians. But the history in question—the history revealed in any case to the narrator-trekker[15] of the text—is shown to be less a voyage in the homogeneous time of an epiphany than a progressive, dizzying disorientation (*dépaysement*) on the way to the desert:

> But one fine day, the boundaries surrender to the sand, the water sinks deep into the earth like a frightened scorpion, the horizon collapses like an old fence—and the *aimless wandering without landmarks* is taken up again. Days and nights merge, men and beasts fuse. . . . Yet it is up to him to find water, the word that reinvigorates; it is up to him to *reveal the territory*—to *invent it* as needed. [Ibid., 122; my emphasis]

Little by little, the territory that it is to be invented distinguishes itself from the territories customarily marked out by the geographer and the cartographer and from the sites (of memory, for example) that historians are fond of inventorying. Whether it is the vastness of the Arabian desert, his "head," the playgrounds of his childhood, or again, the unmarked spaces of texts he crosses, in making, as if backwards, Rimbaud's journey and/or Ibn Toumert's in Abyssinia, Yemen, and elsewhere, Djaout never allows his reader to make definitive decisions about the nature of this territory. Just as he has difficulty sorting out what in himself comes from Ibn Toumert or Rimbaud (71), so too he has difficulty gaining perspective on crossing through the real desert and the perilous exploration of Algeria's history, or crossing through his own mind: "He is furrowing not the desert of sand and sharp stones, but the perilous desert of his head," he says in just such a moment in his peregrinations. (Djaout, 123) Elsewhere, "The waterwheels are spinning in his head, spilling over the sand of his brain" (88); whereas still elsewhere, the "history" that "crumbled in its course ... comes down to us in ruins." (82) Countless are the passages in which Djaout enjoys spinning out metaphors to the point where the borders between text, desert, mind (head), but also cities, temples, dwellings, and the surrounding walls "against which the centuries ricochet and admit their powerlessness" are no longer distinguishable one from the other. We move imperceptibly from one space to another, from one site to another, without ever being able to decide in which space or site we find ourselves exactly. But are we still talking about space here? What kind of space? What is the nature of these sites?

If we follow Bhaba's notion of the necessary tension between the pedagogical and the performative, the desert invented here proves to be none other than the liminal figure of the nation's history as a space to be discovered (uncovered and explored)—or, if one prefers, as a space with which only a new approach to the text (of reading/of writing) can contend. By making this detour through what Jameson sought in postcolonial texts, I hope to have shown that they can be reduced neither to an allegory nor to a simple fictionalized history. Above all, we may need to question the conditions under which Algeria can enter modern history, rather than to search for what conditioned a history that is stuck in religious archaisms. The multiplicity of the lines of flight crossing Djaout's text and the ambiguous character of the metaphors overdetermining the main signifiers—the desert, of course, but also the text and history—demand a radically new position from the reader. We must still read, and read with caution, but with the clear stipulation that henceforth, "to read" no longer consists merely of searching for a signified hidden behind the words or fragments of narratives that have come from nowhere. Rather, to read is to undertake a voyage more like that of Tarkovsky's Stalker than like that of a tourist, even a tourist who appreciates Francophone literature. The territory that Djaout invites us to cross resembles the Stalker's "Zone" more than it does those of the suburbs or zones of the first world that have, in contemporary literature, come to be called the countries of the third world.

Indeed, as we know, seen from the outside, this zone displays no particular marks: it resembles any other space or landscape in the world. Yet, seen from the inside, as Guy Gauthier aptly shows in the beautiful article he devoted to Tarkovsky,[16] in the zone, "all measurements of time and space are without value [and] geometry has no meaning. The straight line is not only the longest path from one point to another: it is impassable."

What Djaout has tried to do is initiate us into the veritable zone that Algeria became in the 1980s. For this zone, too, became impassable. At any rate, we can no longer cross there, travel there, live there without being constantly threatened with finding ourselves without warning or sign in a time, a place, and a world of customs that no longer belong to the present we occupied only a few minutes before we entered this other vector of time and space. Like Tarkovsky's zone, Djaout's desert "controls the progression, alters the course, dictates the rules, and punishes [often brutally, unjustly] those who transgress them." (Gauthier, ibid.) In both cases, in the zone, "the misfortune is that there are [apparently] no known rules, and one does not know if the zone [or the desert] accepts, represses, or punishes by death."

In Tarkovsky's "Stalker," only "the unfortunates with pure hearts" could pass. Djaout surely did not have Tarkovsky's film in mind when he wrote *L'invention du désert*, and he was no doubt far from thinking that his "desert crossing"—let us string out the metaphor a little!—would be compared to Tarkovsky's crossing of the zone. Still, there is more than a simple analogy between the filmmaker's zone and the Algerian writer's desert. In the desert as well, one must go through tunnels, navigate waterfalls, and come face to face with deserts that are different yet always the same. And like Tarkovsky's zone, the desert also seems at every moment to "determine the progression, alter the course, and even dictate the rules," while it simultaneously creates mirages and blurs the borders between the past, present, and future, the near and the far, the Algerian territory and its doubles. Here is yet another passage in which the "becoming-Stalker" of the narrator is produced before our eyes:

> *I insinuate myself in the desert,* wed its grain like a rattlesnake, find a way around the rising winds, and I arrive at the stony heart of the Giant. *I have the greatest respect for the desert, for its unpredictable moods,* its scorching caresses. I take care to prostrate myself before the desert fells me onto its vast pebbled carpet. I know the cruelty hidden by its gentle slopes and its nonchalant façade. [Djaout, 42; my emphasis]

At another point in the book, the narrator finds himself in the bus that will carry him across the desert in the Hoggar region. His fate is in the hands of Amar Nedjm, an experienced bus driver and pathfinder, who explains to him that he orients himself in the region thanks to the color of the dirt and sand. He knows that the dirt is white in the direction of Tamekrest, and brown or reddish brown elsewhere. But he also knows that, despite the fact that he has the "sixth sense of a desert animal" (47), the desert is unforgiving when it comes to errors. He himself was lost for twelve days with his friends Hamid and Azzi. The narrative of their wandering in the desert makes a great impression on the narrator; but what strikes him the most is the word that Amar invents to describe their ordeal. Because his French is not fluent, Amar does not say that his friends and he "se sont égarés" ("wandered off"), but speaks instead of their "égaration" ("wanderment"). This word delights our narrator all the more, since the neologism somehow perfectly coincides with the site where he finds himself—a site that seems to infect words with its multiple phonetic and semantic resonances: Hoggar, or in Tarqui, the language of the Touaregs, Ahaggar, and the disorientation of careless tourists who are found completely "haggard" in the desert (41)—all somehow miraculously find their concept in the phonetic changes that lead to "l'égaration." As if the desert were taking revenge on all those who do not abide by its law:

This is how the desert sometimes takes revenge on those who refuse to acknowledge its harsh law so that they see only the ultimate paradise of the eternal holiday, a vacation spot where one can wander about at leisure, get a suntan, and photograph the unfamiliar. *Yes, the desert sometimes takes revenge.* For having been smoothed over! [Djaout, 42; my emphasis]

Yes, the desert sometimes takes revenge, as does Algerian and Maghrebi history, because they have so often been smoothed over. And as we have seen, this is not the tourist's desert here. It is more like that of Victor Segalen's "exot," the traveler with the ability to "sense the Manifold":[17]

The territory *is not delimited in a precise and definitive way;* the homeland will continue to be invented from the unions and births that rarely bear fruit—a bitter fruit when it comes forth, like that of wild orange trees. The winds that rise from the sand, the unceasingly altered edicts, beget new frontiers— imminent evictions or new prohibitions to wandering. The land's entire history is the story of being surveyed. . . . But one fine day, *the boundaries surrender to the sand, the water sinks far into the earth like a frightened scorpion, the horizon collapses like an old fence*—and the aimless wandering is taken up again. [Djaout, 121; my emphasis]

Are we back in the allegorical? Undoubtedly; now, however, it seems clear that what opens up to a given regime or register of metaphor and leads to one place of thought or representation or another has become essentially undecidable. The meaning has now been disseminated in the trails and footpaths of a written crossing that knows no more frontiers. And in this sense, what characterizes the work of third-world writers is not so much the political-allegorical dimension of what they write. Rather, this work is better characterized by their renewed challenge of anything that tends to reduce the history of the third world and consequently the history of their countries to a kind of picture postcard, a case or a simple moment in the master text of Western reason's history. Not having inherited a preordained history, or perhaps because they inherited a history that a certain rationality has always already allegorized, these writers placed themselves almost instinctively on the side of a writing of difference rather than on the side of a history of identity/sameness. Wherever the dominant models were those of simple, rational recognition and prediction—wherever all that is real is rational and all that is rational is . . . Western!—they had to, almost of necessity, mobilize writing's resources to promote a conception of history no longer grounded in a simple recognition of oneself or prediction of the future. Their aimless wandering is no longer simply due to disorientation or misorientation; it has become a constitutive element of a reasoning process that radically calls into question what seemed to represent the very essence of history, namely, continuity, linearity, permanence—in short, one form or another of the absolute. For them, "the features of nonlinear changes, emergent properties, spontaneous self-organization, fractal becoming, and so on are perceived to represent not the abnormal condition of physical, chemical, biological and even socio-historical processes but rather their 'normal' conditions of existence."[18] And this is what, to my mind, explains among other things the distress we find in the works that have counted in Maghrebi history, or in those that have attempted to take charge of the history of a territory that, as I have tried to show, comes more to resemble Tarkovsky's zone than a country whose territory can be surveyed,[19] its trails located, its progression controlled.

> This is why [for example] Tehouda is not even a remnant. . . . Tehouda, den of the Kahina. Mirage place that escaped inventories, without even a plaque to name it. Yet it is here that so many paths cross. It is strange, moving, to look at Tehouda today entrenched in its anonymity and its desolation as if in the continuance of an eternally renewed battle where the cadavers and debris are cleared away with each turn. One has the impression that History has fallen asleep here. [Djaout, 31]

No places of memory, then, and no landmarks; no more ancestors either,[20] or symbols or allegories to wrap it all up and make a beautiful story, to offer itself up as a beautiful totality. Like Tehouda, the city blotted out by history, the Algeria of today "is not a place of history." It is a place in the process of becoming, a place to be made, constructed, (re)written. In order for this place to happen, to be able to enter history, however, it is imperative that we wrest it from the commonplaces that have been stuck on it; we must wrest it as well from the allegories[21] that made it lose its way in the desert. And this is what gives meaning to the enigmatic title of Djaout's novel: "to invent" the desert is to be given the means—those of the Stalker—of tearing Algeria from the desert or rather, of making a map of the cultural and political desert that contemporary Algeria has become. By following the trace of erased time, by locating the overlapping of different times and places, Djaout managed to survey a territory where a true cultural and political history of independent Algeria could begin to be inscribed. We know at present that the map of places—geographical, cultural, rhetorical, political—in this country can only be established at the price of an authentic desert crossing. The desert: "The margin without limits that hunts the Text beyond its bounds." (Djaout, 81)[22]

This essay was originally written for the ACLA Annual Conference held in Montreal from April 8–11, 1999. It was published in the special volume of *Research on African Literatures*, ed. Danielle Marx-Scouras. I have reworked it slightly here.

5

(Hi)stories of Expatriation

Virtual Countries

1. Assia Djebar's *La Nouba des femmes du Mont Chenoua*: Introduction to the Cinematic Fragment

In an interview with an Algerian journalist who asked about the difficulties of understanding her film *La Nouba*[1] *des femmes du Mont Chenoua*, Assia Djebar replied, "My film is not a difficult film. What I ask of the viewer is some effort."[2] Indeed, what struck Maghrebi viewers when the film came out was the absence of points of reference that would allow them to become engaged or taken by the film. *La Nouba des femmes du Mont Chenoua* offers viewers none of the classic narrative perspectives that would enable them to close the circle and enter fully into the subject matter of the film: there is no story, no continuous narrative; nor is there a dominant main character—is *La Nouba* a film about the martyrdom of Zouleikha? about Lila's quest? Or is it a tribute to the numerous Algerian women who participated in the Revolution? There is certainly no single thread to guide the viewer toward a definitive meaning or a final synthesis. Instead, the film seems to take a perverse pleasure in thoroughly disappointing any desire on the viewer's part to tie up loose ends or to reach closure.

Constructed as a "musical suite"[3] that is itself made up of heterogeneous fragments, the film proceeds through a succession of delocalized, denarrativized, and/or detemporalized images that are not summed up by any overarching signifier. Overall, the film presents itself as a succession of disparate elements that are joined together neither by plot nor by a unifying theme. The result is immediately evident: The universe that *La Nouba* invites us to contemplate is offered not as a closed or fully realized world but rather as a world in progress, in gestation. In other words, this universe is not a totality that preexists the elements that constitute it; rather, it is an apparently chance juxtaposition or dissemination of dispersed fragments (of [hi]stories and events) in search of a unity to come (or to be created). This explains, among other things, how rapidly the film takes on the feel of a disturbing interrogation or, more precisely, of a terrifying announcement: the annunciation, which hangs in abeyance until the end of the film, of the end and/or the beginning of a world. There is no doubt that this aspect of the film is affected by a certain philosophical and political bias on the part of Assia Djebar, and indeed Djebar has never pretended otherwise: *La Nouba* is a film essentially geared to the investigation of a world that was as yet virtually unknown in Algeria—the world of space and time as perceived by women, the world of body and thought as experienced by Algerian women (and Maghrebi women in general) and of their relationship to the world, to sociality, politics, morality, intellectual identity. The film's disjointed construction and its feminine viewpoint set it formally and thematically apart from Algerian cinematographic and cultural production and make *La Nouba* utterly unique.

But to read *La Nouba* as a film made solely about or for women would be to considerably restrict the film's political and ideological weight.[4] In fact, the focalization of Djebar's film around the feminine gaze or women's thought functions less as an exclusively profeminist bias or apology than as a sort of experimental working hypothesis: a phenomenological reduction that enables the filmmaker to imagine the fiction of a world in which the male gaze and the ascendancy of men have been for the time being suspended or, perhaps better, set aside for the duration of the film.[5] For us as viewers, this time is the space of a dream or an experiment (psychological, sociological, and political all at once). Apart from the fact that such a reduction was in itself still difficult to imagine within the Algerian political situation of the time, this setting aside of the male gaze never amounts to a pure and simple cancellation but rather—from a cinematographic and thus symbolic viewpoint—is meant to declare the male right to gaze temporarily out of bounds, outside the film's field of vision.[6] This seems to me to have presented the greatest obstacle to understanding (for men?): apprehended for the first time systematically by a female eye, the relationship to time and to space had abruptly changed in nature and was now being transmitted in a radically new mode to the eyes of an audience that was completely unprepared for such a shift in values. Indeed, in Djebar's film, space is revealed as much more complex than had ever been imagined: It is laid open to experimentation, sometimes as a closed container coiled around itself (like an "envelope," as Irigaray might say), in which the female body is inscribed in its multiplicity, sometimes as a space opening out onto infinity, bounded only by the gaze cast upon the horizon. In contrast to the way domestic—one is tempted to say domesticated—space fosters a turning inward of the self, an involution, what emerges now is a turning outward, an infinite unfolding toward the external world and toward others: slow film shots along the ridges of Mont Chenoua, shots of the ocean, the forest, of underground or undersea caves, and so on.

But what is even more interesting is that the relationship to time is itself subject to the same disjunctive movement: "Time is out of joint!" Time in its turn becomes dislocated, fragmented, and made infinitely plural; it is broken into discontinuous moments or snapshots that alternate with slow repetitive periods. In these rhythms, there is a more than superficial analogy between Djebar's approach and that of author-cinematographer Marguerite Duras, to whose work Djebar's film is deeply indebted both cinematographically and thematically. Indeed, rather than exploring the psychology of one or more characters, *La Nouba* functions first of all as a painstaking, so to speak, "geo-thetic" survey of *feminine places*, not only in the geographical sense but also in the rhetorical sense of *commonplaces*: home, hearth, bedroom, window, but also speech, memory, song, scream. This is the necessary detour that must be taken if we are to avoid committing the gravest mis-understanding of Djebar's film, which would be to seek a single meaning, to plot a fixed course, where what is called for is to open new paths, ride a line of light, draw a map instead of a carbon copy graph; to seek a "(hi)story" where, rather, an attempt is being made to try out a new way of relating to time, to memory, to the different places where women have lived for all time and invested their presence, places that traditional cinema had never been able to reconnoiter. In this sense, *La Nouba* presents not just a simple (hi)story of feminine space, but, one might say, the lay of the land, its topography. It is a matter, above all, of making a *topography of feminine places*, the map of a continent as yet undiscovered, at the same time as inventing a new *chronotope*: that of feminine time(s). And this is what makes it possible to understand the mode of construction and the rhythm, or better yet the tempo and cadences of Djebar's film.

This dimension, in any case, explains the lack of action, prop-erly speaking, in *La Nouba*; instead of plot, there is ceaseless rambling, constant circulation. Indeed, the film depicts much walking and endless movement from place to place by various means: on foot, on horseback, by boat, by car. All these displacements are undertaken not so much in order to accomplish a specific action as to mark out the terrain, to locate its secret or unknown borders or to create new ones. What deter-mines the unfolding of the film is not action-images but rather time-images. In this sense, the film does not function as a sensory-motor trigger.[7] The characters do not act or converse in order to propel the story forward or to resolve a personal conflict. They seem, rather, to move and to speak in order to encounter other people and other words—always moving toward what is unknown, what is new to them. Furthermore, there is not a great deal of dialogue in *La Nouba*, and what there is appears not for the sake of idle chatter or palaver but rather out of a desire to learn to listen, to ask questions, to glean some-thing from or about others by listening to them.

In *Istikhbar* (the prelude), while several measures of a Bartók suite are heard, we hear the female narrator's voice chanting these words in the background:

I seek nothing, but I listen
How I would like to listen!

Later, in the *Meceder* (adagio) section, the narrator resumes her narration with these words:

We must stay awake
Keep watch for fear that the nightmare may return
Say nothing, let others speak
Is it the past, is it the present that comes back to us?

Or again:

I was seeking nothing any more, but I listen
I listen to memory in tatters.

Here speech is no longer an instrument of communication, but has become a sporadic and open-ended exploration of a past buried or repressed in the limbo of a still inchoate memory; or else a passionate sounding of the present, which is constantly haunted by the violence of a past that has not yet found its voice and that is pregnant with a thousand potentialities. Speech here is not yet revelation, but preparation for the only labor that counts: that of recalling (recollections), and, above all, that of anamnesis. When an accident immobilizes her husband and leaves him aphasic, Lila is able to detach herself, affording herself the means to meditate, to dream, to wander. She is able to forge anew not only the bonds that link her to other women but also those that re-connect her to herself. And if we are attentive to a certain linguistic and musical economy in the film, to the rhythm with which its polyphonic elements unfold, and of course to the demeanors of the film's main characters—to their *chansons de geste*—we realize that all of these point us toward an utterly unique instancing of the return to the self.

In this sense, what Lila pursues is not simply a withdrawal into herself but rather something on the order of what psychoanalyst M. Masud R. Khan has aptly termed *lying fallow.*

Land left fallow is "ground that is well-ploughed and harrowed, but left without crops for a whole year or more."[8] The fallow state depicted in Djebar's film is that of an individual who, in Khan's terms, feels "the basic needs of the person to be private, unintegrated" for a time (398–9): "It is not an idle moronic state of being. It is a cogent capacity in a well-established, disciplined, and personalized individual." (400) Or again: "Lying fallow is a way of being that is above all the proof that a person can be with himself unpurposefully."

It seems to me that in temporarily wresting Lila from her wifely responsibilities, in freeing her from her maternal duties, Assia Djebar has created the conditions that allow her heroine to lie fallow. This heroine can at last explore her own privacy and come face to face with herself and with others without having a specific purpose, without needing to justify her actions—without, in current parlance, having an agenda. And in this sense, Lila transgresses the taboo that governs the relationship of the Maghrebi woman to the Outside (the *Kharidj*), by venturing out from her home "without good reason(s)," unpurposefully.[9] What is striking is the degree to which Lila's capacities correspond to the three conditions Khan identifies for lying fallow (402): (1) "acceptance of self as a separate person": as I have already mentioned, Lila is always on the move without showing any clear sign of alienation from others; (2) "toleration of noncommunication," evident in Lila's listening stance: what interests her is getting others to speak, listening to them, providing a forum for their expression, rather than imposing her speech upon them; and (3) lastly, "putting up with reduced relatedness to and from the environment": very often Lila gives every appearance of wandering from place to place, but something tells us that this rambling is not totally arbitrary; something indicates that her displacements are not those of someone who is lost or who does not know where to go. Quite the contrary, her apparent indolence exudes strength, her idleness is a vast sigh of freedom.

In *The Primacy of Perception*, Maurice Merleau-Ponty describes a similar psychic situation:

> In adults, ordinary reality is a human reality and when use-objects—a glove, a shoe—with their human mark are placed among natural objects and are contemplated as things for the first time, or when events on the street—a crowd gathering, an accident—are seen through the panes of a window, which

shuts out their sound, and are brought to the condition of pure spectacle and invested with a sort of eternity, we have the impression of acceding to another world, to a surreality, because the involvement that binds us to the human world is broken for the first time, because a nature "in itself [*en soi*]" is allowed to show through.[10]

When Lila enters into a fallow state for the first time, she undergoes an experience of the kind that Merleau-Ponty describes. The links that connect her to the human world seem to be broken, and she accedes to a state of nature in which things are revealed to her. By choosing to lie fallow, Lila is (temporarily) removed, in a way, from the symbolic terrain that enclosed her, and she gains the freedom to encounter a *sur-reality.*

I hope I have articulated enough elements of the phenomenology of lying fallow to allow some of the benefits that it entails to be identified. What effect does the fallow state have on someone who experiences it? The answer, as one can imagine, is unavoidably paradoxical. To lie fallow is to experience simultaneously both nothing at all and the essential. The power of fallowness lies in the rhythmic beating—that of the *Nouba?*—between plenitude and nothingness, fullness and void, between saturation or plethora ("too much!") and the white of emptiness. We might as well say that it partakes of the realm of Tao or satori.

As Masud Khan has shown, the capacity to lie fallow is "a nutrient of the ego and a preparatory state. It supplies the energic substratum for most of our creative efforts, and through its unintegrated, psychic suspended animation (which is the obverse of organized mentation) allows for that larval inner experience that distinguishes true psychic creativity from obsessional productiveness." (400) In transposing these parameters to what happens in Djebar's film, we might say that Lila's experience of lying fallow establishes the conditions necessary to recuperate her creativity as an Algerian woman: for the time being, she is behaving not as a mother, wife, mistress, or economic agent but rather as a woman who—perhaps for the first time in her life—*lives with herself* and finds the strength to plumb her own depths. She has been granted the means to live without a mask, without pretensions. Lila could be said to be in labor—not with another child of Ali's, but with herself; she is pregnant not with a child but with her own becoming-woman and through her own experience with the becoming-woman of all women, of all man, if we recall Deleuze and Guattari's formulation: "A woman has to become-woman, but in a be-coming-woman of all man."[11] That is to say that, for Djebar, becoming-woman takes place through a becoming-minority that is itself a highly political matter and that "necessitates a labor of power [*puissance*], an active micropolitics." (292)

I see this "micropolitics" at work in the treatment to which Assia Djebar subjects the time of her film. She is interested above all in what, for women of today, the present owes to the past and entails in the future; for her, time as becoming "cannot be conceptualized in terms of past and future" (292), but moves between the two. For Djebar time is above all a "force," an intensive force essentially made up of miscellane-ous events and instants not yet gathered together in a final synthesis or in a teleological concept of the future. And this approach to things is, it seems to me, what has caused *La Nouba* to be considered a "difficult" film that demands "effort" on the part of its viewers: never asking ques-tions of meaning or purpose, it always aims at questions of *use* (in a Deleuzian sense, use of the senses, of the gaze, of memory or of words) and of listening (to the other, to others) as rhythm, music, words yet unheard (of) in space and time. This approach, to my mind, is what determines the aesthetic bias of *La Nouba*.

An Aesthetic of the Fragment

In her attempt to render such an apprehension of time and space with-out betraying it, Assia Djebar deliberately opted for an aesthetic form that had long been spurned, even unknown, in Maghrebi films: this is the fragmented work, whose originality and effectiveness cinematogra-phers such as Alain Resnais, Marguerite Duras, Chantal Ackerman, and Peter Handke have taught us to appreciate. Indeed, all of these film-makers are preoccupied, to varying degrees, with abolishing classical narrative continuity, the protagonists' psychological identity, and the unbroken thread of meaning, all previously taken for granted. In their work, the story and the psychological life of the characters are brought into relief primarily through the careful exploration, executed with the detail of a full-fledged geodesic survey, of the different places where the principal events of the characters' lives are supposed to have taken place. These places include those of memory, associated or identified with geographic or architectural places: palaces, cellars, castle hallways, columns, public squares, wastelands, to name a few, all opening onto the abyss of memory; verbal rhetorical places—bits of speech, bits of dialogue, recollections, lines of poetry, in which viewers can, little by little, recognize scenes of language that transport them; places or figures of music and sound—songs, nursery rhymes, short sonatas—imposing a rhythm that serves to unearth a buried memory, to reactivate lost affective bonds; quicksilver images, or signifiers that make it possible to resuscitate certain patches of childhood, to mark the passage of time.

Formally, the most characteristic feature of this type of film is its organization by series. *La Nouba*, for example, is a film comprising at least five series of elements that are not subsumed by any superior instance: (1) the couple series, built around Ali, Lila, and their little girl Aicha (fiction), (2) the series based on the women and children of Mont Chenoua (documentary?), (3) the series of dreamlike or poetic illustrations inspired by the stories of the women of Mont Chenoua (documentaries and fiction), (4) the land and sea series (documentary and fiction), and finally, (5) the series incorporating archival documents on repression during the war of national liberation (documentary).

What must be noted straightaway is that there is no logical or chronological hierarchy to govern the organization of these series. Although after the several archival shorts that begin the film there are scenes depicting the places where Ali, Lila, and their daughter Aicha live, there is no a priori reason to accord more importance to the sequences of this series than to the sequences or shots of the various other series. The composition of *La Nouba* is such that no element can be labeled subordinate to or dependent on another. While the various elements combine to define some form of unity, they do not act as parts of a single whole or as moments of an ultimate synthesis. In this sense, and certainly for the first time in Maghrebi cinema, there is no dialectical conception of the work as a totality to order the arrangement and the progression of elements that constitute the work; quite the contrary, the fragments seem to point to a primordial chaos, and no sum total preordains the constituent units. Consequently, if we are to understand what is played out in *La Nouba*, we must invoke a completely novel type of totality and unity, for what we are faced with is not totality but multiplicity.

Indeed, in terms of form, *La Nouba* was initially conceived on the basis of a threefold fragmentation. The first consists in the division or, better, the dissemination, of the film's principal elements into five series or, perhaps better, five fundamental syntagms or constituent phrases. The five elements of this first fragmentation, which have been enumerated above, reflect what we would call the thematic material of the work.

But what has perhaps not been sufficiently observed is that this first fragmentation has repercussions for the syntagms themselves, which it breaks up or atomizes to carnivalesque effect by creating a *second-degree* fragmentation: indeed, each series is governed by parataxis, or the rupture of logical and grammatical subordination between the fragments that constitute it. The result is that the film, composed of five heterogeneous series, functions in a register that is not homogeneous to them: that is, as a distributional chain of atopical fragments or dechronologized segments that alternate and overlap in the film—elements divorced from place and from time. There is thus a displacement of the work's center of gravity, which moves imperceptibly from the continuous sequence to the fragment and—from a purely cinematographic point of view—from the sequence to the shot and, at times, from the shot to the photogram.

La Nouba does not always move from one phrase to another according to a rigorous logical chain, but rather shifts from one image (or shot) to another, from one word to another. At certain moments, the image itself is frozen in a still frame. This is because, within this logic of multiple series, reliance on classical techniques of coordination and subordination are no longer necessary. Now it is the shot as *punctum* that signifies, not by referring to a whole that is supposed to precede or predetermine it dialectically but as a sign of primordial chaos from which there may emerge some images that will move us, a few words that will prod us to think about that which cannot be conceived within the old categories of meaning or of being: consciousness, the self identical to itself, sexual difference. Thus, we can say that the world of *La Nouba* is not, or is no longer, an organic or dialectical whole but a universe essentially constructed piecemeal from irregular blocks that no conception or vision of the world (*Weltanschauung*) has yet succeeded in representing or totalizing. The world itself lies fallow. The universe of *La Nouba* is not, has not yet become, a cosmos, and is still less a (hi)story. It has not yet been taken up in a narrative. There is no grand narrative: It is a universe before or after the era of grand narratives. And it is for this reason that the series are not really connected by a relationship either of resemblance or of analogy, and that they reflect above all a primordial *chaosmos*: fragments of stories, of remembrances, of primordial questions and quests, which must be continually run through in the tentative hope of seeing them one day, through chance convergence, come together to constitute a world.

To my mind, this approach is what gives *La Nouba* its aspect of a desperate, open-ended, multiple quest: a quest for the identity or the transparency that are lost to Lila; a quest for Zouleikha, the Martyr; a quest for a brother killed during the war of liberation, who seems to have taken with him the secret of the present; a quest also, perhaps, for the meaning of colonization; a quest for the voice of woman, of women; and lastly, a quest for the meaning of the history of the Algerian Revolution. This in any case is the sense of the investigation that Lila pursues among the women of Mont Chenoua, and it explains the fascination their lives elicit in her throughout the film. What Lila seeks through these women is not merely some (unattainable) comfort, but the origin and meaning of her own life.[12] Moreover, it is perhaps for this reason that all these women limit themselves essentially to the telling of past stories; for this reason that all of them *must* tell a story! From a certain point of view, they seem to have been called upon solely to fulfill this task: to bring a slice of history, from the immediate or distant past, to the surface. But as we know, far from converging, these stories never coalesce to make a single story, never merge into a single memory. The many stories remain scattered and fragmentary, eternally juxtaposed, forever pointing back to two blind spots: Zouleikha's disappearance and the brother's death. But herein lies one of the film's most important lessons: that no (hi)story is possible without a true anamnesis, and that the conditions required in order for the latter to occur include the setting aside of meaning and short-term goals—in short, a period of lying fallow. In this sense, *La Nouba* may be interpreted as preparation for (the labor of) essential mourning and for anamnesis, both indispensable if we are ever to be emancipated from the past.[13]

Filming *La Nouba?*

The third type of fragmentation has to do with the treatment of the film's sound track, in particular that of the musical score. Dedicated to Béla Bartók,[14] Djebar's film was conceived, as its title indicates, as a type of musical composition: that is, as a *nouba*, "an everyday story of women," but at the same time as a discontinuous suite of heterogeneous musical fragments. Indeed, in musical terms, *La Nouba* is conceived as a pure suite of intermezzi, that is, as a series of four musical pieces of varied conception and rhythm that are set between an *Istikhbar* (prelude) and a *Khlass* (a rather lively and dynamic finale). Opening musically with a *Touchia* (overture) while we are introduced to Lila, Ali, and Aïcha, the film moves immediately thereafter to the four modes that precede the finale: a *Meceder*, then a *Btaihi*, followed by a *Derj* and a *Nesraf*. But contrary to what we might expect, although there are as many musical pieces as narratives or documentary series, there is no term-for-term correspondence between a given narrative or documentary series and a given musical series. The music neither follows nor illustrates the image. By and large the music, like the images, is not redundant: for it to be so, there would have to be a correspondence between the visual series and the musical series, on the one hand, and on the other, each of the two series would have to be continuous internally. Now, as we can observe in viewing the film, whichever of its aspects we choose to consider, the film constantly sends us back to a primordial atomization. Thus, contrary to our expectations, the music does not serve to make up for the loss of continuity and the dispersion of visual and dramatic units. Consider by way of example all the various audio and visual segments that enter into the part entitled "Istikhbar" (see Schema 1).

Dialog / Image	Sound Off / Music	Series
Lila in the doorway: to her daughter: "Go and play" (S1') Lila, to Ali outside; "I am going to see Djamila's mother" (S1") Lila "sing to us, sing us something, Djamila!" Djamila "I am not from here: I have been your neighbor only since Independence!" Lila: "Ah well, then sing us a song . . . of the South!" (S1''')	Istikhbar

Voice-off Voice-off; Lila, at the potter's house: "I am seeking nothing. . . . I remember only that I used to be!" etc. . . . | Series I (fiction) " " " " " " " " " " |
| The Potter's story (S2')(S"2) | Djamila's Song | Series I |
| Scene with pigeons in the barn (S'3) | B. Bartók, Dance Suite No. 4

Istikhbar | Series II (documentary) |
| Scene with mother and child on the bed: Lila to the child: "Do you want to hear the legend of the pigeons?" (S1"") Little Aicha: "Mommy, I hear them!" (S1"") Lila: "They have fled! They are at your house . . . Here!" (S1"") etc. . . . | | Series III (fiction)

Series I (fiction) |

Dialog / Image	Sounds Off / Music	Sound Track
Games-Laughter All gazes from afar. (S1""") The child falls asleep (S1""") Lila, after some comings and goings, falls asleep under Ali's gaze and dreams of yesterday's war. (S1""")	Istikhbar	Series (Fiction)
Image of events presented as images from Lila's dreams (S'5) (S"5) etc. . . .		Series (documentary)

Schema 1. Istikhbar (Prelude)

Transposed into a diagram, this analytical reading of the *Istikhbar* gives the following schema (see Schema 2).

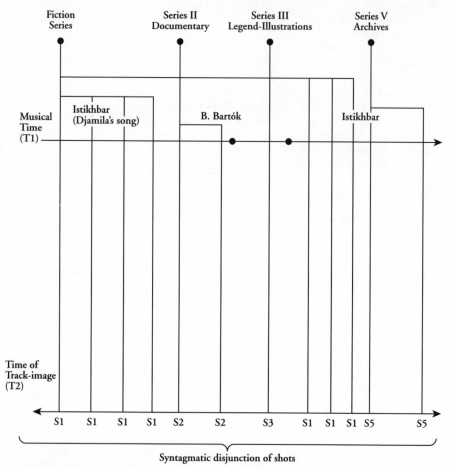

SCHEMA 2. Diagram of Istikhbar (Prelude)

What the diagram shows is that musical time (T1) is not at all congruent with the time of the image (T2). Actually, where the music is arranged according to a relatively continuous tempo (Djamila's Andalusian chant, extract of a Bartók piece, return to the Andalusian chant), the images, in contrast, are multiplied and fragmented at an increasingly rapid pace. Alongside the relative discontinuity of musical series is the systematic disjunction of narrative and documentary segments in a series of irreducibly erratic, disjointed shots. The immediate result is that music—a medium that is often considered one of the most powerful unifying instruments in the construction of narrative coherence and psychological cohesion—begins to falter and actually to unhinge or derail the meaning of each sequence. But what is even more interesting is that the intervals that separate the interspersed segments of each narrative, discursive, or documentary series are never "consonant": the film does not progress in arithmetic order (1–2–3–4 and so on), but rather according to a very idiosyncratic system that distributes small differences within each series: 1', 1'', 1'' ', then 2', then back to 1'' '', 1'' '' ', and so forth. It is not surprising that *La Nouba* contains over seven hundred shots! Instead of classical narrative development, it emphasizes tone: to borrow Roland Barthes's words, "[S]omething articulated and sung, a diction."[15] What dominates and guides the film is no longer meaning or directionality but rather timbre. The word functions less as a word within a sentence than as a sound, a cry or interjection, a password. Made up of fragments (short, discrete shots), which imply an "immediate delight" (Barthes, 98), the film moves forward by fits and starts of the imaginary, by bursts of memories and recollections wrested from the past or appeals projected into the future; it progresses by spurts of images rather than by smooth "phrases" that are nicely organized hierarchically.

This pattern of distribution is what makes the line of force that pervades the film possible: that of a woman who chooses to lie fallow and who allows everything that was submerged in silence by the war to bob to the surface again—women's voices, women's dances, women's laughter. These elements will make it possible, perhaps, to take stock for the first time; this is the chaos that engenders the true labor of mourning and anamnesis, and perhaps of reconciliation with Algeria's painful past.

6

Multilingualism and National "Traits"

I. "Translating or Whiting Out¹ Language": On Khatibi's *Amour Bilingue*

In a passage from his journal dated October 24, 1911, Franz Kafka made the following comment:

> Yesterday it occurred to me that I did not always love my mother as she deserved and as I could, only because the German language prevented it. The Jewish mother is no "Mutter," to call her "Mutter" makes her a little comic (not to herself, because we are in Germany), we give a Jewish woman the name of a German mother, but forget the contradiction that sinks into the emotions so much more heavily. . . . Mama would be a better name if only one didn't imagine "Mutter" behind it. [*Diaries*, 111].

Closer to our own time, in an open, unfinished letter "to an American adult" (1945–46), Bertolt Brecht meditates on the relation to the "spoken American language" that his exile in the United States has forced upon him:

> I have absolutely no hope of ever learning this language. It's not that I don't want to; nor is it that the opportunities to do

99

so are lacking, *it's something else. I've already been trying for some time to express myself like a native.* I realize that, in discussions, I do not say what I want to say, but rather what I am able to say. As one can imagine, this is not the same thing. One will assume that it is merely a matter of a *troubling but temporary state,* and that further study will remedy the problem. It is, alas, *pointless to have hope. It is not just a matter of vocabulary and syntax.* We should speak instead of a *certain habitus,* which I do not foresee the possibility of my acquiring. With a bit more tenacity in the end I might be able to say, using American sentences, that in certain American paintings the sky and the trees give the impression that they are wearing makeup, as if they were worried mostly about their sex appeal. But I would never be able to take on the proper attitude to express these things without shocking [others]. I would have to learn to become a "Nice-fellow." [My emphasis; the word "Nice-fellow" is in English in Brecht's text]

More recently, Abdelkebir Khatibi's book *Amour bilingue* gives a contemporary twist to these semidisillusioned, semitragic reflections. And indeed we cannot help but be struck by the muffled yet insistent presence of a series of formidable problems that each of these writers must face in exile: Can one (learn to) love in a foreign language? Can one think, write, dream, sing in a foreign language? These questions may appear trivial on the surface, yet they have continued to haunt the consciousness and thinking of Maghrebi and African writers (both Francophone and Anglophone) since independence. What is particularly striking in both Kafka and Brecht—and what we find in Khatibi's work in yet another, original guise—is the recurrent use of certain traits to characterize the problems caused by the confrontation of two languages in a diglossic situation. For each of these writers, the question of bilingualism or, more precisely, the question of one language's dominance of another is never posed in the psychological and abstract terms of *expression,* but always rather in the concrete (vital) terms of *Umwelt,* territory, of "ways of *being in the world*": the "feeling" for Kafka; the "*habitus*" for Brecht.

True, Kafka's situation was not the same as Brecht's. Kafka's exile was internal, the result of his situation as a Jewish writer and intellectual living in Czechoslovakia who had to *speak* in Czech (or Yiddish when possible) and *write* in German. Kafka brilliantly analyzed and exploited this impossible situation throughout his entire work, and we find some marvelous echoes of it in his diary: no *Mutter* in German, you see, that just isn't possible, it's ridiculous even, and it rings false! Something else must be found, something else produced. The *basso continuo* of the German language humming behind the mother tongue—the Czech language (which Kafka was one of the few Jewish writers to speak fluently), or Hebrew and Yiddish (a language that "makes us afraid," as Kafka said), which he studied fervently. Kafka was at the crossroads of several languages, and this first "impossible situation" takes on catastrophic dimensions throughout his entire oeuvre: to write burning what one writes while moving forward; writing as "war machine" (in Deleuze's terms) rather than as machine of "expression." It is no longer a matter of finding equivalents of *Mutter, Vater*, and so on; no longer a matter of sending language "to the nursery." It is a question of literally and patiently destroying all the elements of this linguistic primal scene: no more "Mommy-Daddy"; instead, an unprecedented deterritorialization of the cultural anchoring of Papa Goethe's German language and the production of lines of flight in the wake of which words and, more generally, language, "cease to be representative in order to reach toward their extremes or their limits."[2] "To be like a foreigner in one's *own* language," to lead language slowly, step by step, *into the desert*. To use syntax in order to scream, to "give a syntax to screaming." (Ibid., 48) Schizophrenia and language!

Because Brecht's situation was contingent and temporary, it was perhaps easier. After the war, Brecht returned to Europe and found himself rid of the problem that he had been able to capture in its most convoluted aspects during his exile, revealing the rift created deep within the speaking subject by a particular bilingual ("*bi-langue*," or "bi-tongue," as Khatibi calls it)[3] situation. What is remarkable in any case is that while Kafka seems to tone down the "unreasonable" nature of his remarks—*Mutter* is not ridiculous *in and of itself, since we are in Germany,* he says, not without some ambiguity—Brecht makes no bones about it: losing the use of one's mother tongue leads to a veritable *conversion,* one that entails a "Becoming-Nice-Fellow" that does not leave the subject intact: I might be able to say that sky and trees give me the impression that they are wearing makeup as if they were more worried about their *sex appeal* than anything else, but I will never be able to go any further than that. Noon! The hour of the shortest shadow!

These two texts (Kafka's and Brecht's) allow us to situate clearly what is at stake in Khatibi's *Love in Two Languages.* First, for Khatibi and other Maghrebi writers, it has become impossible to write in French, while it is just as impossible to go back to writing in Arabic or, as we shall see in other instances, Berber. And second, it has become necessary to go beyond—even at the risk of madness—the dualism of first-order languages (French and Arabic), and to define a new space of writing and thinking, without being obliged to become a "Nice-Fellow," that is, someone who speaks well, writes well, has mastered the colonizer's language better than the colonizers themselves. For Khatibi, the task at hand is of another sort entirely: Maghrebi writers must begin with the fact that they are not French and that, as Artaud might say, "behind" the language used for the sake of the cause, there will always be another "language under the trees." They must tease out a "rhizosphere" to counter the logosphere that had a tendency to pull them under the rule of signs or strata of expression and always led them to a black hole: the loss of identity, the search for authenticity, and other figures of colonial entrapment. Writers now need to forge instruments that will allow them to say what they *want to say, what they mean,* rather than merely what they *can say, are able to say,* in the language of the former colonizing power; in other words, they need to find a way to escape from the prison house of (colonial) language. This is a problem of translation if ever there was one, and Khatibi has greatly contributed to its painstaking elucidation, stamping it with his immense talents as writer and poet.

Indeed one of the most crucial problems that has dominated Maghrebi (and African) thinking since decolonization has been that of defining a national entity or character, which necessarily implies redefining the geolinguistic space in which the work is produced. It has become imperative to choose among the different languages occupying the terrain: Arabic, promoted to the rank of National Language; French, which for a long time remained the dominant vehicular and referential language (at least in the Maghreb); and the various vernacular languages that, from a certain perspective, also *made you afraid*. For most of the writers concerned, the Gordian knot had to be cut: some stopped writing altogether; others opted for one language or the other; still others moved from one language to the other; but the problem has never been solved. Above all, the internal and external conflicts have never ceased to haunt Maghrebi consciousness.

What is striking in Khatibi's work in general, and in particular in *Love in Two Languages*, is that the sort of *Kampfplatz* represented by the question of (two) languages in the Maghreb suddenly appears to us as *history*. That is, with Khatibi—or, more precisely, *after* Khatibi—it seems that we are faced with something like a BEFORE and AFTER in the history and thinking of North African writing. The intervention or the inscription of *Love in Two Languages* in French-language Maghrebi literature is in this sense an *event* to which we must pay close attention if we hope to be in a position to understand the upheavals that have occurred on the contemporary Maghrebi cultural scene. On the eve of the euphoria that would turn into madness, Nietzsche said that his Zarathustra would "split the history of humanity in two." *Love in Two Languages* is the same kind of gesture; it splits the history of Maghrebi thinking and being *in two*. Not in two camps, or clans, or sides—that had already occurred and no doubt will continue to occur; rather, it splits history in two eras: BEFORE/AFTER. And not for the ever contingent reasons of (greater) beauty or artistic and stylistic genius, but essentially because this time the false transparency or obviousness of the bilingual problem itself is profoundly called into question.

In other words, with Khatibi—and this is the originality of what is at stake in his book—the dilemma is no longer whether one *must* write in Arabic or in French, whether the choice is necessary or contingent, politically right or wrong. Rather, the point is to make visible another (infraliminal) level of writing and thinking that renders the dualistic opposition that has dominated Maghrebi literary production completely obsolete. An agonistic thinker, one who engages in "class struggle in the Taoist's style" (the title of one of Khatibi's works), Khatibi rejected this dualism from the outset, attempting instead to conceive and, literally, to stage a space that had remained unthinkable until then. This is a space where both languages (Arabic and French in this instance, but we shall see that this move does not exclude other languages, such as Berber) can *meet without merging*, where the two graphic gestures confront each other *without* a reconciling *osmosis or synthesis*. If indeed this is a translation, it is not one in the usual sense of the term. The originality at work here (an originality not subject to any *worldly* appreciation or value judgment, we might add) stems from the fact that, for the first time in such a radical and concerted way, the question of belonging to (at least) two languages bursts *theoretically and practically* upon a *space of writing that had previously been dominated by a Manichean vision of language and (cultural, ethnic, religious, and national) identity.*[4]

What is immediately striking in Khatibi's book is that, starting from premises that on the surface are almost identical to those I pointed out in Kafka and Brecht—their bilingual situation at the intersection of at least two cultures and three civilizations—he opens the work by radically overthrowing the dualistic framework of those premises. As he elaborates his notion of the "bi-langue," Khatibi immediately presents himself as that fortunate writer who can (only) love, think, take pleasure in the space or interval opened by his need—*ab initio*—to hear/ see/write in both languages *at once*:

> *Bi-langue?* My luck, my own individual abyss and my lovely amnesiac energy. An energy I *don't experience* as a deficiency, curiously enough. Rather, it's my *third ear*. Had I experienced some kind of breakdown, I liked to think I would have developed in the *opposite direction, I would have grown up in the dissociation peculiar to any unique language*. That's why I admire the gravity of the blind man's gestures and the desperate

impossible love the deaf man has for language. [*Love in Two Languages*, 5; my emphasis]

We will need to return to the specific nature of this gesture and to the love—desperate, impossible—that such a move implies. For now, let us simply state that, while it may cause forgetfulness or amnesia (anamnesis?), the "bi-langue" ability the narrator-reciter has to see, hear, and write *double* is never a source of anguish, of destruction, or loss of identity in disjunction. The narrator always sees double, that's all there is to it: the one/the many; the spoken word/the written word; the body/language; the same/the other; Arabic/French, and so on: "From that moment on, the scenario of the doubles was created. One word: now two: it's already a story." (5)

It is immediately necessary to note, however, that by this very gesture, Khatibi strikes out with one stroke of his pen all the guilt that attends the Maghrebi writer's need to write in French, to translate his or her local situation into French. In other words, *"need" here takes on an active meaning*: by exposing the target language (French) to a process that turns it completely upside down, the writer who is (writes in) bi-langue no longer suffers the use of the French language. Instead, he or she needs it desperately as a means to an end: to delight in it (*en jouir*), obviously, but at the same time to extract from it something that, without it, could never occur: to spell, to *translate* "the no-name and the no-foundation," as Khatibi calls it, that the nonworldly treatment of the question raised by the bi-langue carries in its wake:

> I baptized you: *bi-langue*. And now *pluri-langue*. To sum up, a question of translation, to be deducted from my sleepless nights. I spelled out the no-name and the no-foundation as elements of my ordeal, everywhere where the incommunicable held me close. Then I passed through the innocence of things, the confusion of tongues and every preceding language of revelation. [101]

Under these conditions, we might expect to see Khatibi write in such a way as to subvert the syntax and vocabulary of the target language (French in this instance). In other words, we might expect him to employ multiple references to Arabic, to "dialectize" or "Maghrebize" French with the intent of making it *render* what it had a tendency to drive out of its own sphere.[5] Yet nothing of the sort occurs in *Love in Two Languages*. Khatibi's writing is classical. He does not mix the two languages. On the contrary: Affirming his belonging to two cultures, his bias toward the words of both languages, Khatibi seems at first to give French every possible chance of performing with the greatest transparency:

> A certain unity of language was achieved in her body. Her moods, which changed from day to day, were limpid, considerate, prodigiously unexpected. Was the great suffering ended? How about renunciation? Affirmation, there was only affirmation? [107]

So there is no suffering, no heartbreak, no renunciation: There is affirmation, nothing but affirmation! And in point of fact, we won't see any of the "technonarcissistic" devices that characterize so many so-called modern Francophone works. No typographic affectation, no portmanteau words, no conspicuous lexical or syntactical contortions. The text—opaque at times but always "smooth," "flowing,"—never lets itself get caught up in those games of syntactical pyrotechnics or lexical innovation that characterize so many contemporary European and African texts. "All was white with the day's thudding brightness"! And yet, as we read and reread the text (a single reading, as we shall see, is by nature faulty), we cannot help but hear a kind of creaking noise that constantly short-circuits the French word, haunting the vocabulary and making French syntax vacillate according to a rhythm and a scansion whose purpose remains unclear. Something is moving, constantly shifting, thereby scrambling our reading of the text so that we cannot assign it (or bring it back to) a (geographical or rhetorical) place. "Un mouvement de déport" (Barthes)—a "trans-lation" interferes with our reading, making our access to the text even more difficult. At every moment, we have the sense of having switched languages, having moved from one language to another, without our being able to say how (by means of what artifice? what magic?) this has happened: "This time he closed his eyes before paying concentrated attention: he felt a presence there, invisible, inaudible. No hissing , no sound, but presently a silent music, a song within the sea." (31)

A question arises here: Have we changed languages, or is this simply a new way of translating? In *Love in Two Languages*, the narrator mentions an author of whom he is fond, and we might apply what he says here to Khatibi's own writing: "I once read a bizarre author: to rid himself of his teacher, he *switched languages*. A stroke of genius, that rare mutation." (115)

It may indeed be more economical to say that Khatibi has *switched languages*, but he has done so in a breathtaking move that does not consist in either a reterritorializing return to Arabic or an Arabicization of French, but instead allows language to *see double*, making it "loucher" in the active sense of that French word, which means "to peer, to eye." He subjects the French language to a system that enables it to *translate the untranslatable*, to express the inexpressible. In a word, he wrests it from the metaphysical and precritical state in which it was supposed to be merely a *secondary* tool for the expression of a single and/or unified mind, culture, or subject. Among other things, then, Khatibi wants to make language *loucher* (to look cross-eyed), to make it *louche* (shifty):

> LOUCHE (Lathe): "A tool used to enlarge pre-existing holes."
> [*Littré*]

Khatibi's project is to write like a turner (of foreign languages) and to turn French into a language that *makes you afraid*. Again, not by fooling with typography or manipulating syntax and vocabulary, but by putting the French language in the position of a supplement, that is, making it undergo a dual movement that once and for all wrests it from any possible metaphysical salvaging, any expressive co-opting. This dual movement consists of the following:

1. Pulling the French language toward calligraphy, the grapheme, the interval. In a word, making constant use of "spacing,"[6] something that the French language's normal mode of functioning precludes. I shall come back to this point.

2. Making it see/hear the other language (Arabic) in the *between-two-languages*, in the breach opened by this very spacing, without ever returning to a simple point of origin.

This kind of translation is much more revolutionary and effective than any that involves making language howl or putting it in a state of exhaustion. The end of the longest error, the culminating point of humanity: INCIPIT ZARATHUSTRA!

I would first like to attempt to support this particular reading by analyzing the layout of the various elements that can be read/seen even before the reader plunges into the narrative itself. In order to do so, I shall begin with a short description of this layout.

On the binding—visible, readable only when the book is closed upon its secret and placed on a bookshelf—we can read *Amour bilingue* and Abdelkebir Khatibi printed in black; nothing in particular draws our attention to this. As soon as we become interested in the cover, however, we inevitably notice a certain number of features that slow our reading down and which we must take into account.

First, the placement, or more precisely, the even distribution of proper names and titles as they appear on the cover (somewhat like film credits): ABDELKEBIR KHATIBI in black capital letters; then, just underneath in blood red bold letters, AMOUR BILINGUE; then, under that, in a position of anamorphosis, an elegant interlacing of Arabic letters—unintelligible for the person who does not read Arabic—an arabesque that the bilingual reader can *easily* decipher as the literal translation of the book's title: *'Achk Ellisanain* [Amour bilingue]. A final comment on this point: Whereas there are no vowels in the calligraphic translation of the words of the title into Arabic, the dots that allow us to distinguish a Kef from a Fa, for example—in other words, the characters that determine the system of graphic differences in Arabic and make each entity a discrete character—are marked in red. The red of *Love in Two Languages*: a metonymic transfer that opens the play of vertiginous shifts that, from one language to the other, constantly refer to a spacing (*espace-ment*) that does not legitimately belong to either language individually. This is an exercise in *translation*—in the legal rather than literal sense here—that constantly forces each language to appear before the court of the other,[7] signaling now the separate elements, now the gaps, now the distinguishing intervals. In this case, it is color that is the distinguishing feature.

More striking still, however, is that this complex process of translation or anamorphotic (nontautological) transformation somehow even sweeps along in its movement and its fury the name of the series in which the book was published. If in fact the cryptic, *unreadable* (for the monolingual reader), supplementary sign is nothing more than the deferred or displaced translation of the title, there is no real reason not to read the title of the series, FATA MORGANA—written on the cover in a position *perfectly symmetrical* to Khatibi's name and in the same font—as if it were a coded translation of the author's name: Abdelkebir Khatibi/Fata Morgana.

> Morgan le Fay: Castle of Morgan le Fay; name given to the *mirage* on the Italian coast, *where* castles, palaces, cities, etc., seem to appear over the sea. . . .
> ETYM: Celtic name. M. de la Villemarqué offers Breton MOR, very strong, and GAN, brilliant, *ital. Fata Morgana*, a mirage. . . .
> *Morganatic*, adj. From Germanic law. Morganatic marriage, *marriage of the left hand*, a marriage in which a man marrying a woman of inferior rank gives her his left hand in the wedding ceremony. [Littré]

Above I said that there was an appearance before a judge—the language of the other; but the encounter here—both fortuitous and necessary—between the French, German, Celtic, and Italian languages allows us to discover that the *bi-langue* is also the celebration of a marriage—"Morganatic" indeed!—between a language of inferior rank—a minor language, let's say—and one of superior rank, a "major language: a marriage in which the writer marrying a foreign language gives it his left hand in the writing ceremony."

Now let us attempt to translate some of the expectations that accompany such premises. We are immediately struck by the fact that a certain economy of signature and paternity is challenged by the metonymic circulation of the proper names: ABDELKEBIR KHATIBI/FATA MORGANA/THE MIRAGE. The mirage of the proper name and (the transparency) of the origin is always already doubled, always already entwined with the other, with *its own* subversive other: "the mirage of androgyny," as Khatibi so rightly calls it, opening thereby a theme to which we shall return.

And in fact, at the end of the short epigraph, we find this very important remark (in parentheses): "(This beginning of a text seemed to consume the storyteller, who read it ceaselessly. Each time he approached this beginning which excluded him: a story with no protagonist: or if there was one, it was the story itself, which heard itself utter the lone command: Start over)." (5–6)

Here we are only on page 6 of the book, and page 4 of the narrative proper—four pages of writing are taken up by the epigraph that began on page 3 with this sentence that "wrote itself": "(He left, he came back, he left again. He decided to leave for good, the book close upon itself)." (3)

This is the first of Khatibi's *invitations au voyage,* and it serves as a kind of user's manual for, or initiation to, reading (this text). For we, too, begin reading the book casually, only to discover, with each turn of a page or a phrase, the need to go back *to the beginning,* and we risk seeing the *book* this time close upon itself. And so we have been warned: at any time the text may slip away from the reader, may withdraw because of our blindness to its mode of functioning or our deafness to the rhythm that constantly marks, unmarks, and re-marks the slightest sign. FATA MORGANA! A morganatic movement of temporalization or temporization—of delay and withdrawal, but also of eternal return—does not allow us to doze as we read, and requires us to find a new way of reading.

It must be repeated: once again, any transparency between word and thing, name and being, the signifieds of one language and those of another, is immediately blocked or blurred, as is any impulse we might have to relate the mode of spacing of the book's constitutive elements to a simple origin. The nonsymmetrical (anamorphotic) reflexivity brings pressure to bear on each signifier, and thus the self-presence of the enunciating subject, as well as that of the addressee, is challenged. Indeed, if each word always and immediately refers to a *double* that transforms it and transports it elsewhere (to another language, another writing, another culture, and so on), what becomes of the present (of reading), the future (of interpretation), and the past (of an always deferred belonging to a culture or language of so-called origins)? This is sheer reflection, reverberation, and dissemination as far as the eye can see: "permanent permutation," as Khatibi writes, with no hope of any dialectical reterritorialization. Once we realize this, we understand why this attempt *to write with the left hand*, why this enormous effort to do battle with what Khatibi calls the "bi-langue"—and the dual scene that it requires—necessarily implies a constant detour through and return to the figures of death, emptiness, and dream. For one does not choose one's bilingualism: rather, it is thrust upon one; and one is seduced by the bi-langue and its destructive dissemination:

> He didn't forget that in his own lexicon, the word for "seduction" (*fitna*) is a homograph for both the word for "war" and the word for "seduction" itself, for that knightly passion celebrated by those who go off alone into the desert, a passion for the unknown beloved.
> In this respect, seduction carried them to a dual stage, delighting in language's sensuousness. What could they know? . . . How to determine from the smallest word, the least deed the order of mortal law—or its disorder? Death: and to find a way to live in this word, it was necessary to go over all the bi-langue's power of destruction. In his mother tongue, death is a child's idea of heaven, a celestial hereafter. It was his duty to reseed himself not with this charming reminder but rather with the illusion of invisible angels, thereby glorifying, celebrating every loving encounter. [*Love in Two Languages*, 11]

The love of language thus necessarily refers to a *double scene,* one that both enchants the reciter and, simultaneously, bears within its seductive *fitna* nothing less than death and the void: the morganatic book as a topography of the desert!

And so, the book has never begun (to be read): in any case, it is obvious that, however we approach it—as monolinguals or as bilinguals, for example—the book has always already been aware of notions of beginning, middle, and end. The slightest inattention to the play of permanent transformation and translation, and we risk finding it closed (to all readings). In the case of *Love in Two Languages*, beginning is always *beginning anew*. To decipher a word or expression is always to *translate*, that is, to transport the reader into another space, a space that is *other*. We have already identified this gesture. But is this all? Can we assume that we are "quits" with what the frontispiece monogram has to tell us about the perpetual displacement of which the least little sign bears the disseminating trace? In other words, can we ever open or close a book that asks to be read in the mode of deferral? To answer this question, we must open the book yet again, and *return* to the beginning(s), where new mirages await us.

Indeed, after the (blank, white) flyleaf in the French version, the book opens on a page where we find only the two words of the title: *Amour bilingue*. This time, they are written in smaller (black) letters than the (red) ones on the cover. The rest is blank. Yet once we reach the fifth page, one particular element attracts our attention: page 5 is almost a *replica* of the cover. But this time, whereas the ("proper") names Abdelkebir Khatibi and Fata Morgana have changed neither format nor color, the title, inscribed in the same place—in other words, mirroring the title on the cover—is black on white. The monogram punctuated with red has disappeared, replaced by the name Abdeslam Genouni (the calligrapher) and the word *Calligraphies*. There are two calligrams in all: the one on the cover and the one on page 7, where it takes up almost *all the available space*, haunting almost transparently with its shadow and/or its number, the place left vacant by the suppression of the ʿACHK ELLISSANAIN on the cover.

I do not believe I am giving in to some kind of interpretative delirium when I insist on the fact that the way these elements of the text are laid out on the page is neither gratuitous nor fortuitous. They act out a *mise en abyme*, referring essentially to the text's own mode of operation; they refer to what in the text and from the text must remain literally intractable. They mark the place of a difference or, more precisely, of a *différance* that only a patient reading can, not domesticate or co-opt, but perhaps simply render perceptible or possible. In sum, the third ear in Khatibi's work is primarily the ability to read not only *between* the lines but also *through* the lines and even *through the pages*:

the power to fade in and fade out, to move through the pages and to reveal—in the theological or theophanic sense, rather than in the sense of what is hidden *behind*—or at least not just that—like an X ray, that which until then had escaped from the naturalist (expressive) and instrumentalist (communicative) vision of language.

However, we should not jump ahead; rather, we should rephrase the question. What does page 5 propose for our reading? What does it propose for our rereading? Except for the colors in play (and the appearance of the calligrapher's name), page 5 first proposes that we "read" (?) an absence, that we "see" a blank—the empty space left open by the disappearance of the monogram '*Achk Ellissanaïn*— that is immediately taken over by its magnified shadow. For in fact, written in thick calligraphic characters—but can such metaphysically charged notions of "character" or "discrete line" still be used in this case?—the new form of the Arabic translation of the title cannot help but show through the great blank space that has been produced by the disappearance/appearance of the monogram from the cover. This aspect of things is of course not without consequence; at the same time that it overcodes the *visible* dimension of what is *readable*, because of its very absence, the transparency of the monogram designates, all the while canceling it out, that which should remain *un*apparent: the blank/ white space, the irreducible gap that separates and divides *each letter* of the other language, the silent difference without which the language could not happen. We might point out that it is this supplemental trace—which in its very evanescence brings blankness, nothingness to light and opens the text—that constitutes one of the fundamental processes of the Khatibian text.

Like Mallarmé's fold, wing, feather, page, veil, and so on as Jacques Derrida has described them for us in his "La double séance," the "excess of mark" and the "margin of sense" of the monogram that opens Khatibi's work "is not simply one valence among others in the series of Arabic words transcribed and translated into French in Khatibi's text, although it is also inserted there." (*Dissémination*, 283) Because it translates without returning us to the same, since, due to its appearance/ disappearance, it causes blanks and gaps to appear in what the target language obliterates, the monogram constantly alludes to that which *exceeds* any language, *all the while designating* the law of its mode of operation *in an atopical cipher or mark*. Henceforth, the writing machine of the bi-langue will take charge of putting this impossible logic to work. So *blankness/whiteness*—and then what?

> All was white with the day's thudding brightness. He felt extremely tired. Only a little while before, sitting silently, he was meditating or dreaming *with an open book before him*. The slide of light: as the day wore on, he had the impression that the pages he turned were blank.
> ... He began to read again. His glance passed over the letters, so much so *that he grew dizzy among their graphic traces, with each folio of the magnificent book*. [*Love in Two Languages*, 38–9; my emphasis; translation modified]

In order to (begin to) read the book, perhaps we should first have folded the cover in two, thereby obtaining a figure that might have resembled a Rorschach inkblot if the images were symmetrical after a simple fold, and if the colors (ink and script) mixed and mingled. However, as we've already seen, the *morganatic projection*—left-handed or gauche—from the upper to the lower half of the cover does not return to the same; the morganatic projection mixes neither colors nor languages. As a sort of "geometric plane" ("géométral") of these two heterogeneous languages, the projection means that the color of one—the color that adorns its blinding expression—re-marks the pertinent characteristics of the other, that is, it makes it *pertinent*. So the Book (of writing) is a morganatic test, an a-psychological, a-topical text of the bi-langue.

This is where we were when we started the book. But now (on page 5) we are faced with a lateral translation, not a fold or projection of a page onto itself based on a nonlocatable center, but rather a print, a double exposure of an entire page in tinted laid paper, a deforming trace or magical block. Anamorphosis. Fold upon fold; between-the-two (pages) another blank page—*Fata Morgana*. It clearly appears that even if it is in permanent withdrawal or retreat, the monogram overdetermines the text by forever postponing any attempt to drive it toward a single sense or theme, or a unified space (here and now). At every moment, *and due to the very fact of its initial appearance,* "plans are overturned." (Kateb Yacine) There is no longer any self-presence (of the narrator, or the reader), nor is there any transparency between the text and its signs. There is only infinite permutation, endless reverberation, and the play of blinding mirrors. It is true that this aspect of things (only) concerns the arrangement of the first seven pages, pages after which no calligrams appear to haunt the text with their intrusive presence.

So what of the text itself? That is, how can we claim that the text is overdetermined by a monogram that *all in all only appears twice* and, moreover, is not even legible to a monolingual reader? It is here that we must be less attentive to the frequency of a word or a sign and more attentive to its *syntactic* status in the overall economy of a text, in the *code* that is at work. Georges Bataille said that one had to attend to the "toil" (*besogne*) of "words." With Khatibi we must give our undivided attention to the toil of signs and their disposal within the general economy of the text.

What occurs when the text opens is part of a complex (metonymic) mechanism of displacement—a veritable *transference*—of the differentiating power of the monogram to the foreign language. One of the major effects of this transference is that it restores the foreign language—transformed by this very operation into the target language—to the original spacing that silently deployed discrete signs, semes, and punctuation marks and consigned them all to the symbolic.

In order to illustrate what I have just stated a bit too succinctly, I will refer to a passage characteristic of the writing in *Amour bilingue*. Let us go back to the epigraph once again: It is dark, the narrator is at home, in bed. Perhaps he was sleeping and is suddenly awakened by a nightmare or an epiphany:

> It was then that the words fluttered in a parade in front of him, then they came crashing down on top of one another: language was mad.
>
> Get up? He couldn't: instead of the fragments of a word, there was room for nothing visible: the sea itself had sunk in the night. And in French—his foreign language—the word

for "word," *mot,* is close to the one for "death," *la mort;* only one letter is missing: the succinctness of the impression, a syllable, the ecstasy of a stifled sob. Why did he believe that language is more beautiful, more terrible, for a foreigner?

He calmed down instantly when an Arabic word, *kalma,* appeared, *kalma* and its scholarly equivalent, *kalima,* and the whole string of its diminutives which had been the riddles of his childhood: *klima.* . . . The diglossal *kal(I)ma* appeared again without *mot's* having faded away or disappeared. Within him, both words were observing each other, preceding what had now become the rapid emergence of memories, fragments of words, onomatopoeias, garlands of phrases, intertwined to the death: undecipherable. *The scene is still silent.* [*Love in Two Languages,* 3–4]

I have cited this long passage in its entirety because it so marvelously stages what I have called the transference of the *Dunamis* of the monogram to the text. Khatibi give us a deciphered version, spelling out word for word the disseminating logic of this phenomenon of the destructive contamination of the foreign language's transparency. Yet this time, not only are the blanks and gaps that the foreign language had to repress (to shut out) in order to express (itself) exhibited, but language becomes crazed at the end of the morganatic test, since *in French the* mot *(word) is always close to* mort *(death).* "Behind" it all—but still *trans*-parent—is that which forever disappears and reappears *in the holes already begun,* yet another sign, another word of the other language.

Are these once again the effects of the turner's tool? In what sense? The monogram displays the invisible by erasing itself, by withdrawing; the blank, the margins, the folds, the gaps moments ago were insignificant; now they haunt each word, each tiny interstice of the foreign language, which now begins to signify between the lines, or if one prefers, *between the letters.* As Khatibi says, "[T]he word for 'word,' *mot* is close to the one for 'death,' *la mort;* only one letter is missing." Such is the power of the monogram's *eruption* between the lines and letters, and through the transparent pages of tinted vellum. This monogram—always about to surface as it meets the characters of the foreign tongue, its mode of appearing being by definition unpredictable and uncontrollable—may *at any moment* cause one or several figures of the inferior language to loom up *in the blank spaces that it clears*. Like the syncategoreme "BETWEEN" that Derrida analyzed, the monogram's role cannot be reduced to a purely syntactic or semantic game. This is because "beyond its syntactic function, by re-marking its semantic void (illegible for the monolingual; literal and redundant translation for the bilingual), it begins to signify. Its semantic void *signifies*, but it signifies spacing and articulations; its meaning is the possibility of syntax and it structures the play of meanings. *Neither purely syntactic nor purely semantic, it marks the articulated opening of this opposition*" (Derrida, op.cit., 251–2), between two languages, or more precisely between two systems of intervals that forever return to the void, the breach, and the blank that condition their appearance. In terms of typography, the monogram belongs to the category of BLANKS and determines a strange, "other" writing practice. (Khatibi) We are now in a position to name this practice by referring to a sphere that *Amour bilingue* has never stopped secretly seeking out—precisely that hidden art of typography and calligraphy.

"When it is necessary to move one line away from another, or to separate, as with footnotes, a more important from a lesser text, it is with a lead—blank lines composed of quads—that we increase the spacing. This is called 'to white out' (*blanchir*) or 'to cast white' (*jeter du blanc*). (J. Claye, *Manuel de l'apprenti compositeur*, Paris, 1931, 21)

If the above definitions did not really exist, one of Khatibi's readers would have had to invent them to account for the kind of writing we find in *Amour bilingue* for the first time. What characterizes the power and the beauty of Khatibi's text is perhaps most of all the art of "casting white," of "whiting out" the French language that he loves, and *through which* he tells of his love (otherwise inexpressible) for the other (language), *his* other language. He *whites out* language not (only) in the simple metaphorical sense of the term—for example, by wresting it from a history in which it had become synonymous with deculturation and/ or acculturation—but also in the *most technical* and *formal* sense. Since his project is to *separate* one language from another and to *detach* the (erstwhile) superior text from the inferior one, Khatibi calls upon the disruptive power of Arabic calligraphy *in a French linguistic context*; by "increasing the intervals" of the "foreign" language, he clears an unprecedented space where what is called the mother tongue can make itself heard. In a way, it is as if he were sideswiping the French language to make it exhibit characteristics that in customary usage remain completely excluded: on the one hand, its own system of blanks and gaps, but also, more important, the repression and exclusion that French has represented for the Maghrebi (or African) Francophone writer. Whiting out the French language consists essentially, then, in *relieving the guilt* Maghrebi writers feel when they resort to the "paper language" (Kafka) that French represents for them. It also makes the French language the instrument of a new mental topography, what Khatibi calls *une pensée autre*, a way of thinking differently or otherwise.

Perhaps now it is easier to understand what we mean when we say that a calligram is never a simple translation of the terms of another text or language; to pursue the metaphor a bit further, we might say that Khatibi makes the Arabic calligram play the same role as quads in typography:

> Thus there are, in addition to fonts and characters, various devices that are not apparent when printed and that are part of the blanks: quads, em quads, en quads, the spaces we have just mentioned.
>
> The spaces separate the letters; they come in many strengths or thicknesses. The em quads go at the head of the line, and the quads at the end of the line, when the line is not completed by text. [Claye, 18–9)]

Morganatic writing, the staging of the bi-langue in *Amour bilingue*, consists in adding one more quad to the bi-langue writer-compositor's kit, but this quad—a space, a gap—is not content merely to intervene between words or to arrange the empty spaces between lines of text. Rather, this other quad, while not apparent in the printing (of the text in the strict sense) and content to work in the margins, subverts the entire economy of the foreign language. In sum, it makes it do and say the impossible. It almost makes it speak Arabic, Pidgin, Pied-noir, and so on. Having whited out French, Khatibi now finds himself in a position to claim for himself the saying Kafka attributed to Madam Kluge, with a one-word difference: "You see, I speak all languages but . . . in French!" "Il se calma/Kalma/Klima/Kal(i)ma."

Now we can return to the text we had to set aside a moment ago. It explains much better than we ever could the necessity and the toil of the calligram:

> He began to read again. His glance passed over the letters, so much so that he grew dizzy with the blackness of each word, with the magnificent folios of the book. Instantaneously and at the same time, it seemed to him that although he understood and could decipher what he read, nevertheless at the heart of his reading was an intangible word not in the text. Worrisome intangibility with which one blow destroyed pages, words, lines, and punctuation through the agency of a black spot floating between his eyes and the book.
>
> Soon, the book would light up around this word he still couldn't make out, this word which left the book to seep away from its pages and to mark by its passing the squint his glance produced so that the sign of the night would shine before him. Night entered and exited the book, somehow erasing the white with the black. Still, he could not tear his eyes away. [*Love in Two Languages*, 39]

Signifying the spacing, the fold, the interval opened by the whiting out of French, the calligram makes use of a logic, that of the bi-langue, that a *purely statistical analysis* can no longer account for. As Derrida said, the "between," strictly speaking, does not exist; it is by nature plural, pluralizing *and* disseminating, itself disseminated. And so the power of the monogram is in no way dependent on how often it appears. And whether Khatibi was or was not the compositor of the mock-up for the book makes no difference. The reference to the calligrapher, the repetition of the calligram after the flyleaf, and the particular way the elements are laid out: all these are summoned by the text itself, just as they summon the reading and cryptic writing of the text they order. We might also note in support of this hypothesis that while

Arabic words, handwritten or printed, are always *linked*—"entwined to the death," as Khatibi says—this is only rarely the case of *printed* French. Thus the intralinguistic and interlinguistic gap between the two languages now makes the rules for a (new) game of languages. At stake in this game is not only the life and death of the narrator/reciter, but also, as we shall soon see, his (psychological and sexual) identity, his (national and cultural) belonging. This is the paragrammatic dimension opened up by whiting out language and by bringing the bi-langue into play.

"He calmed down instantly when an Arabic word, *kalma*, appeared, *kalma* and its scholarly equivalent, *kalima*, and the whole string." This example plainly shows that the *ana*grammatic or *para*-grammatic interplay at work in *Amour bilingue* is neither contingent nor illusory: separating the letters of the foreign tongue is always a dangerous game that, even within its mad gesture, still touches upon a Reality:[8] that of *homophony*: Where the monolingual writer/reader can and must hear/see nothing (between the lines or the letters), the bi-langue writer watches (the whole economy of) language collapse. "That's why I admire the gravity of the blind man's gestures and the desperate impossible love the deaf man has for language," says Khatibi. This demands a veritable "mutation of thought."

Now my previous remarks on the alteration of time that becomes a *temporization* and a forever deferred gesture can take on their full meaning. The whiting out of French hollows out the word (*mot*) and outlines there the death (*mort*) that lives within it as it gives the narrator (always doubled by the reader and the writer) the capacity and the ability to always see double, in a *mise en abyme* of words beneath words. At the same time, it establishes a new relation to time in general, *and to the time of reading in particular.* For reading is sometimes *slowed*, sometimes greatly *accelerated* by the telescoping effect of letters and their accompanying phonemes; the bi-langue thus becomes a matter and an instrument of speed, a divinity of *word-processing.* Writing-reading, but with two hands, listening, but with a third ear. Writing and reading in this case are not only stereophonic or stereographic, but above *all stroboscopic and strobophonic:* a reading or writing *between* the lines, *between* phrases, in margins, and so on.

Nostalgia he liked to think about and pronounce in Arabic: *hanîne*, anagram for a doubled pleasure. He broke the word down into its elements: "h," an aspirant from the pharynx, then a murmured "a" before the "n-î-ne," modulation sustained by the long "i." Pronouncing this word, repeating it was a breath of a kiss in his throat, a regular unbroken breath. A vocal ecstasy; a euphoric call, for him alone a song. [*Love in Two Languages*, 7–8]

Like the calligram that conditions its appearance, Khatibi's *anagram* also reveals itself to be ambiguous; as J. C. Milner says, "[O]n the one hand, the anagram tells of how homophony belongs to language, but on the other, it also tells of how it is inassimilable"; or in Khatibi's terminology, it tells of the "intractable difference." Because it is always necessarily constructed with (at least) two languages, two graphic systems that are deaf and blind to each other, and because it can only occur (or not) in what *exceeds* any language, the Khatibian anagram is always a manifestation of a dehiscence (in the being that speaks, writes), of an "even more," as Milner says, that will always fill the breath and cut off speech: "Bearing the weight of an invisible god, a single gesture: to interrupt him, render him speechless." (*Love in Two Languages*, 24) Thus the need to invent another way of writing, to create a new "style," as one says, but also to cross barriers that separate different modes of writing and different literary genres, precisely by *doubling* writing with writing: two languages, two writings, two thoughts working *at once*:

> Later on, I learned Braille and the languages of the handicapped. Perhaps I'm capable of writing only for bilingual cripples: in any case, it will be too late to get back together with me. Did I lose you before I ever met you? I must definitely have my story translated into Braille before the computer has swept up everything into the communicable. [*Love in Two Languages*, 24]

As I said earlier, it's all a matter of speed, but of course in a relative sense, since "handicapped bilinguals" can always go more quickly (or more slowly). Their favorite place is one that monolinguals generally bypass, since they don't possess the *bi-langue*'s formidable machine for exploring time and space, and its gift of double vision.

By immediately inscribing the dissolving figure of the calligram in an act of anamorphic translation, Khatibi not only has undertaken to make a dent in the domination of one language or one culture by another; he has dedicated himself as well to an even more revolutionary task, that of founding a "different, other thought" (*pensée autre*). In his own words, this thought is "essentially MINORITARIAN, FRAGMENTARY, and INCOMPLETE." In short, the task is to establish a way of thinking the *milieu*—middle and between—that is not "neutral"; to establish, again in Khatibi's terms, a mode of thought that is "riddled with margins, gaps, and silent questions." (*Maghreb pluriel*, 17)

> "Our" thought, toward which we are turning, is not located and does not move within the circle of (Western) metaphysics, nor according to Islamic theology, but at the margin of them both. It is a margin *on the alert*. [Ibid.]

For the *bi-langue*, then, writing and thinking definitely do not imply a return to or within the self, but "nothing, nothing but critical transformations." (Ibid., 24) This new shift in priorities, places, properties, and reappropriations (of word, thought, language, and civilization) cannot take place without putting into effect a new economy of sexual identity. Indeed, if everything (in language, in the Maghrebi self) is always composed of at least two languages, two cultural scenes, and two bodies (*Habitus*), then no boundary can be drawn to separate one sex from another. In whiting out the relationship to language (to languages in general), Khatibi simultaneously whites out the relationship to sexual difference. To simplify, one cannot venture to change the status of language (use) without also "changing (its) sex" (here I am only putting into perspective this very important theme of Khatibian "poetics"):

> One day—and this only recently—he loved a woman, changed sex. Sex in circumcised sex, two-tongued sex, like a snake. From his anus emerged the face of an invisible god. He was then violated by the foreign tongue. Thrown to the ground, he suffered hideously. But—bizarre sensation—he was behind his

violator, not taking his turn as penetrator but rather pene-
trated by the tongue's orgasm—his homosexuality filed in the
dictionaries of the whole world. [*Love in Two Languages*, 47]

*Mam ware ein besserer Name, Wenn man nur hinter ihm nicht
"Mutter" sich vorstellte!* " 'Mama' would be a better name, if only one
did not imagine 'Mutter' *behind*" this word, said Kafka. One day someone will have to write the history of this *sich vorstellte*, of the "one
behind" who haunts our languages and our discourse, of this invisible
God who violates the transparency of language (to itself) and calls into
question the self-identity of all things. The atopical figure of the androgyne in Khatibi's writing is one of those histories, inseparable from
the shifts brought on by the *bi-langue*: "To translate impurity into purity, prostitution into androgyny was an adventure which had to be
lived without holding back in any way. He wandered from country to
country, from body to body, from language to language." (*Love in Two
Languages*, 23)

Such an adventure demands to be lived to the fullest, because
here too it is not so much a question of adopting one sex or the other,
plunging into one sex or the other—this would not in itself constitute
an adventure, and would assume the question of sexual difference resolved. Rather, it is more a matter of maintaining oneself *between* the
sexes, all sexes. Not bisexual or transsexual, but androgynous; not one
and the other, but the other of both sexes (of both languages). Since
the two sexes do not exist as such by nature, the situation of the androgyne—as well as that of the *bi-langue* writer—is essentially connected
to its mixed status (*metaxu*), as Plato said of the sophist. The mix is a
fold *in relation to which* there is man and woman, male and female,
being and nonbeing, and so on. The wandering that such a figure, or
such a writing, calls for, and the expenditure they require, result precisely from this mixed status. To echo Alain Grosrichard's analysis of the
status of the Eunuch—another mixed figure that has haunted Western
writing on the Orient[9]—we might say that in the logic of multiple displacements that the *bi-langue* mobilizes, the androgyne

> is neither the non-being, nor the being-like-all, but the very
> figure of otherness itself, the Other that arouses all others, the

initiator of their desire, the link or the break that puts the sexes [languages] in relation to one another, and makes this relation both necessary and impossible, since the androgyne (is that not its very function?) is always between one and the other and, so to speak, in the middle of the bed—even and especially when we are sure that it is not. [Grosrichard, 201–2]

What then is an androgyne, Madam, if not also a specialist in mimetics and a producer of simulacra, a being who belongs to the fantastic, and produces before your eyes mirages that leave you lost in wonder?

Who cannot see henceforth that I have taken a route by which, ceaselessly and effortlessly, I will continue as long as there is ink and paper? However, the reader should make no mistake about it; in proposing this reading of Khatibi's book—really just a few of its pages—I have not really interpreted it; rather, I have lined my fantasies up alongside those of Khatibi, Derrida, Mallarmé, Milner, Montaigne, Yacine, Grosrichard, and the devil.

2. On Khatibi's Notion of the "Professional Traveler"

One of the abiding features in Khatibi's work is his emphasis on the *gap* that exists for Maghrebi writers between the languages they *speak* and the language they *write*. In my analysis of *Amour bilingue* in the previous section, I attempted to underscore some of the stakes inherent in his problematic of the *bi-langue*. In this section, my hypothesis is different: I would like to show that it is the specific geopolitical position accorded to the *bi-langue* writer that determines the way he or she treats history whenever it is conceived as the history of a *people*, a ("real") *individual,* or a ("fictional") *character.* If we accept the idea that Khatibi's work is not really fiction *stricto sensu*—can *Un été à Stockhom, Le tryptique de Rabat,* and *Le livre du sang* really be classified as novels?—and if we acknowledge that his work belongs equally to the poem, the essay, and the autobiography, we are led to draw certain inevitable conclusions: The *bi-langue* writer is above all someone who, because he or she lives between at least two languages, two borders, and thus two different *ethos*, can no longer belong to *a single* history, people, or country, but is instead a passenger—or perhaps, better yet, a frontier runner (*passeur*)—of a space-time that, while it *is* the product of artistic creation, is not for all that a simple fiction or myth. Just because it is not yet actual does not mean that this space-time, this world, is not real. As I suggested in the introduction to this book, the writer must experience a virtual space and the site of a very specific experimentation that will transform him or her into what Khatibi calls a "professional traveler."

And so, using several of Khatibi's texts, I would like to show how they are inscribed in a problematic that is attempting to redefine traditional boundaries of national, cultural, and ethnic *belonging*, and how they refer to one of the most *actual* political realities: the emergence of what certain contemporary sociologists have called "global ethnoscapes," that is, those transnational spaces of identity that are becoming increasingly important in the politics of old nation-states. My working hypothesis will therefore be the following: The notion of the professional traveler that we find in Khatibi's work closely corresponds to the changes that have occurred in the cultural and political life of third-world intellectuals in the last quarter of a century.

We have long been accustomed to thinking of literature in ethnic, national, and, obviously, linguistic terms. Even today to be a professor in a French department generally means to be able to recite the names and works of the "great" French or Francophone writers. Teaching a course on Francophone literature still often means *smuggling* in a certain number of works that, while written in French, are not French. What seems important to me in Khatibi's work is the fact that it radically challenges this kind of division, so that the criteria that have been used for carving up what can be termed "literary nationalities" simply do not apply. If the act of writing in French affiliates a writer with a particular linguistic community, it no longer necessarily, if at all, links him or her to an ethnic or national community. It is this position that led Khatibi to articulate certain destabilizing questions in his essay "Nationalisme et internationalisme littéraires":[10] "What is the homeland of a writer? Is it only his language, the hospitality of the language in which he writes, whether it be his native or extra-native [*sic*] tongue? Is it the conceptual unity between a native soil, a language, and a cultural identity of body and mind? Is it the mosaic of an exile and of a universal transposition?" (206)

As the context from which I took this quotation clearly shows, for Khatibi the homeland of a writer does not refer to a specific land, native soil, or culture but to a *circulation*—even a migration—among lands, languages, and cultures. What happens, then, to the nation? Does the writer have a nation? Here too Khatibi's answer is clear and incisive: "One often says that the writer's nation is his language. Could it be then that beyond the idiomatic varieties of *francophonie*, a literary nation, or rather a *transnation* is at the very heart of *francophonie*?"[11]

For Khatibi, recourse or reference to the idea of (the) nation could have been effective had not the very idea of nation become plural and problematic: "Every nation is, in its very principle, a plurality, a mosaic of cultures, if not a plurality of languages and founding genealogies, either through the text, oral narrative, or both at once." ("Nationalisme et internationalisme littéraires," 209) So the question is revived yet again, for as Khatibi explains it so clearly, the different components of this plurality are "never in a truly egalitarian relation," but instead are "in a hierarchical and dissymmetrical relation." The paradoxical principle of the function of the state is to manage, "with or without pertinence," this dissymmetry. And he continues:

> *But what is a literary nation?* We can dream of a literary nation that would respect plurality and the art of dissymmetry, a nation in which each component would have a place of emission and reception in language, as an active and affirmative force in the whole of the nation and the *internation* [*sic*].
>
> Yet you can imagine that respect for this plurality is probably rather discreet and fragmentary, if not entirely *absent*, belonging to the *utopia of an ideal city*, a *cosmopolis*. [209]

I have allowed myself to reproduce his line of reasoning *in extenso* to underscore the kind of impossibilities and contradictions that Khatibi patiently pressed home in order to put forward his own positions on the questions of homeland, nation, people, and national culture and identity. His approach to these questions clearly shows that he has reflected on the idea of the "professional foreigner/stranger" with full knowledge of the theoretical and political impasses that exist in the present world. This idea was forged in a moment of history—*our* history—when the defensive (or better, reactive) idea of the nation, cautiously directed toward the quest for a single identity, could no longer play the role that had been attributed to it in a still recent past. As they are confronted with the upheavals that affect both the countries of the Maghreb and those of an expanding Europe (and I shall return to this shortly), as they face the globalization of trade and modern technologies, writers must change their tactics vis-à-vis questions of language and ethnicity; change position vis-à-vis problems of identity (both their own identity and that of their audience); and adopt a strategy that is no longer defensive, but active and flexible. This strategy, writes Khatibi, must be "adapted to a double principle: one of *respect for idiomatic variety,* and one of *a plural universality,* with several poles. *The illusion of a center, of an ethnocenter* as generating force of French civilization, integrated around a territory, State, or ideology is over." ("Francophonie"; my emphasis)[12]

At the end of this trajectory, many questions remain unanswered and new ones arise:

What is exoticism? The literary nation and internation? Cosmopolitanism? To write? to write about the foreign man? the foreign woman? the secret to be shared? him? her? the all-foreign [*le tout-étranger*]? What are you doing with *francophonie*? Maghrebi literature? Belgian literature? Canadian literature? Swiss literature? Where is the "black continent"? Negritude? Where on this planet can the Franco-French be found? [Ibid., 213]

Regardless of the angle from which we address the problem, we find ourselves confronted yet again with an extraordinary bursting apart of the idea of the center, and a mixing of languages, peoples, and identities. The difficulty of determining a center—and even an ethnocenter— renders classic notions of race, culture, and nation completely obsolete and invalid. People, nation, audience, language, foreigner, border—all are concepts that can no longer function without being reexamined. On the contrary, everything points to the need to rethink them, or to create new concepts to account for a radically new situation. We are no longer dealing with peoples or even with distinct minorities, but with *diasporas*: the Francophone diaspora(s), some would say. The expression is appealing in that it seems to offer an answer to the problem that we have been discussing, but it doesn't quite cover all the ground. For example, the notion of a Maghrebi diaspora—unlike the model for the Jewish diaspora that refers to the idea of the presence in a "foreign" land of a people from elsewhere who form, in emigration, an extraterritorial cultural community (Galissot)[13]—takes on an entirely different political and philosophical meaning: no longer national, it becomes transnational, "not only because it plays a role among several national states (which was also the case for older immigrations), but *because the ethnic reference is no longer national*." (Galissot, 122; my emphasis)

In the countries of the Maghreb there are Moroccans, Algerians, and Tunisians, but there are also Arabs, Berbers, Touaregs, and Mozabites; and in Europe, there will be Maghrebis, just as in the past there were the North Africans of the metropolis and just as today there are men and women who identify themselves as Maghrebis from France or Beurs in order to emphasize a double distance: a distance from French nationalism and racism, but also a distance from the nationalisms of the countries of the Maghreb who are paying the French back by playing the card of fundamentalism or Arabo-Islamism. (Galissot, 122) This is what leads Galissot to make the following statement, which is important for our argument:

> To identify oneself as "Maghrebi" is not only to refuse to align oneself with a state nationalism; it is also to avoid being identified as Arab or Muslim even, and thus it is a mark of detaching oneself from community norms by proclaiming a new identity and inventing a culture in diaspora. [Ibid.]

And here again we find the question of cultural pluralism about which Khatibi speaks. Now we can better situate this pluralism from historical, sociological, and political points of view. Indeed, what characterizes it is the challenging of "any genealogical identification" that linked nationality and citizenship, race and culture, people or community specificity, and exploded identitarian specificity. We are no longer dealing with one specific ethnic group or another, but with cultural mixes. For a long time in France, the same populations were treated by turns as Kabyle or Arab, North African, and today, as Muslims, but what we can see today is that

> these identities are simply identifications inscribed in an ideological field of altercation, [that they are] both attributed and claimed, stigmatized and emblematic. They discriminate in the greatest proximity to precariousness and social exclusion. It is because they are part of the same economic and cultural misery that, in the name of nationalism and race, certain groups lash out against others who exhibit their difference, playing on ethnicity in a racial way. [Ibid., 125]

Galissot also remarks in the same text that while there are no longer "dangerous classes" today, there are "dangerous ethnic groups," gangs and young men, workers, intellectuals who are dangerous because of their difference as it is related to an origin that is other. These "dangerous" ethnic groups are precisely those cultural mixes that I mentioned earlier, those mixed populations—Maghrebis, Beurs—that can no longer be segregated in ghettoes and are exhibiting increasingly clear signs that emphasize a radical distance from the dominant French symbolic and the nationalisms of country of origin. Another change is also apparent: in the nineteenth century, these *métis* were limited to a minoritarian and marginal intelligentsia (underclasses, Jews, socialists), but have today become millions of people who have broken with national stereotypes and traditional community senses of identity. As the anthropologist Arjun Appadurai has argued, the "landscape" of group identities, or what he calls a "global ethnoscape," has completely changed in today's world.[14] In any case, these groups no longer represent the familiar, classic anthropological and sociological objects of study, since as groups they no longer present those characteristics that made them entities firmly attached to a strictly defined territory and/or a homogeneous culture. More and more what we are seeing today is a widespread process of deterritorialization that obviously translates into the transnational movements of large corporations and financial markets, as well as into ethnic groups, religions, and political and religious configurations. Clearly, though, deterritorialization does not stop there. It also affects the displacement of entire populations from one country to another. It provides cheap labor to wealthy societies while impoverishing the countries from which this labor is taken. We find the deterritorialization of Hindus and Sikhs in India, Palestinians in Israel, Ukrainians in Russia, Maghrebis or Africans in France and Belgium, and increasingly in Spain and Italy as well, and still recently Haitians and Cubans in the United States, Kurds in Great Britain, France, or Italy, with the creation of pockets of internal resistance to imperialism and its counterparts, fundamentalism and nationalism, in the countries of origin.

In the media sector, the globalization I mentioned has determined the setting up of planetary systems in the arenas of advertising and television, with the creation of international conglomerates in Europe, Japan, and America that have resulted in the recent megamergers between the Time-Warner groups, and, even more recently, between Viacom and Paramount.[15]

The speed at which the shift from the international to the global occurred has masked a phenomenon that did not escape the theorists of geo-economy and communications. I have already made reference to the work of Appadurai; now I would like to refer to the analyses of Armand Mattelart. In his article "Comment résister à la colonisation des esprits?" [How to resist the colonization of the mind?], Mattelart remarks that what we are seeing today is not a simple "massification," but rather a contradiction between two different logics: globalization on the one hand and widespread demassification on the other. One of the consequences of this phenomenon has been the creation of "transnational segments," that is, large groups of individuals who share, *beyond their national borders*, the same points of view, the same systems of values, priorities, tastes, norms, in short, similar "sociocultural mentalities." In this sense, globalization and localization become two sides of the same phenomenon. "Since the early 1980s," Mattelart writes, "the dynamics of globalization have set off another, antagonistic movement, the revenge of unique cultures. The tension between, on the one hand, the plurality of cultures and, on the other, the centrifugal forces of market universalism have revealed the complexity of the reactions against the emergence of a planetary market."

As the world-system deployed itself, connecting different societies with productions and networks functioning on the global model, culture itself underwent an effect of transnationalization. Simultaneously, digging deep into local cultural traditions, civil societies each offered different responses to the project of the reorganization of social relations, accelerated by the new systems of communication. And as we know, these responses sometimes took the "form of resistance, reversal, parody, adaptation, reappropriation"; and sometimes the form of an extremely "powerful nostalgia for differences and the mechanisms of differentiation. Everywhere we are seeing a return to specific cultures, to tradition, territory, specific values, [or] the rebirth of nationalisms and fundamentalisms." (Mattelart)

It is this twisted dialectic that led nongovernmental organizations (Green Parties, human rights associations, associations for the rights of women, prodemocracy movements) to attempt to locate what Mattelart has called a "third space," that is, a space that would place itself "between intermarket logics and interstate logics, mediating market pragmatism and the *Realpolitik* of the prince." (Mattelart)

I believe that it is in just such an international and/or global sociopolitical context that we must understand the kind of thinking in which Khatibi was trying to engage in his essays on the Maghreb, the Gulf War, or in a novel like *Un été à Stockhom*.[16]

When he created the concept of the professional traveler, Khatibi showed himself to be entirely aware of these changes and upheavals, and especially of the impact of the internationalization of the culture industries—new markets for large film companies, international travel agencies, television, and recently the new communication highways—on the formation of these new *ethnoscapes*: while American families from Key West are relocated to the mainland to make room for Cuban refugees, Algerians are pirating French television with satellite dishes, Beurs are listening to American rap, and young African Americans are tuning into Algerian raî.

"Why," Khatibi pointedly asks, "should we make a distinction between *literature* and *paraliterature*? Because paraliterature is not supported by a secret and a force of writing. It is a monumental reproduction (pastiches, imitations, parodies, simulations) determined by the book market, media circulation, and commercial exchange. Paraliterature is the entropic circulation of words in an economy of interchangeable objects. *An economy in which writing no longer has a space of its own.*" ("Nationalisme," 211; my emphasis)

It is perhaps this kind of *disappropriation* of the space of the Maghrebi writer's nomadic writing that can best explain the need to introduce the paradoxical figure of the professional traveler and the means and ends that are connected to him or her.

First, a few words on the *means*:

1. A new relation to language, to languages and writing as a means to opening oneself to plurality and difference; this is what Khatibi has called the "laws of hospitality in the language":

> If writing is the exploration of the unknown, whatever it may be (native or extra-native, natural or supernatural, cultural, intercultural, and transcultural); if to write is to give shape to the power of life, death, and survival, then the (writing, speaking, loving) other should be welcomed in his or her capacity to move through these differences (of sex, language, culture, imaginary). [Ibid., 206]

2. A new relation to (cultural *and* ethnic) *identity* as well, which, in Khatibi's work, no longer refers to an ontology of the one, the self, or even of us, but to a logic that is itself paradoxical, the logic of the third term—just as we find, for example, the concept of the "neutral" in Roland Barthes,[17] that of the "tiers-instruit" [The third-instructed] in Michel Serres,[18] or, even more relevant for obvious reasons, that of a "poetic of the Relation" in Edouard Glissant[19]—that is, a logic where the relation is more important than the opposed terms:

> Yes, a stranger is always a stranger for the other, but BE-
> TWEEN THEM, there is a COMPLETELY OTHER [TOUT-AUTRE],
> the THIRD TERM, the RELATION that maintains each of them

in their uniqueness and that is in one way or another UN-TRANSLATABLE. ["Nationalisme," 204]

We are now on the way to understanding what could have led to the creation of the main character, Gérard Namir, in *Un été à Stockhom*. Namir is, as you may have guessed, a *translator* by profession. He is a character, Khatibi tells us, who was constructed on the basis of three cultural features:

> In Arabic and in Berber, Namir means "tiger," "panther." The Berber referent is the legend of Hammou or Namir, known primarily in Morocco. In this story we see the young hero, in love with an angelic fairy whom he impregnates and whom he pursues between heaven and earth. Namir has other names as well: "Agnaou" (in Guinea), which means in fact "THE MAN OF UNINTELLIGIBLE LANGUAGE," in other words, the *foreigner*.[20]

Or again:

> I stared at this horizon, its mobility. I did so, I believe, very calmly. Should I attribute this calm to my profession [as a translator]? Am I not a *professional traveler* who wants to cross borders with a flexible mind? A flexibility that is not always granted to me with each change of climate, country, language, and—how can I express this?—at each exchange of glances and words. [*Un été*, 9–10]

To leave, go out, to let oneself be seduced. To become several people, to become someone else (with others), to become, to become, to face the outside, fork off elsewhere, make a rhizome with others, discover oneself to be a foreigner, to create a new identity for oneself. These are some of the odd, foreign elements, some of the varieties of alterity and exposure that the professional traveler encounters. He or she has to be a simultaneous translator because he or she knows that there can be no apprenticeship without exposure to or encounter with the other, without loss. Professional travelers can never know in *advance* who they are, where they are, where they come from, where they are going, or how they will or might get there. It really does not matter to them, since what they most want is to expose themselves (to the other), to expose themselves to their own strangeness/foreignness, to the foreigners in them. What they want is to become (other, foreign, more foreign than the foreigner); in a word, to become (with others, not like others). This is their work, their passion, and their secret: to be done with gregariousness:

> I thought of my work for a moment. A life, an entire part of my life spent traveling. How can I return to myself? recenter myself without losing my points of balance? I conceive my birth into the world at a speed that increasingly separates me from my past as it veils it, detaching me from my native city and its gregarious roots that are almost motionless at the edge of an oceanic square. Ah, to grow old, ripen without succumbing to this distance. [*Un été*, 10]

What, finally, are the *ends*?

Since his objective is to "liberate thought from the imaginary" and to release "the imaginary from thought"; since the ultimate goal of his writing is to inscribe "dissidence" as a "desire to consolidate the living force as a work of art and to explore the unknown of language" (*Nationalisme*, 211), the new Francophone writer will have to commit himself or herself further by transforming himself or herself into a "professional stranger," that is, into a writer for whom writing will simply be an "exercise in cosmopolitan alterity capable of traveling through differences." (*Nationalisme*, 211) And in this sense, he or she is a *paredre* of the philosopher about whom Serres speaks in *Le tiers-instruit*: the "professional stranger" who has no "methodology" at his or her disposal; exodus is his or her sole sojourn and his or her blank book. He or she does not travel by following a map that covers an already-explored space; he or she has decided to wander. It is true that this wandering carries risks of error, of getting lost. But this is the price one must pay if one wants to have the opportunity to touch the men and women who form the new cultural space in which one gravitates, a *global ethnoscape* as third space that rises from the ruins of the community world of old and of identitarian nationalism. For the professional stranger or, in Segalen's terms, the *exot* who is Khatibi, it is not the assimilation of customs, races, and nations of others that is important; it is rather, on the contrary, the "enduring nature of the pleasure of feeling [and I would add of "causing to feel" and of sharing] the Diverse." The other is the one who cannot be assimilated and whom one must learn to preserve, to protect against a global market whose logic is to assimilate him or her. A *bi-lange writer*, A. Khatibi's "professional writer," like Hermes—the god of translators—is like the messangers who

> belong to two worlds because they put them in communication with each other, flying from one riverbank to another, but who can also be found on earth or in the sea, on islands or paths; these *third places . . .* of the most intellectual, learned, or cultural project, and of a tolerant ethics, of *third instruction*, a harmonious middle/*milieu*, a daughter between two banks of scientific culture and of knowledge culled from the humanities, of expert erudition and of artistic narrative, of the gathered and the invented, conjugated together because in reality the single reason of universal science and of singular suffering cannot be separated. [Serres, 164]

3. Writing Metafiction: On Khatibi's *Le livre du sang*[21]

> Since Belief, Dogma, Mysteries and Miracles are a theological word-game, it follows that the poet is the guarantor of these games and of their exploration, more so than the theologian; and as the poet himself would say, much more so than any other interpreter.
> —Abdelkebir Khatibi (*Ultime dissidence de Jean Genet*, 156)

Khatibi's *Le livre du sang* proceeds from multiple writing strategies. One of the major difficulties the reader encounters is to locate the site—historical, poetical, or rhetorical—in which such a text is inscribed or, more precisely, the site from which it attempts to tear itself away.

I would argue that the apparent hermeticism of this book, the extreme complexity of its composition as well as the mode of its invention, come directly from the literary tradition of Arab mystical poetry and narrative. From such a perspective, *Le livre du sang* presents itself simultaneously as a radical attempt to rewrite and surpass such a tradition. What is original about Khatibi's work is that this same attempt to rewrite and surpass does not start from some outside or neutral point of view, but deliberately from a real fascination for—or even a primitive seduction by—the form this tradition has historically taken, in the Hikayat, or mystical epic genre.

What strikes and unsettles readers of *Le livre du sang* right away is the disquieting feeling of strangeness that seizes them as soon as the narrative begins. The narrative first resembles a meditation book in the manner of Swedenborg or of the metaphysical poems of El Hallaj—as suggested by the Retreat into the Asylum of the Inconsolables, the presence of a spiritual Master and his disciples, and by the Narrator's flights of lyricism. Little by little, however, the presence of the androgynous Echanson ("Cupbearer") and his/her sister Muthna comes to corrupt or "gangrenate" the narrative, to jam the reading and throw its rhythm into a turmoil:

> The Cupbearer has been lent to us by Destiny to weaken our bloodthirsty genealogy. Blessed be this pining! Blessed be the form of the androgyne, delivered to our angelic rage! (22)

We see how rage and the most unbridled sexual hubris can quickly contaminate a narrative that seemed destined for higher ends. It is as if the Marquis de Sade, by some trick of an erotic genie in the form of an ambiguous androgyne, had surreptitiously infiltrated a devotional text.

> The wandering of the winds adds to our enchantment,
> isolating the Asylum on a low hill, a landscape almost violet
> because of the force of the sun on the bushes, rocks, and
> wildflowers. From there the land descends toward the town
> in the valley, where Muthna shall await us, sprawled on the
> canopy bed. (20)

The constant drifting of the narrative toward the failure to surpass itself—the failure to reach the ecstasy that the learned "Inconsolables" desire—leads to my second hypothesis about this incandescent book. The mystical tradition must be rewritten and surpassed because the seduction it has exercised upon Arab peoples has provoked a real decadence in their ethos. It is as if, for Khatibi, a certain kind of decadence in Arab culture were indissociable from the epic poem (*Epos*) that has prevailed in its literary tradition.

Le livre du sang will not spell out such a thesis in so many words, even though it is inscribed cryptically throughout the book. For this reason, I would like to take a detour by way of a text where Khatibi, quite conscious of the difficulties his book poses, tries to explain, to lay out some of the stakes implied in it. I am referring to the text that opens his *Ombres japonaises*:

> Tell me a beautiful tale or I will kill you: the supreme principle of the 1001 nights, the principle of the narrative as an absolute seduction: this will be our mode of writing, the axis of our narrative delight. A mode, let us say right now, that will be accompanied by the scene of the white night [*nuit blanche*].[22] And then, above and beyond this series, this scene: no more Scheherazade, no more of this account of death, of this tattered marriage, of this sleepless night. (11)

The setting is established right away—the retelling of a story, apparently *One Thousand and One Nights*. But this rewriting of the story (is it really *One Thousand and One Nights*?) is not done from a distance. It cannot be neutral. It is, on the contrary, contemporaneous with a seduction that, we are told, conditions the "writing motif" (and the "reading motif" as well).

Caught between the initial seduction provoked by the vision of an androgyne, and an infinite narrative climax, the text will no longer present itself as what Roland Barthes would call a "text of pleasure," or as a text that "pleases, fills, gives euphoria," but, in Barthes's terms again, as a "text of bliss," because it has broken with the dominant culture and with the type of comfortable practice of reading upon which such a culture is dependent. It is what Barthes describes in *Le plaisir du texte* as a text "that places the reader's historical, cultural and psychological givens in a state of loss, disturbs and shades the solidity of his/her tastes, of his/her values as well, and maybe of even his/her memories." (25–6)

Likewise, just like the Asylum collapses after the betrayal of the Master (or is it the opposite?), the narrative should also collapse:

> Go, my story, above all these ecstatic ruins this is how insomnia leads all Asylums toward their definitive destruction and how each brick of the narrative—on the edges of the din flares up. One must choose the mortal work to destroy all, as fast as the slash of a knife. The words must disconnect from each other and fall upon me like a pile of bricks. [LS 156–7]

A writerly rather than a readerly text, *Le livre du sang* is a text that will not be read in the traditional sense of the word, because it does not limit itself to simply telling a story (the sordid tale of the gory seduction of the Master of a mystical fraternity by an androgyne and his sister, Muthna).[23] Rather, the unreadable text is constantly being made to exceed any inscription of plot. *Le livre du sang* is a book that demands to be rewritten or, one might say, written in concert.

Indeed, written "Under the Gaze of Orpheus" (the title of the book's last chapter), this narration of crazed poetic drunkenness demands on the reader's part an underwriting, a sub-scription without which it could not even take place. *Le livre du sang* demands a dramatization of reading similar to that which the Narrator has employed to tear this multivoiced narrative from the silence that seems to have preceded it, and to integrate the multiple genres that run through it: lyric, poem, dirge, oratory, spiritual meditation, lamentation, epic, exhortation, and so on. Between the reader and the Narrator there must be a sacred pact of unconditional, unstinting coproduction, with the goal of bringing the text to its highest point of incandescence:

> Reader, do not close this book so soon it holds a cadaver. And do not be angry with me if I gallop fast, faster than my broken feet, if I fall at your feet over and over, begging you constantly to finish me off. I implore you, my beloved, isn't it true that you will never forgive me! Because forgiveness would be the false ransom for my death.

Would you desire such a pact? Now that I am above everything, do not forgive me. By betraying you, I have drained the last of my strength. Look at me closely from my shattered bones, from my oozing marrow, from my emaciated face, what remains if not the empty image of a cadaver in chains? (155–6)

"Never Another Scheherazade"

As a reader, I let myself be taken in when I proposed to clarify certain areas, or loci—both rhetorical and physical areas of the body, of memory, of the body text—from which the text is generated and takes off. In the passage about the "nuit blanche" quoted earlier, Khatibi continues:

> But first, let us take the time to love Scheherazade, to listen closely to her voice, to follow the rhythm of her body-story. Only this immense body will now matter, spoken from time immemorial by nobody's voice, a voice that comes from nowhere and a fabulous procession of stories that exceed every law of writing, a procession of stories within stories whose characters' only worth is how they can narrate or die. [OJ 11]

Khatibi then poses the question that seems of the utmost importance to the subject at hand:

> And what if dying precisely meant saying no to this supreme principle, if dying meant for us the decadent Arabs of today—to say no, if dying for us (above and beyond morality and metaphysics) was this unheard-of negation, still unspeakable: never another Scheherazade? [OJ 11]

"Never another Scheherazade," because the point will no longer be to imagine Scheherazade as a real body tattooed with pearls and intoxicating perfume in a paradisiacal harem where "houris dance and princes (principles) have orgies, concubines and slaves engaging in serial coitus." (LS 11) But also because it is urgent to deconstruct the "cheap Orient" ("l'Orient de pacotille," OJ 12) that has nourished the imagination of the West and of Arabs as well. From then on, the metaphor of the Asylum of the Inconsolables and the latter's bloody destruction in *Le livre du sang* means that the problem is not only to extricate the Orient from orientalism, but literally to tear both the Orient and the West from the metaphysics that haunts them. In fact, reading too quickly through what Khatibi writes on the Orient, one might think that he is mainly against what he calls the "haunted thinking" of Arabs, who are seduced by mystical narrative:

> Enchantment and seduction both imply haunted thought, and such was, moreover, the literary destiny of Arabs sung by the poetical prose of the Koran, by the lave of tales and poetry. (OJ 12)

At stake in this drama is not so much the pleasure Arabs might have felt by telling tales and reciting epic poetry as the absence of discrimination that presided over such choices. What is at stake is the absence of vigilance over the metaphysical foundations that explain the persistence of such narrative forms in Arab culture. Khatibi does not take issue with the fact that Arabs have let themselves be seduced by tales and poetry, or that they have not distinguished between Mythos and Logos—this he leaves to Hegel and Western metaphysics. He takes issue with the fact that Arab people were unable to distinguish between theological narratives that always situate real life in an inaccessible or transcendent future, and narratives that can no longer distinguish themselves from their ends. The latter would place us from the outset at the heart of "real" history but would reconcile us to that which, in history, is no longer amenable to sublation (*Aufhebung*)—with that which, in our history, cannot be sublated—the body and the narrative. Such a history would be recounted in the future perfect, and freed from the ends that we would have formerly assigned to it.[24]

Pensée-autre

There is a problematic in Khatibi's work that is fairly similar to that of J. F. Lyotard in *La condition post-moderne*, when the latter tries to think out the "intelligible of our (postmodern) time" as marked by the advent of the end of the "grand narratives"—those of the sense of history or the end of history, those of the sense of "technique." Khatibi adds to the chain of speculative and emancipatory narrative—the so-called "legitimizing" narratives Lyotard had deciphered for Western society—the missing link of "Salafism"[25] that presents itself, this time for the Arab world, as "metaphysics turned doctrine" and as the "surpassed" historicism upon which it depends. But it is not in this addition that the originality of Khatibi's project lies. In fact, if Khatibi's work is important, it is not because of its capacity to link another grand narrative to the train of Western metaphysics. Rather, as "pensée-autre"[26] ("thought of otherness"), it has given itself an exorbitant objective: to open up our thinking to the point of thinking difference as the surpassing of both Western and Arab metaphysics. And this according to the modalities of a double criticism and a double writing that goes hand-in-hand with a double objective—commitment in "today's social and political struggle" (*Maghreb pluriel,* 34) and in opposition to "the absolutes of theology and of the theocentrism that hold time, space, and the whole edifice of Maghrebi societies in shackles." (Ibid., 33)

Khatibi describes this "intractable difference" in *Maghreb pluriel*:

—The essence of technique[27] is doubled in relation to the metaphysical foundation of Islam and of its values. We were saying earlier that Aristotle's God came into Islam before the latter's emergence. The same goes for his *organon*, prelude to the universal destiny of technique. That is why we must direct our attention to the encounter between these two metaphysics (Western, Islamic), which erase each other. We are caught in their gap, unheard-of gesture. It is not in order to read such traditions over and over that we thus speak but rather in order to provoke a crisis, to put ourselves in crisis within the unthinkable which is our lot, or rather within this need to differentiate oneself. For difference is not just granted to the first rebel.

—Is this what you call the "intractable difference"?

—Yes. And there are other gaps, other ruptures that are unleashed in the violence of some and against others. In the

Arab world, the submachine gun of theology bespeaks a sinister unleashing of metaphysics. Examples of this are plentiful all over the Arab and the Iranian world. The intractable difference lies in the relinquishment of metaphysics by a double criticism, a double combat, a double death. (38)

In Search of the "True" Orient

It is on those gaps and ruptures that Khatibi establishes a radical distinction between two types of stories/histories (*récits/histoires*). One of these, according to Khatibi, has presided over the decadence of the modern Arab ethos: the metaphysical history contaminated by the myth of a single and unified narrative—a narrative thereby ahistorical, or even antihistorical. The other is a metafictional history, a history in the future perfect, in harmony with the linguistic, cultural, and political plurality that permeates the Arab people, and that is in search of a true Orient of thought. Such an Orient cannot be circumscribed on maps nor associated with people who live in Eastern countries. The Orient Khatibi envisages—in keeping with the Orient of the mystics whose meaning he nonetheless subverts—is no longer a racial notion and owes nothing to what Western romanticism called "Volkgeist"—the spirit or genius of a people or a race.[28] The Orient will not be the origin (*Oriens/Origo*) of being as light, either, or even immediate presence, unveiling intuition of the heart or of the spiritual eye, as it is for a mystic like Sohravardi. It will be free of any ethnic meaning, including the Arab ethos. The Orient will be, rather, an intermediate knowledge that undermines all simplistic dualism:

> The Orient is not a simple movement (dialectical, speculative, culturalist . . .) toward the West. [The Orient and the West] are, each for the other, the beginning and the end. We are thus trying to turn toward global and pluralistic thinking, toward the thought of Otherness that is built step by step and without a guaranteed end. That is why the Hegelian metaphor of the two suns (the outer sun of the Orient and the West's inner sun of universal thought) is a metaphor still caught in metaphysics. [MP 37]

Khatibi will give the dichotomy between the two types of story the appearance of a schism between two textual regimes, two works that will affect in turn two regimes of the body and thought, as well as two distinct temporalities:

> Whereas in the Koran mankind's path follows a circular movement definitively sealed within the above and beyond—dying, living, dying, living forever—in the thousand and one nights, the narrative principle introduces death's performance, the narrative becomes the absolute performance of death, a performance without which it could not exist. Welcoming death, the narrative becomes the sojourn of the immemorial, or more precisely, it becomes the trajectory, the inscription of what will have been: the narrative is in the *future perfect*. [OJ 12–13]

Such are the parameters within which the essential of *Le livre du sang* comes together. It is the principle of circularity and its collusion with the above and beyond that Khatibi wanted to throw into question in the book, but not so much from the vantage point of a theoretician as from that of a poet. Indeed, once Khatibi has seen it as his duty to write *Le livre du sang*, he rediscovers as already occupied, so to speak, the metafictional terrain he had previously cleared. For mystical Arab and Persian writers had already explored history as a "tearing away of the past from the past" (Corbin, 163) or better yet, history as a metafictional story. As I mentioned earlier, there is a specific genre that corresponds to this—the Hikayat, or mystical epic.

As Corbin has noted, the Hikayat designates above all a history that is a mimesis as well as a repetition and re-creation—which is what makes it a recital in the complex sense of the word: poem, song, and myth at the same time. Indeed, the Hikayat is a recited story, but one in which the narrator (*le récitant*) is also a mime—an actor in the real and active sense of the term. The rule of the Hikayat is such that the distance between author, narrator, hero, and narratee is abolished. (Ibid., 163) This is due to the fact that the event narrated is never folded upon itself but becomes a story only as far as it becomes an event understood or acted out by all participants, especially the narrator. The act of understanding—the goal of the Hikayat, designated by the word *hermeneutic* (Ibid., 165)—is in this case no longer the work of any universal reader, but the work of each one of us, from generation to generation. Henceforth, it engages our responsibility without any possible alibis.

At least this is the case as far as The Book—the Holy Koran—is concerned, a text where one must reactivate the real meaning over and over in the present by means of the interposed Hikayat. To understand The Book is to make sure that the past continues through us, and that some equivalent of destiny always obtains.[29]

Once he has sensed it his duty to write *Le livre du sang*, Khatibi envisions a "primitive" scene—one that comes back to us from the eternity of the angelic Hikayat. But for the primal Adam and Eve and the heroes of epic poetry, Khatibi substitutes the destabilizing figure of the androgynous Cupbearer followed by his double, Muthna—a double visage that cuts off the Hikayat from its metaphysical and theological foundations.

In fact, Khatibi uses all the resources of the mystical Hikayat—not only the kind of symbiosis it establishes between the narrator, actor, and reader, but also the principles of tearing away and the reversibility of time to completely overturn the expectations of dialectical and anthropological idealism upon which its articulation is founded. Indeed, by replacing the reconciling, theological figure of the primordial couple (Adam and Eve) with that of the insane and intractable, incestuous and androgynous Cupbearer and his sister Muthna, Khatibi breaks with a whole secular metaphysical tradition, showing that he will no longer play into the hand of the idealistic adamology we have inherited. Henceforth, an unprecedented rupture takes place, for the narrative will no longer break up positive history according to the tearing away of the mystical and theological principle. The tearing away of the past is no longer the issue. The goal will be to overthrow the history of Arab thought and the rules of its *Epos* according to a law of disturbance of all the senses, in relation to the *nuit blanche*—the thousand and third night. The raconteur becomes the accomplice to an initial seduction that comprises the risk of death or insanity.

Le livre du sang thus presents itself as the book of an "insane" narrator writing the mystical Hikayat at a time when the figure of the androgyne as Imago Dei—as idea, *genos*, or intelligible, incorruptible, and incorporeal seal—is undergoing the process of degradation or mutation.[30] The book's incandescent narrative attempts to capture, in a quasi-hallucinatory gesture, the moment of the so-called fall, the moment when the doomed idea finds itself invaded, little by little, by the flesh—the moment when Eros and Thanatos become bound to the body (of the reader) as a dazzling mutation, and when, henceforth, sex proves bound to death. But this time, what we are given to experience is no longer a transitory stage, but destiny itself—our "historial" destiny ("destinée historiale").

In one of the most beautiful passages in *Maghreb pluriel*, Khatibi suggests that as subjects of the new materialist narrative—the new Hikayat—"no gods will attend our deaths, no angels, no devils. Our subversion . . . is to make heaven and hell come tumbling down in a thought of Otherness." (21) It is therefore no longer being that Khatibi wishes to paint, but becoming, the becoming of the body, of the flesh—the eternal "passibility" [*sic*] of man. And in this case, the image of the primordial androgyne that haunted the deeroticized and desexualized world of the mystical Epos will appear only (in the best of all possible worlds) as an "Imago," but an irreverent and especially unsublatable Imago. Belief in the grand narratives of the mystical epic, which Khatibi incorporates in his narrative and transforms into a *nuit blanche*, will not appear as anything more than one story among others. According to Khatibi, the mystical epic—and the history of the Arabs seems to him its historical accomplice—wanted to conceal itself from history by denying the future and becoming. Such was the fatal, destructive seduction. Such is the corpse both the narrator and the reader inherit from this *livre tombeau* ("book as mausoleum") of all traditions.

By overthrowing once again the "normal order of time" and by introducing "cosmic time into the very duration of the narrative" (OJ 16), the new Hikayat surreptitiously introduces a fatal disruption in the economy and modes of functioning of the classical Arab narrative. A radical shift now affects the heroic epic, calling into question a certain ideological history of the Arab ethos. From now on, one no longer contrasts the eternal light of mystical revelation with history. Rather, it is according to the principle of the *nuit blanche* that one tries to account for the duration and becoming of life. However imperceptible, the difference is one that, if taken seriously in the highly theoretical game (OJ 12) set into motion here, will touch off the incandescent creativity inherent in the narrative principle of the *nuit blanche*:

> It is now sufficiently clear that the whole scene of the sleepless night, the principle of the sleepless night as narrative and theoretical principle, as mutual attraction between death and narration, night and day, conceals another scene, the backstage of seduction, or rather that which precedes and lies ahead of seduction. [OJ 19]

We can now more easily understand why *Le livre du sang* cannot be analyzed in narratological or even poetical terms, and why, in a certain sense, it does not even fit in the category we call literature. By mobilizing the mimetic and dramatic power of the mystical Hikayat, the narrator and the reader become the actants as well as the actors in the metafictional narrative. The story is not "told" to them: they are its agents, its actors, and its active subjects.

Like Scheherazade, who is the prisoner of the *nuit blanche*, readers must allow themselves to be seduced first, and, as much as they can, play the game of infinite seduction the narrative invites. It is a never-ending narrative no longer guided by the tearing-away principle that brings us back to a beginning that would also be an end. It is what Khatibi describes in *Ombres japonaises* as

> repeated abolition of time in the *bewitching of the body*, coming out of fatigue, out of boredom and drowsiness to enter the brilliance of the white night, conqueror of confusion, of desires, or words and unexpected tales. [OJ 17]

The hermeneutic principle is no longer "Recite the Koran as if it had been revealed to you alone" (Corbin, 187), but, as I suggested earlier, "Tell me a beautiful story or I will kill you." For Khatibi, there no more exists an original text to be interpreted than there is a hermeneutic circle where explanation and comprehension would be coterminous with the appropriation of the Self. As the singular, original text disappears, so do the safeguards that used to be coterminous with the appropriation of the text and the Self. The subject of the utterance and the subject of the uttered (*le récit*) are still coterminous, but in a new way: the "absence of the text" (OJ 17) now entails a permanent wandering and a permanent danger of the fading of the subject.

Reading, writing from the self onward, beginning from a self that is invisible even to itself, a guarantor of or even guaranteed by the absolute of the Text—the Koran—is no longer the point. The point is now writing/reading,

> at the end of the self, at the end of the devastated earth, at the end of every disaster, begging for the hallucination of its clandestine life, to celebrate it, forever captive, toward the consuming fire of Destiny. [LS 28]

Amor fati! To burn up! Such is the main characteristic of Khatibi's highly paradoxical thought. As he departs from a tradition in which The Book exists and where all exists by The Book, he discovers that he is the traveling companion of the Rommys—the gypsies—who formed the epic of their people by refusing all books, or, in Franz Liszt's words, "by singing their say." (Corbin, 170–7)

The task of poetry in *Le livre du sang* is to rediscover a state of utter nakedness, of extreme passibility between two languages, between two texts—between two sexes as well—by opposing once and for all the chiaroscuro of the *nuit blanche* to the light of revealed truth. Such passibility will no longer occur through any sort of elevation, or transcendence or conversion, but rather by an excruciating return to the "skin tunics." And the well-known *tunica pellitia* of which Jean Scot Erigène speaks,[31] when he evokes the differentiation of the sexes and the creation of the physical body, are the garment of which the poetical androgyne becomes the burning sign, the androgyne whose "principle . . . unifies, in the blazing void, gods and men, angels and demons, heaven and earth—for the love of a rotating star." (LS 148)

This essay was originally written for an international colloquium, "La traversée du français dans les signes littéraires, culturels, et artistiques marocains," organized by Hedi Bouraoui, Yvettes Benayoun-Schmidt, and Najib Redouane, that took place at York University, Toronto, April 20–23, 1994.

7

The Cartography of the Nation

Mouloud Feraoun's *Le fils du pauvre* Revisited

Mouloud Feraoun was one of the first writers to have experimented brilliantly with the idea of the future nation. Although he was long overshadowed by Kateb Yacine, Feraoun was in fact one of the first to have understood the obstacles Algerian Francophone writers had to overcome in order to rise to the different demands made on them on the eve of Revolution: to give *voice* to the nation, when it existed only in a virtual state; to *bear witness* in writing to the sufferings of his people, when an audience of readers worthy of this name was as yet being formed; and finally, *to write* the first page of a history freed from colonial rule. It seems to me that Feraoun accomplished all of this in his deceptively modest novel *Le fils du pauvre*.[1] Because it did not live up to certain critical expectations, the novel was all too readily categorized as "testimony" or "ethnological narrative." The fact that it radically questions received ideas about postwar Algeria was completely overlooked.

What is it that *Le fils du pauvre* forces us to think about, once we allow ourselves to read it without bias and stop trying to force it into a category where its political stakes are completely eradicated or, conversely, where its formal strategies are wholly ignored?

As the critic Christiane Achour has shown in one of the first serious studies of Feraoun's work,[2] the initial revolution carried out by this pioneer of Maghrebi Francophone literature was his decision to write: by deciding to write, he freed himself from the constraints and obligations of orality (*l'énonciation orale*).

In addition, because he chose to write this novel *in French*, he also distanced himself from his own community. If, as Jack Goody has said, writing and, more generally, print culture is "the possibility of the play of the intellect upon language,"[3] and while it represents "progress" for creating an "archive" in relation to oral culture, *writing* is nonetheless a "mark of rupture and distinction with an ambiguous status." (Goody, cited in Achour, 32) Writing both valorizes the person who is able to write (and to read) and allows the group to which this person belongs to use him or her to communicate with the outside.[4] At the same time, written traces (*in French*) are the best proof of the changes already taking place in the country and of an inscription in the country (to come).

There are several different kinds of text in *Le fils du pauvre*. We have the text Feraoun wrote on Kabylia, on Kabyle customs, on the colonial school system, and so on. We also have the letters that the father, who emigrated to France to support his family, sends to his wife and children *when he doesn't even know how to write!* And we have the letters that Fouroulou, the book's hero, begins to write to his father, as well as the compositions he has to write to get ahead in his studies and obtain a scholarship that will allow him to become a schoolteacher. It is these letters, like everything that is written in this novel (Fouroulou's journal and compositions, but the text we are reading as well), that little by little constitute a *political and social cartography* that will serve as an identity card, a map of the heart, a cadaster, and finally an inventory of cultural and geographical sites.[5] In this sense, Feraoun can be said to belong to a group that Geneviève Mouillaud-Fraisse has called "mad cartographers," that is, writers whose madness was to try to make a "shape sketched on a map of the earth by the tracing of borders and a proper name, coincide exactly, without remainders, with [their] belonging to a human community and even with [their] very being."[6]

Feraoun—alias Fouroulou—is not "mad" because he is seeking at all costs to *anchor himself* in his village or, as Mouillaud-Fraisse says, to find for himself "landmarks in the places of the earth." (Ibid.)

Nor is he mad because "the violence of History [may have] deprived him of a place and of a *we* to which he was attached." (Ibid.) We need only reread the first part of Feraoun's book to see that, on the contrary, he is completely aware of his belonging to a specific village, a community, a language, and customs. "Vanity is one of those faults that *we* mock the most, perhaps because *we are all close relatives*," writes Feraoun in the first pages of the novel, clearly indicating thereby that he is seeking neither a "we" (already taken for granted) nor a reconciliation between the "lower city" and the "upper city." Rather, he is seeking a way out *not from a "we"* but from whatever it is that makes the belonging without remainder to this "we" impossible. It is not—oh diabolical paradox—absence of belonging, loss of identity, or exile that makes Feraoun/Fouroulou a mad cartographer. Rather, it is his internal adherence to the impossible imperative of coincidence without remainder (Mouillaud-Fraisse). In this sense, Fouroulou does not adhere to the *paranoid* version of the quest for self but to the *schizophrenic* version. The schizophrenic blames neither his own people nor the colonizers for what he is lacking or for the misery of his people; he does not project onto others the suffering he feels because of his noncoincidence with or nontransparency to his people. His madness—and this is why it is more of the schizophrenic variety that Mouillaud-Fraisse pinpoints— can only manifest itself, as we shall see, by the elocutionary disappearance of the hero of the book: a silence that cannot be relieved by the intervention of an extradiegetical narrator who seems to appear miraculously out of nowhere.[7]

Indeed, one of the most striking formal aspects of Feraoun's novel is its narrative bipartition. Whereas the first part of the text is narrated by an intradiegetic and homodiegetic narrator (in Gérard Genette's terms) (the narrative of Fouroulou's childhood and adolescence is presented as if it had been written by Fouroulou himself), the second part of the text is narrated entirely by a classic extradiegetical and omniscient narrator, that is, by a subject who is supposed to know what happens to Fouroulou after a scholarship has allowed him to pursue his studies and become a schoolteacher. And so we are faced with two radically different texts. Yet this aspect of the novel's structure has never been commented on by the numerous critics who have analyzed this supposedly minor work of Feraoun's. It seems to me that if we read it from the perspective I am proposing here, the novel reveals much more than the customs of a small Kabyle community on the eve of the struggle for liberation. This 1940s' novel had much greater ambitions than merely ethnographic or populist ones. And it is in the "schize" to which I referred above that we can find the key that allows us, despite the failed readings to which the book has been subjected, to understand what it is that has made this novel resist time and survive these simplistic analyses. This perhaps offers an explanation of the ways in which this novel becomes symptomatic of a very specific (political, ideological) unburdening (*dédouanement*) that can only enable us to read it in a new light.

1. Fouroulou writes his autobiography. In principal, however, this autobiography is not destined to be *published*, that is, to *become public*. In addition, we are told that it is incomplete and/or "aborted." Indeed in the preface to the chapter entitled "The Family," the extradiegetic narrator describes Fouroulou's found manuscript as an "aborted masterpiece lying *forgotten* between a *cahier de roulement* and preparatory note cards [among other texts!] like the fifth egg of a warbler that the mother and her chicks scornfully leave behind in the abandoned nest." (*Le fils du pauvre*, 6)

2. Also striking is the fact that, as I mentioned earlier, the parts that make up the novel are not homogenous. In the first part, we find primarily a description of the Kabyle village, families, and customs *as they are experienced and transcribed by Fouroulou*, whereas the final part that describes Fouroulou's fate *once he has left his village* is recounted by a narrator whose identity we don't really know. It is this narrative "divide," or, if one prefers, this veritable "division of the narrative work" that must be emphasized if one truly wants to understand the novel in all its depth, to wrest it from the banalities of a simple *Bildungsroman*. What animates the first part of the novel is Feraoun's desire to provide a true idea of what life in Kabylia was like for a child growing up under colonization. It is only in the second part that the logic of inclusion and exclusion that leads our hero to leave his village and cut himself off from his community in order to succeed can be put in place. Once again, Feraoun's novel clearly demonstrates that it is only at the

cost of a loss of self or an alienation from one's freedom—in the Marxian sense of *Entfremdung* as loss of autonomy—that the colonial subject can accede to any social status. So it is not surprising that school—education—little by little becomes the novel's dominant theme. Generally speaking, we can say that in the first part the community takes precedence over the individual, and orality takes precedence over the printed and the written. And in fact it is only *symptomatically*, when the father emigrates to France, that the *written*—and therefore *school* and what goes with it (to know how to read and write letters, a document, a newspaper)—will take on all its importance.

Nonetheless, by not completing his narrative, by aborting it in a sense, Fouroulou/Feraoun proves that his goal was not to distinguish himself, not to tell an edifying story about the success of a young Kabyle child. On the contrary, his goal was to bear witness for his community through the very modest story of his own life. And although Fouroulou was able to bear witness by writing his *Journal*, there was a remainder, since he did not tell his story to the end! By breaking the narrative in two, Feraoun—and this is his genius—draws the cartography of what makes the colonial subject incapable of reaching transparency (with himself or with others) the moment he is metamorphosed into an assimilated subject.

Feraoun plainly shows that learning how to write cuts the colonial subject off from his community. By breaking the text in two and giving himself two opposing voices, however, he provides himself with the means to inscribe something that could, on another level, be used to fight against that which threatens the "enunciating subject" with the loss of his community and himself. And we can show that Feraoun was acutely aware of the strategy he used in his novel by referring to the signs of *schize* that he attributes to Fouroulou/Feraoun during the entire first part of the narrative—signs that Feraoun translates (consciously?) by means of the irruption of the third person in a narrative that in theory should have been narrated entirely in the first person: The hero speaks of himself as if he had (in the meantime) *become someone else*:[8] "Khalti's character *suited the little Fouroulou very well*" (41), he writes. And, later, "My uncle called me at each of his meals. Even Helima herself was surprised by her desire *to spoil Fouroulou*." (56) In fact, the more time passes, the more Fouroulou's relation to writing, and to written culture in French in general, becomes deeper, penetrates him, and little by little alienates him, distances him from his own culture *without for all that providing him with another culture that he can call his own; without arming him with a map that would allow him to be or to feel at home.*

We find no parousia in Feraoun's work, no final synthesis or reconciling *Aufhebung* at the end. By making the novel's "informer" (Feraoun's word) mute, Feraoun emphasizes the fundamental paradox of colonial alienation: assimilation always refers to a particular situation—and to a *topos* as well—that makes any reconciliation between heterogeneous belongings impossible.[9] We are then faced with a "blurring of identity" and, as Derrida has shown in a similar context, the very formation of the "speaking I" (*dire-je*) or the "me-I" (*moi-je*) refers to the "site of a *situation* that cannot be found, a site always referring elsewhere, to something other, to another language, to the other in general."[10]

This is what Feraoun has managed to translate by giving his text its particular form, in which the "I" of the first part and the "I" about whom the "he" of the second part is supposedly speaking no longer coincide. What reveals this noncoincidence of voices and personae to *us* is the fact that "this same 'I' is also someone for whom access to French *was also interdicted*, in a different, apparently roundabout, and perverted manner."[11]

In order to get out of this impasse, Feraoun splits both himself and his work in two. He delegates to Fouroulou the task of narrating the period when he was (supposedly) still a member of a community, and to a narrator X the task of narrating the events that would forever separate him from his community, making him a "mtourni," that is, someone who can never again live within his original community.[12] In this way, Feraoun provides himself with the means of experiencing that which is spectral in the colonized's relation to France, in particular for those who are evolved (*les évolués*).[13] At bottom, it is as if Feraoun had found a solution to the problem that all evolved people will come to know—that of being aware of the fact that just as assimilation will provide them with a way out, it will also distance them from their culture and the customs of their community. And it will do so radically and, in a certain way, *definitively*, because assimilation very quickly reveals itself to be Orphic in nature: the price to pay for coming back with an education, a degree, or a future even—an identity in other words—is never again to be able to turn toward who one was and forget everything.

In the second part of the book, the narrative uses indirect discourse or a third party. In a certain way, Fouroulou wanted to remain faithful to the community to which he belonged, and this no doubt is why he did not dare bring his narrative to the *point where it breaks off.* In fact, he is presented as someone who has experienced rupture as destiny; but this destiny is in its turn revealed as the pure product of the colonial policy of educating the natives. And so, as Feraoun clearly demonstrates, to speak of destiny—and to make destiny speak—proves that the departure of our hero, his break with his community, was never his *own doing.* Rather, it was the result of a logic and a history that go well beyond the freedom of a single individual.

In this context, the name "Fouroulou" Menrad becomes emblematic, or even symptomatic, of the drama to which I alluded at the outset.[14] As his name indicates, Fouroulou will be *the man who cannot speak his own name*, the man/writer who must remain hidden and who can only be himself (?) *clandestinely*, because the act of writing—because of the existential and cultural situation that is made of it—has been transformed into alienation, both a breaking in (*effraction*) and a deterritorialization *at once.*

In and of itself the structure of the novel is thus a denunciation of colonialism's misdeeds. It was colonization that turned emancipation, learning to read and write, into the equivalent of "cutting oneself off from one's community," becoming alienated, acculturated, and deculturated precisely at the point where one was supposed to enter into culture and become emancipated.

Had Feraoun not chosen the structure of a *divided* narrative, we would simply have been faced with an edifying narrative, in the rather trite mode of Pagnol-like populist novels. True, Feraoun's writing is "simple" and at times seems to be in the style of a legal document: Is his writing blank or neutral? Is it the writing of a schoolteacher (?) or a good student? It seems, rather, to be a writing that offers a choice: to write neutrally is to let one's readers have leeway to form their own opinions, to provide a way of not forcing them into something.

When Feraoun describes misery, hunger, and illness, he does not do so for ideological, apologetic, or edifying purposes; and this no doubt is what explains why there is no happy end to this novel, and, in fact, no end at all. It is the extradiegetic narrator who informs us of Feraoun/Fouroulou's fate. He (?) is the one who provides the truncated, incomplete narrative that Feraoun had deliberately left to posterity with a continuation.

Yet something that is just as striking and important is the fact that there is no real hero in *Le fils du pauvre*; the hero is the people, the small community of Tizi: Ramdane and Omar, the emigrants; Khalti and Nana, the two women who struggle alone to survive adversity; Fatma and Helima, the mothers who face the difficulties of all poor families; and the others.

The two-voiced structure of the novel clearly demonstrates that colonialism is the social, economic, political, and cultural regime that, while it allows some of its "native" subjects to be saved, always does so to the detriment of the community to which these individuals belong. One hundred and thirty five years after the conquest of Algeria, the country was still 85 percent illiterate. Feraoun was conscious of all this, and thus he did not turn his alter ego into a hero, into a self-made man to the glory of the colonial education system. By lending his voice to an anonymous narrator to continue the narrative, he wanted us to meditate on this tragedy and understand that one survivor among millions is not a success story.

Feraoun has been compared to Jack London, Maxim Gorki, and even to Jean Giono (on the back cover of the book, for example). But these comparisons do not take into account what this deceptively simple narrative tells us about a history that continues to weigh upon the fate of the French and Algerian people. When he wrote *Le fils du pauvre*, Mouloud Feraoun may have had the hope—no doubt idealistic—that one day Fouroulou's destiny would no longer be a privileged one, but that his fate would some day be shared by his friends from

Tizi, his sisters, and all the other boys and girls of all the other Algerian villages. Certainly he could not have imagined that he, one of the rare survivors of the system, would be assassinated on March 15, 1962, a few days before the country's independence, in the very school where he was a teacher. This terrible event may be interpreted as the result of fate; but given the circumstances of his life, it is easy to view it as a symptom. For having dared to represent the unrepresentable and risked breaking the taboo (*l'interdit*) regarding any attempt to aspire to the culture of the other, Feraoun had to pay with his blood. Because he transgressed the fundamental taboo of fiction and of what can be said (*le dire*), Feraoun apparently went too far, crossing a boundary in a way the colonial regime could not tolerate. This is what gives his work its exemplary meaning, power, and beauty.

8

By Way of a Conclusion

In the final chapter of her book on contemporary postcolonial theories, Ania Loomba asks the following:

> Are academics located in the West, or working in Western conceptual and narrative paradigms, incapable of opening up the perspectives within which we can view the non-Western world? Or have they adopted reactive perspectives which lock them into a reductive position whereby they can return the colonial gaze only by mimicking its ideological imperatives and intellectual procedures?[1]

In the context that interests us here, it is obvious that a question of this kind is not innocent and deserves to be considered in all seriousness. *Are* scholars who live and teach in the West—specifically in the United States—capable of transcending Western critical and theoretical frameworks and paradigms so as to create an original, *critical* work? Do they have the means to turn the tools with which Western culture has provided them to their advantage, to make them serve the peoples from which they come? Or are they forever condemned to ape the ideological imperatives of their previous masters, as Dipesh Chakrabarty and many other contemporary postcolonial critics would have it?[2] For these critics, because postcolonial scholars have for the most part been educated in Western colonial institutions, they are unlikely to be able to overcome the handicap that is, so to speak, ontologically inscribed in European critical and theoretical protocols. What is troubling here, however, is that, just when they are formulating questions in this way, these critics seem to have forgotten that they themselves have done everything possible to put us on our guard against the dangers inherent in all attempts at cultural, political, or ideological generalization. They also tend to neglect the fact that their theoretical baggage has most often been inherited from the philosophical and scientific figureheads of Western thought: Marx, Freud, Nietzsche; but also Kant, Hegel, or Heidegger, depending on the situation. Furthermore, isn't one essentializing things in one's turn when one speaks of postcolonial scholars and academics as if they formed a homogeneous category? Isn't it a kind of excessive generalization to say that men and women who have been educated and who teach in Europe and the United States are condemned to repeat the values of the ex-colonial power or that they are, willingly or unwillingly, in all circumstances, its ideological and political stooges? One need scratch the surface only slightly to realize that beneath such an approach lies a fantasy of contamination: the great fear of having been body-snatched, so to speak, by European modes of thought and transformed into a simple cog in the system of reproduction of Western ideology.

This kind of thinking cannot lead us far, based as it is on a completely erroneous conception of the nature of what is learned (or not), assimilated (or not) from Western culture by the ex-colonial subjects and on a very narrow vision of the notions of borrowing, apprenticeship, and education. It also presupposes that Europe or, if one prefers, the West has a monopoly on the formation of master narratives and that these narratives somehow represent a homogeneous and transparent instance.

As I hope to have shown throughout this book, nothing could be more false. The texts I have studied here make evident that it is no longer possible to reduce the various *protocols of knowledge* and *forms of narrative* to any single hegemonic formation—even one from the West. Furthermore, when Loomba reminds her readers of the content of the works of someone like Paul Gilroy, she herself reinforces the idea that it is no longer possible to isolate black American or African culture from other cultures—in particular European or Latin American—and that the world can no longer be divided into clearly differentiated categories (such as race, language, nation, religion). As we know all too well today, these categories are constructions that do not allow us to account for the complexity of the interrelations that characterize international exchanges in the age of globalization.[3] Thus, the work of the writers I have studied here must be inscribed in the ever-changing "Tout-Monde" (as it has been defined by Glissant), and not in a space that has been reduced to any single ethnic or racial component.[4] To say that postcolonial intellectuals and critics must be more sensitive to the concrete realities of their respective countries, that they must study local situations more seriously, is, *at best*, stating the obvious. For how can one claim to write something competent if one doesn't really know what one is talking about? *At worst*, it implies a serious misunderstanding of what is really happening over there. What, in fact, is happening? In what situation do the intellectuals in question find themselves? And is this "situation," to use Sartre's term, as uniform as all that? Finally, are postcolonial intellectuals—whether they are working in the field or whether they are in "the lion's jaws," as Kateb would say—merely content to borrow, and are they as alienated or as innocent as all that?

To affirm, for example, that "insofar as the discourse of history—that is, history as the discourse produced at the institutional site of the university is concerned, 'Europe' remains the sovereign,"[5] as Chakrabarty does; to present the fact that third-world historians refer to the works of European historians as well as their methodologies as proof of their alienation, based on the fact that there is no reciprocity—none of this makes any sense, because it does not take into account several factors:

1. That history as a discipline was never the exclusive property of European intellectuals. All civilizations—Arab, Chinese, and so on—have their hagiographers, their annalists, and will eventually have their own historians; it is thus absurd to present recourse to history as an act of allegiance to Europe and therefore of alienation from one's original culture. All that postcolonial historians and writers have managed to bring to light since independence should amply suffice to refute such a vision of things.[6]

2. Several things are being confused here: (a) the history that we shall call colonialist, drawn up by the colonialists themselves or by their sycophants, on the one hand, and the history that modern historians have managed to wrest from the servile history of the former, on the other; (b) this also comes down to saying that only Western historians can be scientific, because one then seems to be saying that only by differentiating oneself from them can one ever hope to be free to draw up one's own history.

And so it seems that some postcolonial critics still do not understand, *especially when dealing with literary texts*, that it is not that intellectuals should *distance themselves* from European intellectuals—which is merely a reactive attitude. Rather, they should participate *on equal footing* with them in what, for example, historiography, philosophy, or modern literary theory have bequeathed to us: a historical methodology and protocols of thought that have profoundly contributed to articulating the ideological bases of political *and* intellectual independence movements, as well as the tools for thinking about the significance and meaning of the present. The Algerian War—Algeria, the country of Saint Augustine, but also of Juba II and Ibn Khaldoun—did not lead to Algeria's independence without producing Ferhat Abbas, Abane Ramdane, and Franz Fanon, as well as Albert Memmi, Assia Djebar, and Hélé Béji; that is, historians, sociologists, and writers who would take up the torches of their previous masters and attempt to light their own way, as well as that of their peoples.

All this is to say that if history seemed at one time to be primarily the instrument par excellence of colonization, this never meant that it was essentially the exclusive property of the colonizer or of Europeans. Europeans themselves once had to take over the resources that history—as well as philosophy, poetry, and the art of war—had circumstantially placed in the hands of Arabs, in order to turn it into their own instrument of conquest and subjugation. What we are seeing today is neither necessarily an act of allegiance nor some sort of situation of alienation. Rather, we are witnessing the reversal of a situation whereby those who were dominated in the past regain strength and gradually relearn the importance of what making and relating history means; relearn what narrating, fabulating, and fictioning mean. To reproach intellectuals for being subservient to European methods, to say that what they do depends wholly on a problematic that is foreign to them, is automatically to place oneself in a position where it is impossible both to write one's own history *and* to fight against the history that was written for one. It is as if one had asked the Algerian independence fighters not to use modern weapons because the machine gun, the canon, and the grenade were invented by the French! The fact is that they needed to learn to use these arms—the metaphor is troublesome, granted—while continuing to learn to use the other arms that the colonialist West had used to subjugate them and enslave them politically, culturally, and economically. One need only think of the impact of the introduction and mastery of modern means of communication in the so-called third world countries: telephone, internet, e-mail, dish antennas, and so on. It is by fighting for their independence that Algerians, Africans, Vietnamese, Haitians, and so on managed to rediscover the theoretical arms that they lacked and that they needed to escape their alienation. To think of the relation subaltern/colonizer as a fixed relation that can only be undone—like the Gordian knot—by a return to the self, or a return to one's native land, is to forbid the disciple from being free from the master. It is also to ignore the fact that the intellectuals in question have not always chosen to be in the place where they have landed. One forgets all too easily that, even if they live in conditions that are relatively better in their adopted lands, they are also emigrants, exiles who were pursued by their own governments, driven out of their countries. They have had to adapt, find the means of rebuilding a life, as well as the means of "thinking differently, otherwise" (*pensée autre*), as Khatibi would say. They have had to find the means of understanding what was happening to them and, at the same time, what was happening to their own country. In other words, their work is also the symptom of what has happened to their country, their people, their culture.[7] To say that they are alienated, and that they can only think *like Europeans* is to give Europe a transparency that it does not have and to give them an opacity that they have never ceased to contest. Their works—themselves migrant, censured, exiled—are living proof that their emancipation, and that of their people, has already been moving forward for a long time.[8]

Le Dépays

On Chris Marker's *Lettre de Sibérie* (1957)

I write to you from a distant country. *They call it Siberia. For
most of you, it evokes nothing other than a frozen Guyana, and
for the tsarist general Andreevich it was "the largest wasteland
in the world." Luckily there are more things on the earth and
under the sky, Siberian or otherwise, than all the generals can
dream of.*

*As I write, I am following with my eyes the fringe of a small
copse of birch trees, and I remember that the name of this tree
in Russian is an endearment: Biriosinka.*

*It could be autumn in Ermenoville or New England, if it were
not for the telegraph workers, with boots like Michel Strogoff,
who as high as trapeze artists are working their hands like shoe-
makers. They make you believe in Siberia. Not only because of
the local color they provide—with their boots, fur hats, and
lovely barley-sugar hair. But also because of the idea, for example, that if one of these climbing Cossacks began absent-mind-
edly to roll up his wire all the way to the other end of the line,
he would wind up with an 8,000 kilometer ball.*

—Chris Marker, *Lettre de Sibérie* [Letter from Siberia]; text
from the film's voice-over

It has always been extremely difficult to situate Chris Marker's films, to classify them in one category or another. His *Lettre de Sibérie* is no exception. On the surface, the film recounts the journey of a French filmmaker in Yakutsk. As the images unfurl, however, viewers gradually realize that what they see is not so much contradicted as constantly displaced by what they hear. Rather than making the viewer's task easier, the voice of the narrator-reciter seems to make it more difficult. And while viewers don't really see double, they do *hear* double. Letter upon letter, voice upon voice, image upon words! André Bazin recognized this synesthetic effect when he commented that in this film, it is the "sonorous beauty" (in particular, of the spoken word) that becomes the "primordial element," and it is from this word that the "mind must leap to the image." And Bazin added: "The editing moves from ear to eye."[1] The eye listens.

Perhaps Bazin was thinking of Paul Claudel, whom Marker also quotes on the sound track; but I cannot help be reminded of Henri Michaux's collection of poems entitled *Lointain intérieur*, and in particular his prose poem "Je vous écris d'un pays lointain" ("I write to you from a distant country"):

> I write to you from the ends of the earth. You have to know. Often the trees tremble. We gather up the leaves. They have so many veins. But why? There's nothing between them and the tree any more, and we disperse, embarrassed.[2]
> I write to you from the ends of the earth. We are going deeper and deeper into this endless taiga, where once the Siberians—the enemies of spilled blood—were happy to drive back their criminals. Here no doubt freedom was more likely to kill than a bullet. [*Letter from Siberia*, 42]

In the time of a fleeting citation, double exposures and dissolves fuse two heterogeneous texts, two falsely identical voices, one that comes to us from a distant interior and the other that seems to burst forth from a near exterior. As these two voices merge, they seem to sound the death knell of the travel film, sending the journey out to discover other horizons, languages, voices, landscapes, sounds, and other texts as well. We are witness to a veritable passion for alterity; an alterity nourished not so much by the desire to merge with the other—this would be reducing it to the same or to the self—as by the will to make this alterity seen, heard, and almost experienced in its intractable difference.[3] We are also witness to a veritable passion for what we can call, using Victor Segalen's term, the "Diverse," since to travel is to go toward the other in oneself, to lose sight of the self. But of course there are different ways of traveling:

> There are different ways of traveling—Barnabooth's way, Genghis Khan's way, Plume's way—and for example: accepting in no particular order the rhymes, waves, and shocks, all the bumpers [sic] of memory, its meteors and its dredges.[4]

Whereas in Michaux, Marker finds a *paredre* with whom to journey through "imaginary current events" that allow him to make certain characteristic slippages,[5] in Segalen he finds an alter ego in whom he can nourish his taste for narrative and "true" exoticism. Indeed, Marker does not find his "distant interior" in Michaux's imaginary *Paoddema*, *Pays de la Magie* or *Grande Garabagne*, but in Pyongyang, Tokyo, or Irkutsk—cities in "real" countries that, thanks to the "magic power" (Segalen) of his photographic and cinematographic images, are transformed into what we could call his "Close Exterior." And it is this constant passing between a "Hinter-World" made up precisely of the "bumpers, meteors, and dredges" of memory—"the place one comes from"—and a "Fore-World" made up of journeys to come and of the terra incognita represented by the breathtaking white of geographical maps and film that characterize *Letter from Siberia*. It is a film of passage, in the sense of a rite of passage in Taoism. But it is also a film of conversion, in the sense of a hysterical conversion—provided this expression is understood in more than purely clinical terms. *Letter from Siberia* aims to reveal a presence beneath and beyond the representations of what is there to be seen.[6] The idea is to wrest Siberia from clichés and stereotypes, to return it to its inhabitants, customs, rivers, forests, animals, and above all to its own imaginary and its own folklore. In so doing, some of the strangeness of Siberia in all its diversity is made to pass *through us*; and Siberia takes on for us some of the transparency that it has for Siberians. Soon the encounter between opacity and transparency, the near and the far, the inside and the outside, the old and the new, something like a "pure presence" (Deleuze) of Siberia become both visible and audible. As these different series are paired off and juxtaposed, we are able to experience the Siberian diverse, and to share the feelings of the Yakouts and the Siberian Toungouses. Indeed, for Marker, "geography is perhaps nothing more than feeling in code."[7]

Like Segalen's, Marker's work is that of an *exot*.[8] That is, it is the work of someone whose ecstatic gaze is constantly aimed at the outside and at exile from the self. It encompasses a displacement between two places of the imaginary, one a distant civilization to be tamed and the other a civilization that is curiously familiar and for which one must lose one's affection. This, then, is what Marker magnificently calls not *dépaysement* but *Le dépays*.[9] It is a "virtual" country, somewhere between Tokyo and Paris, Siberia and Arizona, for there are always two image tracks, two savage hordes of words from horizons of the diverse that an atopical word—Biriosinka, Chu-mou, or L(I)ena/S(I)ena—will bring together by multiplying their respective differences. Unlike with words that represent concepts, with the multitude of "bastant"[10] words such as Biriosinka or Chu-mou in Marker's films—words that act like dark precursors and that always mean at least two things, two percepts, two affects that belong to different contexts and cultures—meanings enclosed in one series are never absorbed by the meanings of the other series with which it is juxtaposed. The stories that each series enfolds remain intricately involved with one another, whereas the series themselves remain distinct from each other. As it plays on at least two heterogeneous series of images or texts, the bastant word complicates things by multiplying stories; and within these stories, it provokes and engenders new distinctions, new images, causing each series to branch out in a new series of yet other stories, other imaginaries. At times, too, the process begins from an image that has escaped from the text: a simple medallion representing a boat with paddles, for example, will summon the histories of the two gold rushes—American and Soviet—complicating them with the journeys of Charlie Chaplin and the Trans-Siberian:

Until now, the context was mostly Russian. But once Iénisséi [Tennessee?] had been passed, the décor changed. While the uniformed engineers began to miss Moscow, the American prospectors began to recognize Arizona. Did you expect to find Indians? There were some! [*Letter from Siberia*, 69]

From this point on, other "magical" spaces can easily loom up in the heart of Siberia. The viewer is not dying, he is not delirious. He is jubilant. We continue. And from behind a sentence images begin to rise up, like confessions. A morning in times of peace. A bedroom in times of peace, a real bedroom. A little wood of birches. Real children. Real birds. A bear with the lovely name of Ouchatik. An André Gide. A real horse. Real Indians. Real gold diggers. But also real trappers. The 16th day, at 7:02 A.M., "the cranes begin to move. They are genuine monsters: 30 meters high. And as it should be, each of these monsters is tied to a young girl. She gives it orders in a monstrous alphabet, and the monster obeys."[11]

As I leave the movie theater, for just an instant I think I'm a crane operator in Irkutsk! I too have tasted the monstrous alphabet. True, I was a bit drunk from cold and anticipation. I imagine the Spartak players from Yakutsk finally receiving the Dynamo team from Odessa or, why not, the Olympic team from Marseilles, in underground stadiums with an electronic referee that goes "tilt" when the public whistles. I also imagine going to sit on the terrace of the Escholier on the Place de la Sorbonne to drink a beer, where I could see my friend Ouchatik getting his first taste of the Parisian crowds. And then . . .

And then, straight ahead!

Introduction
Is an "Experimental" Nation Possible?

1. Among others, we could mention—but the list is obviously not exhaustive—texts as varied as Théophile Gautier's *Voyages en Algérie ou Scènes d'Afrique* (1853), Guy de Maupassant's *Au soleil* (1884), Fromentin's *Un été dans le Sahara* or his *Une année dans le Sahel*, and Henri de Montherlant's *Il y a encore des Paradis. Images d'Alger 1928–1931*. We could also add J. T. Merle's *Anecdotes historiques et politiques sur Alger* (1831), Isabelle Eberhardt's *Mes journaliers* (1923), J. Lemaître's *Petites orientales*, etc. For additional details, see Aimé Dupuy, *L'Algérie dans les lettres françaises* (Paris: Les Éditions Universitaires, 1956).

2. Edward Said, "Figures, Configurations, Transfigurations," *Race and Class*, 32:1 (1990), in Neil Lazarus, *Nationalism and Cultural Practice in the Postcolonial World* (Cambridge: Cambridge University Press, 1999), 139–40; my emphasis.

3. See Gilles Deleuze, *Difference and Repetition*, trans. Paul Patton (London: Athlone Press, 1994), 208.

4. Some of the chapters in this book have appeared previously in specialized journals, in French or in English. All have been revised, and only those parts of direct interest to the general problematic of this book have been included here.

Chapter 1
Nations of Writers

1. Gilles Deleuze and Félix Guattari, *Kafka: Toward a Minor Literature*, trans. Dana Polan, foreword by Réda Bensmaïa (Minneapolis: University of Minnesota Press, 1986), 18.

2. Jean Déjeux, *La littérature algérienne contemporaine* (Paris: PUF, Collection "Que sais-je," 1975), 75ff.

3. Albert Memmi, *The Colonizer and the Colonized*, trans. Howard Greenfeld (Boston: Beacon Press, 1991). See in particular the section entitled "Situations of the Colonized" (90–108) and especially the following: "The colonized writer is condemned to live his renunciations [of either mother tongue or colonial language] to the bitter end. The problem can have but two outcomes: either the natural death of colonized literature—the following generations, born in liberty, will write spontaneously in their newly found language; or, without waiting that long, a second possibility can tempt the writer—to decide to join the literature of the mother country [*la littérature métropolitaine*]. Let us leave aside the ethical problems raised by such an attitude. It is the suicide of the colonized literature; in either prospect (the only difference being the date), colonized literature in European languages appears condemned to die young." (111; translation modified) The point here is not simply to state that Memmi was wrong, but to note that the most important Maghrebi Francophone writers were "born" after independence and new talents continue to appear on the scene.

4. We could say the same for the other countries of the Maghreb, Tunisia and Morocco.

5. I rely on Deleuze and Guattari's *Kafka*, and Henri Gobard, *L'aliénation linguistique. Analyse tétraglossique*, quoted in *Kafka*, 23–4, note 19.

6. An expression in which we find words in French and Arabic, with a supposedly Kabyle pronunciation.

7. See Nabile Farès, *Un passager de l'occident* (Paris: Éditions du Seuil, 1971). Specifically, I am referring to the little allegory on page 32: "*Currently Kabylia is suffering from the deepest malaise, what is called the 'fig tree's malaise,' there is even a song that is reluctantly*

sung to show that one knows how to speak but that one does not want to be heard, so precious this song of today! so intimate . . . and this song goes 'our fig tree has always been infested with fungus' and 'the coming of the people from the plains rotted our orchard' and 'if the fig tree doesn't speak anymore, it's because his friend the hedgehog was stolen from him,' " etc. The entire context (and the rest of this apologue) demonstrates Farès's acute consciousness of what Memmi called a "linguistic drama." (Farès's italics and punctuation.)

8. Quoted in T. Brennan, "The National Longing for Form," in *Nation and Narration*, 68, note 14.

9. Anthony Barnett, "Salman Rushdie: A Review Article," *Race and Class* (Winter 1985). Cited in Brennan, Ibid.

10. And, to a certain extent, as we shall try to show subsequently, with filmmakers such as Merzak Allouache, Assia Djebar, and Amina Benguigui.

11. Quoted in Paule Thévenin, "Voir/Entendre/Lire," *Tel Quel*, 42–3 (1969).

12. See Jean Déjeux, *La littérature algérienne contemporaine* (Paris, 1975), 58ff.

13. The period, for example, of Djebar's *Les enfants du nouveau monde* (Paris: Julliard, 1962).

14. Quoted in Déjeux, *La littérature*, 72.

15. Nabile Farès, *Un passager de l'occident*, 35.

16. Because I cannot fully develop this point within the framework of this chapter, I refer to my article "L'exil est mon royaume ou les Devenirs de Nabile Farès. Idéographie et Politique," in *Francographies: Création et realité d'expression française*, Special Number 11 (1993) (New York: Publications de la Société des professeurs français et francophones d'Amérique, 1994).

17. Hélé Béji, *Désenchantement national: Essai sur la décolonisation* (Paris: François Maspero, 1982), 18.

Chapter 2
Cities of Writers

1. Michel de Certeau, *The Practice of Everyday Life*, trans. Steven F. Rendall (Berkeley: University of California Press, 1984).

2. In this sense, the experience of the passerby is very close to that of Segalen's *exot*. Like the *exot*, the passerby in the Medina is someone who is "a Born-Traveler in the worlds of marvelous diversities, and [who feels] all the flavor of the Diverse"; like the "*exot*, the passerby is able to say: 'To see the world and then say his vision of the world.' " See Victor Segalen, *Essai sur l'exotisme: Une esthétique du divers* (Montpellier: Fata Morgana, 1968), 42.

This experience of the old city also has deep affinities with the relation that that particular passerby, the migrant, has with the city. I refer here to Isaak Joseph's marvelous book *Le passant considérable. Essai sur la dispersion de l'espace public* (Paris: Librairie de Méridiens, 1984), where we can read this intriguing passage: "What are the characteristics of [this] world [i.e., the world of the Maghrebi emigrant, for example]? First, he is *delocalized*. Whatever the organization of the city, whatever its social or cultural morphology, it remains *depolarized* for the migrant. How can one orient oneself when one is incapable of perceiving oneself in this new context? The field of vision is irremediably segmented, all totalizing vision has become impossible. The frame shrinks. Confusing accumulation of sights. Absence of perspectives" (74).

3. Elias Canetti, *The Voices of Marrakesh*, trans. J. A. Underwood (New York: Continuum, 1978), 17–18.

4. Hélé Béji, *L'oeil du jour* (Paris: Maurice Nadeau, 1985), 127; my emphasis.

5. Claude Ollier, *Marrakch Médine* (Paris: Flammarion, 1979), 20.

6. This is the case for many writers from the Maghreb after the independence of their country from colonial rule, and in particular, in exemplary fashion, for a writer such as Hélé Béji in her *Itinéraire de Paris à Tunis* (Paris: Noel Blandin, 1992) and *Oeil du jour*.

7. Here I have strung together passages from Claude Ollier, Hélé Béji, and Elias Canetti. I could have considerably added to these references to the "chaosmos" of the Medina by citing passages from A. Meddeb's *Talismano* (Paris: Éditions Christian Bourgois, 1979).

8. Claude Ollier, *Marrakch Médine*, 20.

9. Isaac Joseph, *Le passant considérable: éssai sur la dispersion de l'espace public* (Paris: Librairie des méridiens, 1984).

10. Deleuze and Guattari, *Qu'est-ce que la philosophie?* (Paris: Éditions de Minuit, 1991), 67.

11. Nicholas de Cues created the Idiot and Descartes the Cogito, Nietzsche the dancer, Kierkegaard the seducer, and Pierre Klossowski the couple. See Deleuze and Guattari, *Qu'est-ce que la philosophie?* 68ff.

12. Chris Marker, *Le dépays* (Paris: Herscher, Format/Photo, 1982). See appendix: *Le dépays*: On Chris Marker's *Lettre de Sibérie*. I have included this text in my book because Chris Marker's notion of "dépays" has played an important role in the conception of the idea of "experimental" nations.

13. *Talismano*, 15.

14. *L'oeil du jour*, 103; my emphasis.

15. Chris Marker, *Le dépays*, np.

16. Emily Apter, *Continental Drift: From National Characters to Virtual Subjects* (Chicago: University of Chicago Press, 1999), 2.

17. Pierre Nora, introduction to *De l'archive à l'embleme*, vol. 3 of *Les lieux de Mémoire: Les* France, ed. Pierre Nora (Paris: Gallimard, 1992), 15–16. Quoted in Emily Apter, *Continental Drift: From National to Virtual Subjects* (Chicago and London: University of Chicago Press, 1999), 2. It is surprising that this "sanctioning" by the "foreigner" did not elicit a certain curiosity regarding the viewpoint of immigrant populations in France. Are there not nearly one million Algerians living in France today? And what about the Haitians, Senegalese, Martinicans, and other immigrants counted among France's population? What about the *Beurs*?

18. We are all familiar with Ernest Renan's thesis in "What Is a Nation?" "[F]orgetting, I would even go so far as to say historical error, is a crucial factor in the creation of a nation, which is why progress in historical studies [!] often constitutes a danger for [the principles of] nationality. Indeed, historical enquiry brings to light deeds of violence which took place at the origins of all political formations. . . . Unity is always effected by means of brutality." "What is a Nation?"

trans. Martin Thom, in *Nation and Narration*, ed. Homi K. Bhabha (New York: Routledge, 1990), 9.

19. Laurent Gervereau, Jean-Pierrre Rioux, and Benjamin Stora, *La France en guerre d'Algérie. Novembre 1954–Juillet 1962* (Paris: Musée d'histoire contemporaine-BDIC, 1992), quoted in Anne Donadey, *Recasting Postcolonialism: Women Writing between Worlds*. In the two or three paragraphs that follow, I owe much to Donadey's analysis of the different forms of forgetting the "war without a name" in the works of postcolonial Francophone writers. I will come back to this.

20. Jean-Pierre Rioux, "La flamme et le bûcher," in *La guerre d'Algérie et les Français: Colloque de l'institut d'histoire du temps présent*, ed. Jean-Pierre Rioux (Paris: Fayard, 1990), cited in Naomi Davidson's excellent article, "Naming *La guerre sans nom*: Memory, Nation and Identity in French Representations of the Algerian War, 1963–1992," *Paroles gelées* 16:2 (special issue, 1998), 65.

21. Tahar Ben Jelloun, *Hospitalité Française: Racisme et immigration maghrébine*, 33.

22. Anne Donadey, *Recasting Postcolonialism: Women Writing Between Worlds* (Portsmouth: Heinemann, 2001). I would like to thank Anne Donadey for allowing me to make reference to her work here and to use her excellent analyses in the pages that follow.

23. Donadey refers to this movement of thought in a passage where she clearly demonstrates the analogies between the almost total "forclusion" of "Vichy" and what I am calling here the "scotoma" or "blind spot" of Algiers.

24. See Jean Baudrillard and Paul Guillaume, *Figures de l'altérité* (Paris: Descartes et Cie, 1994), esp. the chapter entitled "La spectralité comme élision de l'autre," 19ff.

25. Paul de Man, "Autobiography as De-Facement," in *The Rhetoric of Romanticism* (New York, Columbia University Press, 1984), pp. 75–6.

26. Martin McQuillan, *Paul de Man, Routledge Critical Thinkers* (London and New York: Routledge, 2001), pp. 77–9.

27. See Amin Maalouf, *Les identités meurtrières* (Paris: Éditions Grasse & Fasquelle, 1998).

Chapter 3
Nabile Farès, or How to Become "Minoritarian"

1. See Leila Sebbar, "Femmes arabes: des citoyennes," in *Le magazine littéraire* (May 1992), 99: "For some years Algerian women have been experiencing a situation unlike any other before. They claim in effect to be essential to a political debate in which they themselves are the stakes. They form a minority that is avant-garde, ready to fight, and that has no intention of letting itself be swindled as did the generation of the war of liberation." See also Sophie Bessis and Souhayr Belhassen, *Femme du Maghreb, l'enjeu* (Paris: Lattès, 1996), and Fatima Mernissi, *La peur de la modernité. Conflit Islam et démocratie* (Paris: Albin Michel, 1992).

2. Deleuze and Guattari, *A Thousand Plateaus*, trans. Brian Massumi (Minneapolis: University of Minnesota Press, 1987), 291.

3. Regarding the status of women in Algeria and the different forms their struggles have taken, see chapter 5 infra on Assia Djebar's "prise de parole" in *La Nouba des femmes du Mont Chenoua*.

4. Think, for example, of the recent events in South Africa where one can see how the white majority—in fact an actual (numerical) minority—is in the process of *becoming* a minority. Thus the desperate attempts of the reactionary, conservative wing to halt the events by means of violence; they are, in psychoanalytic terms, *acting out*. It seems, however, that the white progressive "minority" is, on the contrary, experiencing a *becoming-minoritarian* worth paying attention to.

5. Farès does not state that the hypostasis "Man/Algerian-Man" is the cause of this bureaucracy or patriarchal regime, but it most certainly is for him one of the *transcendental conditions of possibility* of its hegemony. Without this "great bass" (Ezra Pound), it would be impossible to establish a patriarchal and bureaucratic regime. We can easily imagine that, for Farès, the supremacy of the FIS draws from the same "Man" source. The whole "Paganism" theme in Farès's work may be/must be read as an attempt to extract Algeria—even if it is by poetic, and thus *virtual*, means—from the usurpation of all (the) power by this "false" majority, that is, a usurped majority that was arbitrarily imposed on Algeria. "The renewal of ancient Pa-

ganism in a belief in life without obstacles is the route by which an Algerian artistic consciousness will be defined. Any other determination on the cultural level will be nothing other than a false and dull ideological reconstruction. It is the idea that must be made apparent, and not giving an idea to a rotten appearance." And Farès adds, unambiguously: "The true homeland of Algeria is its most ancient past, and the most ancient past of Algeria, AESTHETICALLY SPEAKING, is Paganism. When revolutionary expression meets pagan expression, the life-moment the country is going through will increase in political fervor." (*Un passager de l'occident*, 74ff; Farès's capitalization)

6. For the "molar/molecular" paradigm, see Deleuze and Guattari, *A Thousand Plateaus*, 292.

7. Farès, *Un passager*, 74–5: "The cultural history of contemporary Algeria is still a 'cathartic' history. The recognition of an internal dialectic in Algerian society as such has not yet occurred. After the French decolonization of Algeria will come the Islamic decolonization of Algeria. For whatever our Islamic brothers think and want us 'to think,' the Islamization of Algeria is not a divine phenomenon, but like all phenomena, it is a historical one.

8. Rather, for Farès, they are *contingent*, which is obviously something else entirely.

9. Farès, *Un passager*, 151. The double—or, even better, the *crossed* (*croisée*)—deterritorialization allows us to identify a deterritorializing and a deterritorialized force, even if it is the same force that moves from one value to the other according to the "moment" or the aspect under consideration; furthermore, the least deterritorialized element or force always precipitates the deterritorialization of the most deterritorializing, which affects it even more. During the war of liberation, Algeria (as national entity with a majoritarian vocation?) was the most deterritorializing force; but as soon as the war ended and independence was gained, this force changed valence.

10. Farès, *L'état perdu: Discours pratique de l'émigré* (Le Paradou: Actes Sud, 1982).

11. Deleuze and Guattari, *A Thousand Plateaus*, 4.

12. Ibid.

13. As registration numbers, the drawings as well as the words are symptoms, especially if we think of the affects attached to the registration cards of Maghrebi immigrants, and on an even deeper level, of all the connotations attached to this lexeme: car registration, the registration of Jews in Nazi concentration camps, etc. And let's not forget that registration's goal is always to *identify* individuals.

14. Farès, *L'état perdu*; Farès's emphasis.

15. Things are in fact a bit more complicated than that. The same kind of operation is at work here as the one that, according to Deleuze and Guattari, links the wasp and the orchid. The orchid becomes deterritorialized by forming an image or a copy of the wasp; but the wasp in turns reterritorializes itself on this image while simultaneously reterritorializing itself by becoming a pawn in the reproduction apparatus of the orchid, that is, in a new organization. Yet the wasp also reterritorializes the orchid by carrying its pollen. This process can easily be adapted to the question of languages that are at stake in *L'état perdu*. French (the language, the signs of this language) is deterritorialized by forming an image, a copy of Arabic or Kabyle; but Arabic and Kabyle in turn are reterritorialized on this "image": "3. (4 in Arabic)." (*L'état perdu*, 66) Yet by moving to a regime of signs that is foreign to them, both Arabic and Kabyle are themselves deterritorialized by becoming pawns (one signifier among others) in the apparatus of production and reproduction of meaning in French. Yet they are not themselves metamorphosed as graphic systems, without deterritorializing French, by carrying, not pollen this time, but the materiality of their signifiers that will come to fertilize the French language with their poetic power (the power of their *gesture*, rhythm, written forms).

Thus French, Arabic, Kabyle, Lybic make up a rhizome, but remain heterogeneous. Just as the orchid is said to imitate the wasp whose image it reproduces in a meaningful way, so French begins to "imitate" Arabic, Kabyle, and so on, the images of which it reproduces in a meaningful way.

But this too is merely another relatively simple view of things for, in fact, on another level, something else entirely is happening. It is not only a matter of imitation, but of a veritable capturing of the code that opens onto a plus value, an increase of valence that pro-vokes a series of becomings: the becoming-Arabic or Kabyle of French (see, for example, *L'état perdu*, 65), the becoming-French of Kabyle and of Arabic. Each one of these becomings ensures the deter-ritorialization of one of the terms and the reterritorialization of the other; the two becomings, the two semiotic systems connecting, join-ing each other according to a circulation of intensities that pushes the deterritorialization of the languages mobilized ever further: "[M]ixing signs—enough to move the sun in its 'course' to make one admit that the influence of the moon has not ended at all." (Ibid., 21–2)

16. Here let me point out Deleuze's distinction, in *Cinema 2: Image-Time*, between so-called "rational" cuts and "irrational" cuts in the construction of the "power of the continuous." See *Cinema 2: The Time Image*, "Thought and Cinema," in particular this passage: "The cuts and breaks in cinema have always formed the power of the con-tinuous. But cinema and mathematics are the same here: sometimes the cut, so-called *rational*, forms part of one of the two sets which it separates (end of one or beginning of the other). This is the case of 'classical' cinema. Sometimes, as in modern cinema, the cut has be-come the interstice, *it is irrational and does not form part of either set, one of which has no more an end than the other has a beginning: false continuity is such an irrational cut*." *Cinema 2: The Time Image*, trans. Hugh Tomlinson and Robert Galeta (Minneapolis: University of Min-nesota Press, 1989), 181.

17. For example, the recourse to pictograms, drawings, Arabic letters, or ideograms.

18. See Ezra Pound, *Guide to Kulchur* (London: Faber & Faber, 1938) (first American ed.). Rpt. New York: New Impressions, 1952; and *ABC of Reading* (New York: New Directions, 1960). See also Laszlo Géfin, *Ideogram: History of a Poetic Method* (Austin: University of Texas Press, 1982). It is to Géfin that I owe the main part of the analysis proposed here of Pound's "ideogrammatic method."

19. See the special issue of *Change* devoted to "Montage" (Paris: Seuil, 1968).

20. Géfin, *Ideogram*, 36.

21. Cited in ibid.

22. Ibid.

23. My emphasis. In order to simplify the point of my argument, I have omitted the additional case of Erigena that Pound adds to those of Gaudier, Leibniz, etc. For more details see Géfin, *Ideogram*, 36ff.

24. Pound, *ABC of Reading*, 22.

25. For the nature of the poetic word, see Julia Kristeva's introduction to Mikhail Bakhtine, *La poétique de Dostoievski* (Paris: Seuil, 1970). See also Henri Meschonnic, *La rime et la vie* (Paris: Verdier, 1989), in which he defends the idea of the poem and poetry as a "language of the body" and/or "the body in language." A nice idea, too, of the poem, and in particular of *rhythm* as "great bass." "This is why the poem makes us hear, in the sound of the world and the worldly, the subject's silence. This is its weakness and its strength. It is the allegory of what the sign can never say. *Of what one doesn't hear, which is more important than what one hears. What rhythm is.* Where a pause, which is silence, can count more than words. And so, far from being the opposition of ordinary language, the poem is its most visible representative. It is through the poem that, like in Exodus (20:18), 'all the people see the voices.'" Meschonnic, 57–8.

26. Géfin, *Ideogram*, 36.

27. Ibid, 37.

28. Ibid., 40.

29. "The multiplicity of numbers, the reversals (even: duplicity: X:10:5) is only the umbilical trajectory of a de-order of identity." Farès, *L'état perdu*, 17.

30. See the multiplicity of personalized addresses and dedications, but also all the references to places (streets, bars, restaurants, cities) or precise historical moments in the book. "Vincent was in the heart of his lands in the field-house, while Camille was in the kitchen: how this structure—not house—is mortal: 'I will offer you a cigarillo that belonged to my friend Lagona who died just a little while ago in the area, not far from Cadarache: dead, because expelled, etc.'" (Ibid., 25)

31. Quoted in Géfin, *Ideogram*, 40.

32. Deleuze and Guattari, *A Thousand Plateaus*, 36.

33. See Farès, *L'état perdu*, 17, 21, 29, 41, 43, 53, 75, etc.

34. On the specificity of the paratactic in relation to the syntactic, once again I must refer to Géfin's excellent clarification on this point: "The central method and the main form of modernism I call the *juxtapositional* or, to use the name given to it by its 'inventor' Ezra Pound, the *ideogrammatic* method. To juxtapose, of course, means to situate side by side two or more things. The method may also be called paratactic, based on the Greek verb παρατάδδω, to place beside one another. Parataxis is the opposite of hypotaxis, from ὑποταδδω, to arrange under, which signifies a dependent construction or relation of parts with connectives. On the simplest level such a mode is an asyndetic composition." (xiiff)

35. These last remarks, and everything that relates to the notion of the rhizome, are indebted to Deleuze and Guattari's wonderful text on the "rhizome" in *A Thousand Plateaus*, ch. 1, 80.

Chapter 4
Postcolonial Nations

1. Fredric Jameson, "Third World Literature in the Era of Multinational Capitalism," *Social Text, Theory/Culture/Ideology* (Fall 1986), 65–88.

2. I am thinking in particular of Ahmad Aijaz's "response" to Jameson, "Jameson's Rhetoric of 'Otherness' and the 'National Allegory,'" in *Social Text* 15 (Fall 1986), and, of course, of Homi K. Bhabha's "DissemiNation: Time, Narrative, and the Margins of the Modern Nation," in *Nation and Narration*, ed. Homi K. Bhabha (London and New York: Routledge, 1990).

3. Can works as different as Kateb Yacine's *Nedjma*, Abdelwahab Meddeb's *Talismano*, and Abdelkebir Khatibi's *Amour bilingue* be inscribed under the same generic rubric? What becomes of the concern for *writing* that these authors manifest throughout their works if consideration is given only to what in their texts belongs to "allegory," even if it is "national allegory"? I shall return to this question below.

4. I shall return to the question of the appropriateness of employing a term that is as fraught as *allegory*. One need only think of

the fate of this notion in the hands of Paul de Man! If we grant de Man that "literary codes are subcodes of a system, *rhetoric,* that is not itself a code," and that "literature is not the place where the unstable epistemology of metaphor is suspended by aesthetic pleasure" but "rather the place where the possible convergence of rigor and pleasure is *shown to be a delusion,*" it follows that the category of allegory can henceforth only complicate and make all the more uncertain and unstable the question of what is specific to "third-world" literature. See de Man, "The Epistemology of Metaphor," in *Aesthetic Ideology* THL 65 (Minneapolis: University of Minnesota Press, 1996), 49–50.

5. Let me leave aside for the moment the problems raised by the category *third world,* which at best designates a group of texts sharing the characteristic of not belonging to the West and, at worst, refers to a value judgment that has negative connotations within the hierarchy of literary angels. All in all, these texts would be "third-worldish." Obviously this is not what Jameson had in mind. Indeed, his article is more of a gesture toward integrating this literature, since for him the only hope for a revitalization of literary studies in general is the expansion of the literary canon to include postcolonial texts. For a thorough discussion of the thesis of the three worlds— "first" (capitalist countries), "second" (socialist countries), and "third" (formerly colonized countries)—I refer the reader to Aijaz's article.

6. See Albert Memmi, *Portrait,* and Réda Bensmaïa, "Traduire ou blanchir la langue," as well as "Nations of Writers," *STCL Studies in Twentieth Century Literature,* 23:1 (Winter 1999), 163–78.

7. See Bensmaïa, "Nations of Writers."

8. Tahar Djaout, *L'invention du désert* (Paris: Éditions du Seuil, 1987).

9. Djaout was born in 1954. Having studied mathematics, he became a journalist in Algeria in 1976. He is the author of a number of poems and novels, among them *Les chercheurs d'os,* which won the Fondation Del Duca awarded in 1984. In January 1993, he founded the journal *Ruptures.* He was assassinated in June that same year for his position against fanaticism.

10. I am referring here to Tahar Djaout's journalistic political activism.

11. Paul de Man, "Semiology and Rhetoric," in *Allegories of Reading* (New Haven: Yale University Press, 1979), 10.

12. While in certain passages it is evident that Djaout is referring to the Koranic "Text," there are many passages where it is a matter of the text that Western logic has superimposed on the history of the colonies.

13. Kateb Yacine, *Le polygone étoilé* (Paris: Éditions du Seuil, 1997), 10.

14. Thus the reference to Rimbaud and to the subtext to which it refers. See Djaout, *L'invention du désert*, 71, 103, 124, 151, 191–2.

15. "Narrator-trekker," but also, as we shall see, "narrator-tracker," and soon after, as I attempt to show, "Stalker." See the beautiful passage in Djaout, *L'invention du désert*: "I *track* the disintegrated tribe, I *reconstitute* the pulverized dynasty. I *swim* in the canals of the chronicles, *go up* the apocryphal torrents, I *span* time without milliaries and *stretch across* the frightening deserts. *I must make myself a renowned trekker at all costs.* I *track* with monstrous patience, however harsh the watchful wait." (40–1; my emphasis) While there is allegory to be found in this text with its multiple pathways, we must also inscribe in it the movement of the legend of Osiris. Like Isis in search of pieces of Osiris's body, which was torn apart by Seth, one of the quests of the narrator of *L'invention du désert* is to recover the dispersed fragments of a history of the Algeria that was shattered by colonization—a history whose logic will never really be understood because entire sections of it are missing. Seth the colonist has decidedly and definitively altered the integrity of the body of (the history of) Algeria. Some sections of this history are missing and will forever be missing.

16. Guy Gauthier, *Andréi Tarkovski*, FILMO 19 (Paris: Éditions Edilig, 1988).

17. See Victor Segalen, *Essai sur l'exotisme* (Paris: Livre de Poche, Biblio, Essais, 1986); English translation: *Essay on Exoticism: An Aesthetics of Diversity*, trans. Yaël Rachel Schlick, foreword by Harry Harootunian (Durham: Duke University Press, 2002).

18. See Keith Answell Pearson, "Deleuze Outside/Outside Deleuze," in *Deleuze and Philosophy: The Difference Engineer* (London and New York: Routledge, 1997), 11.

19. The word *to survey* (*baliser*) recurs constantly in Djaout's writing. See, for example, "This is why *nothing can be surveyed* and we can manage to travel a good thousand kilometers with our eyes closed." (44) See also 104, 122, etc.

20. Djaout writes: "I would have liked Ibn Toumert to be planted so firmly inside of me that the sun suddenly could acquire all the properties of liquid between my fingers. I would have wanted my head to be filled with symbols so that everything that flows—sand or water—would merge, so that everything that wounds purifies. *But the ancestor is not at my side. He is merely a distant idea that perhaps one day I will turn into a book so that his wanderings can come to an end*, so that the idea will cease migrating from place to place in my head. I will enclose it in a paper fence so as not to fear it any longer." *L'invention du désert*, 76; my emphasis.

21. Nabile Farès certainly understood this when, almost echoing Djaout, he wrote in *Un passager de l'occident*: "This is why we shall witness (we the inhabitants of the peninsula), the passage from an allegorical reality to an allegory that has become reality. Hence our infinite hope; to see artistic expression offer reality a density that it has not yet obtained" (37). For a more detailed analysis of this aspect of allegory, see Bensmaïa, "Nations of Writers."

22. Obviously, my analysis here does not do justice to everything that is at stake in Djaout's text, particularly the gesture that little by little leads the narrator to rediscover some traces of his identity in his childhood memories. It is in fact through a return to the "country of childhood," by means of writing, that the drifting of meaning and borders finally manages to be eased and appeased. But this identity is fleeting, aleatory, uncertain, and perhaps impossible in the end.

Chapter 5
(Hi)stories of Expatriation

1. The *Petit Robert* gives the following information about the feminine noun *nouba* : "(from Algerian Arabic *nowba*, 'taking turns,'

used to designate a type of music performed by various players in turn in front of dignitaries' houses) 1. Military music of certain North African regiments, played on indigenous instruments (fifes, tambourines); 2. *Fig., pop.* (1897) *faire la nouba* (see *bombance, noce*): to party. 'Just because they're rich doesn't mean they have to *faire la nouba* every day' (Georges Duhamel)."

In this article, the word *nouba* refers to the songs and dances performed by Algerian women in the five movements of Djebar's film. The four modes (*Meceder, Btaïhi, Derj* and *Nesraf*) are framed by an *Istikhbar* (prelude), a *Touchia* (overture), and a *Khlass* (finale).

2. Interview with Ouassila Tamzali, *Ciné-Arabe* 10–11, 64.

3. I would like to point out that, according to the *Encyclopedia Universalis,* "the term *suite* was originally used to designate *a series of dance tunes composed in the same key* (major or minor) but with *different rhythms and styles,*" and that "the practice of *linking dance tunes in pairs, one slow and one fast,* can be traced back to the Middle Ages." Also in the Middle Ages, "the *estampida* or *estampie,* originating in Provence, is divided into several sections—or *puncta*—creating an internal melodic periodicity through the alternation of 'open' and 'closed' cadences" (my emphasis). There is no doubt in my mind that this musical "memory" was ever present in Assia Djebar's mind as she created *La Nouba.*

4. "[T]o say that my film is a film about women is meaningless. I will always be drawn to making films. . . . [W]omen's bodies, women, are my subject matter. It's a little like being a sculptor: one uses one material, another a different material." Djebar, "Interview," 64.

5. "Here we come up against the second problem, which is perhaps more that of the girl in Algiers: that is, moving freely, *outside the male* gaze—here, my camera's gaze." Ibid., 65.

6. "What the movie-going public of Algiers could not tolerate is that I *excluded men from my film.* But how can I respond other than by saying that all I did was show what exists in reality?" Djebar, Ibid.

7. See Gilles Deleuze, *Cinema 2: The Time-Image,* trans. Hugh Tomlinson and Robert Galeta (Minneapolis: University of Minnesota

Press, 1989), ch. 1: "Beyond the Movement-Image," particularly the section "Optical and Sound Situations, in Contrast to Sensory-Motor Situations."

8. *Oxford English Dictionary,* cited by M. Masud R. Khan, "On Lying Fallow: An Aspect of Leisure, "*International Journal of Psychoanalytic Psychotherapy* 6 (1977), 397.

9. Here I have in mind what A. Begag and A. Chaouite discuss in their *Ecarts d'identités* (Paris: Seuil, 1990), in particular the following remarks: "Among Maghrebi immigrants, women go out *in order to perform a useful or indispensable activity:* to go shopping, straighten out administrative problems, visit family members or take the children to school. Going out just to be outside, to get fresh air, to take a walk, or simply to get a change of scenery are considered to take time away from running the household. Illegitimate excursions are even seen as a sign of perversion." (69; my emphasis)

10. Maurice Merleau-Ponty, *The Primacy of Perception,* ed. James M. Edie, trans. William Cobb (Evanston: Northwestern University Press, 1964), 167; cited by Martin Jay in *Downcast Eyes: The Denigration of Vision in Twentieth Century French Thought* (Berkeley: University of California Press, 1993), 305, note 139.

11. Deleuze and Guattari, "1730: Becoming-Intense, Becoming-Animal, Becoming-Imperceptible . . ." *A Thousand Plateaus,* 292.

12. "She is old," says Lila of one of the old women whom she meets. "She is 88 years old, she is young. I call her 'Aunt,' as if my mother had come back to life in her." This quest for an origin is a constant in the film. In the economy of the film as a whole, it may take on a very different significance.

13. Writing these lines, I recall Abdelwahab Meddeb's remarks in an interview with Guy Scarpetta: "All I know is that everyone out there in the field must not let go," Meddeb said, alluding to the ties that bind Algerian intellectuals to the places of their memories. "The intellectual work [of anamnesis] has not been accomplished in Algeria. Intellectuals needed to apply themselves to dispelling the oblivion of tradition, of the ancient Arab trace, and also to the indispensable learning that leads to mastery. To think that a man of the sword and of the word as important as Abd El-Kader went completely neglected

in Algeria. . . . When the labor of memory is not carried out, there is always a price to pay. . . . Another example: understanding, correcting, and moving beyond the effects of colonialism and its crimes would have required a tremendous effort. Was this work done? Were the 45,000 Algerians who were butchered wholesale in the massively traumatic post-war massacre at Sétif accorded an effort equivalent to that of Klarsfeld, who labored for over 40 years to establish the identities of the 70,000 Jews who were persecuted in France? Were the 40,000 Algerians assassinated at Sétif ever identified, their lives recorded or recounted? Has their memory been handed down?" Abdelwahab Meddeb, "Algérie: L'Enfer et l'amnésie," in *La règle du jeu*, October 1994, 293–4.

14. Djebar dedicated the film "posthumously" to Béla Bartók, the Hungarian musician who around 1913 went to Algeria to study folk music, but also to Yamina Oudaï, alias Zouleikha, who in 1956 and 1957 went underground and "coordinated the national resistance in the mountains and in the town of Cherchell." She was arrested and disappeared.

15. Roland Barthes, "The Circle of Fragments," in *Roland Barthes*, trans. Richard Howard (New York: Hill and Wang, 1977), 94.

Chapter 6
Multilingualism and National "Traits"

1. The French word *blanchir* has several meanings: to "whitewash" (such as in the expression to "whitewash a reputation"). It is also a typographical term, as in "blanchir une page," meaning "to white out" a page, that is, to widen margins, increase spaces between lines, etc. It is this latter meaning I have retained here, for reasons that will become apparent. —Trans.

2. For these questions, see Deleuze and Guattari's indispensable *Kafka*, especially chapters 3 and 4, respectively titled "What is a Minor Literature?" and "The Components of Expression." For a "historical" and "political" perspective on the problems raised by bilingualism, diglossia, and tetraglossia, see Henri Gobard, *L'aliénation linguistique. Analyse Tetraglossique*, with a preface by Gilles Deleuze (Paris: Flammarion, 1976).

3. Khatibi coins the word *bi-langue* in his *Amour bilingue* to distinguish it from the more usual *bilingue* (bilingual) situation. The literal translation would be "bi-tongue." Richard Howard, in his translation of *L'amour bilingue*, keeps the French *bi-langue* throughout. I have done the same here.—Trans.

4. I am aware that Khatibi is not the first Maghrebi author to raise the question of bilingualism. However, it does seem to me that he is the first to put it at the core of his thinking and to inscribe its theoretical problematic in the very body of his poetic texts. Pastiching Barthes, I might say that bilingualism, *practically and esthetically born* with writers such as Kateb Yacine, was still waiting to make its *theoretical entrance* in the Maghreb. With Khatibi, this entrance becomes explicit: begun in *La mémoire tatouée* and *La blessure du nom propre*, this problematic finds its strongest expression in *Amour bilingue,* and more recently still, in an even more frankly theoretical form in *Maghreb pluriel* (Paris: Denoël, 1983).

5. I shall try to show a little further on in what sense posing the "confrontation" of the two languages (French and Arabic) in terms of a simple repression is insufficient. In regard to Khatibi's position on this complex problem, see "Pensée-autre" in his *Maghreb pluriel* (11ff). See also, in the same book, the article "Bilinguisme and littérature" on Abdelwahab Meddeb's beautiful book *Talismano.*

(As I write these notes, I realize that Khatibi had in a way already prefaced what I am trying to put in place here—*after the fact.* One can, in effect, read at the very beginning of the article he devoted to *Talismano* something that interestingly takes note of my reading of his book: "As long as the theory of translation, of the *bi-langue,* and the *pluri-langue* has not advanced, certain Maghrebi texts will remain impregnable to a formal and functional approach. The 'mother' tongue is at work in the foreign language. From one to the other occur a *permanent translation* and a constant *mise en abyme* that are extremely difficult to clarify. . . . Where does the text's violence become apparent, if not in that chiasmus, that intersection that are, in reality, irreconcilable? This must be noted IN THE TEXT ITSELF: to take on the French language, yes, to name within it that flaw and that pleasure [*cette faille et cette jouissance*] of the foreigner who must *con-*

stantly work on the margins, that is, for himself alone, in solitude"
("Bilinguisme et littérature," in *Maghreb pluriel*, 179).

6. See Jacques Derrida, part 1, "L'écriture avant la lettre"
(Paris: Éditions de Minuit, 1967); Derrida, *Marges de la philosophie*,
"La différance" (Paris: Éditions de Minuit, 1972), and also Derrida's
development of this concept in *Positions* (translated and annotated by
Alan Bass; Chicago: University of Chicago Press, 1981), 106–7, J. Derrida's emphasis): "I specify again that spacing is a concept also, but
not exclusively, carries the meaning of a productive, positive, genera-
tive force. Like *dissemination*, like *différance* it carries along with it a
genetic motif: it is not only the interval, the space constituted between
two things (which is the usual sense of spacing), but also spa*cing*
[*sic*], the operation, or in any event, the movement of setting aside.
The movement is inseparable from temporization-temporalization
(see '*La différance*') and from différance, from the conflicts of force at
work in them. It marks what is set aside from itself, what interrupts
every self-identity, every punctual assemblage of the self, every self-ho-
mogeneity, self-interiority."

7. In French the verb *traduire* means "to translate," of course,
but it also has a legal sense, "traduire en cours de justice," which
means to bring (someone) before a court of justice.—Trans.

8. Here I am using for my purposes certain aspects of J. C.
Milner's excellent analyses of the status of Ferdinand de Saussure's
Anagrammes in *L'amour de la langue* (Paris: Éditions du Seuil, 1978).
See in particular the chapter "Un linguiste désirant," 85–98.

9. See Alain Grosrichard, *Structure du Sérail: La fiction du des-
potisme asiatique dans l'Occident classique* (Paris: Éditions du Seuil,
1979), and especially chapter 3, "L'ombre du sérail," 153ff.

10. In Abdelkebir Khatibi, *Figures de l'étranger dans la littérature française* (Paris: Denoël, 1987), 203–4.

11. See the pamphlet "Francophonie et idiomes littéraires"
(Rabat: Éditions "al Kalam"), published after the conference on the
state of Francophonie held in Paris on December 11–13, 1989.

12. In this sense, Khatibi's perspective is in keeping with the
theses on "fictional ethnicity" put forward by philosophers, political
scientists, and theorists of the modern nation such as Immanuel Wal-

lerstein and Etienne Balibar. I am thinking in particular of their *Race, Nation, Classe: Les identités ambiguës* (Paris: La découverte/Poche, 1997), specifically of the closing words of Balibar's essay entitled "La forme nation: Histoire, idéologie": "Each 'people,' the product of a national process of ethnicization—is today compelled to find its own voice to go beyond exclusivism or identitarian ideology in the world of transnational communications and relations between global forces. Or rather: each individual is compelled to find, within the transformation of 'his' people's imaginary, the means to get out of it in order to communicate with individuals who belong to other peoples who have the same interests and in part the same future as he does." (143)

13. René Galissot, "Pluralisme culturel en Europe: Identités nationales et identités européennes. De l'intellecctuel métis au métissage culturel des masses," in *Information sur les sciences sociales* (Newbury Park: Sage, 1992), 117–27.

14. Arjun Appadurai, "Global Ethnoscapes: Notes and Queries for a Transnational Anthropology," in *Recapturing Anthropology: Working in the Present*, ed. Richard Fox (Santa Fe: School of New Research Press, 1991).

15. Armand Mattelart, "Comment résister à la colonisation des esprits?" *Le monde diplomatique*, April 1994.

16. Khatibi, *Un été à Stockhom* (Paris: Flammarion, 1990).

17. Roland Barthes, "Les allégories linguistiques," in *Roland Barthes*, 127–8.

18. See Michel Serres, "Naissance du tiers," in *Le tiers-instruit* (Paris: François Bourin, 1991), 26–7. In English: *The Troubadour of Knowledge*, trans. Sheila Faria Glaser (Ann Arbor: University of Michigan Press, 1997).

19. I am specifically thinking of what Glissant articulates in his insightful book on these questions, *Poétique de la relation* (Paris: Gallimard, 1990), especially when he writes, "From the moment cultures, lands, men and women were no longer [objects] to be discovered, but to be known, Relation became an absolute (that is, an entity at last sufficient unto itself) that, paradoxically, *liberated us from the intolerances of the absolute.*

"To the degree that our consciousness of the Relation is total, that is, immediate and immediately bearing on the realizable totality of the world, we no longer need, when speaking about a poetics of the Relation, to add: the relation between what and what? This is why the French word 'Relation,' which functions something like an intransitive verb, does not correspond, for example, to the English word "relationship.'" (Glissant, 39–40) As we can see, the "relation" refers here to a virtual, not actual "totality," but which is real nonetheless. As Glissant says, the Relation "needs the word to produce itself, to prolong itself. But its relatedness does not really come from an absolute, *it reveals itself to be the totality of contingencies [des relatifs] that are placed in relation and spoken.*" Ibid., 40. So it is as a "totality of contingencies" that it "acts," and, in this sense, we can say that it is "virtual"!

20. In Abdelkebir Khatibi, "Extase froide," *La langue de l'autre* (New York and Tunis: Éditions Les Mains Secrètes, 1999), 49.

21. Abbreviations used: LS, *Le livre du sang*; MP, *Maghreb pluriel*; OJ, *Ombres japonaises*;

22. In the French expression "nuit blanche" (sleepless night), several meanings resonate: whiteness, blankness, sleeplessness.

23. In Arabic, *Muthna* signifies effeminate, hermaphrodite, and androgyne. In spoken vernacular, at least phonetically, it also means "we are dead."

24. Concerning the problematics of history in the context of the mystical epic, I am indebted to Henri Corbin's studies on traditional Arab and Sufi philosophy of history, especially *Face de dieu, Face de l'homme: Herméneutique et Soufisme*, ch. 3, "De l'épopée héroïque à l'épopée mystique," 163.

25. The *Salafiya* movement or *Salafism* is a reformist movement that appeared in Morocco after World War I and developed in North Africa thereafter. It "stressed the purification of Islam, opposition to saint worship and defense against Western encroachment." (Ira M. Lapidus, *A History of Islamic Societies* [Cambridge: Cambridge University Press, 1988], 707, 716–7)

26. In Khatibi's work the "Pensée-Autre" is certainly the "thought of otherness," the "thought (of the) Other" and also an "other thought."

27. Earlier in his essay, Khatibi first defines rationalism as metaphysics become technique and thus technique (technology) as "the ordering of the world according to a new will to power that derives its strength from scientific progress." (*Maghreb pluriel*, 25)

28. Here is the complete citation from Corbin regarding the notion of the *Orient*: "In no way is it a question of a principle of racial explanation, of what Western Romanticism called the *Volkgeist*, the spirit or genius of a race or a people. Sohravardi's notion remains essentially sacred, hieratic. Its horizon is dominated by what he defines as the Orient, but it is not a question of the east that is found on our geographical maps, nor of the peoples who inhabit these Eastern countries. It is a question of the Orient as origin (*oriens/origo*) of the Being as Light, of the *succession of Orients* to which each order of light in the hierarchies of beings of light is raised to its respective rank: The *Major Orient* of cherubic Intelligences (the world of 'Jabarût'); the *Minor Orient* of Angels or celestial Souls (the world of 'malakût'); the *Middle Orient* of the imaginal (or the world of 'Hûrqalyâ'). Oriental knowledge designates a knowledge that, rather than being representative of its object and obtained by discursive means, calls for logic, is immediate *Presence*, unveiling [*dévoilement*], the intuition of the heart or the spiritual eye, in sum, a dawn rising in the soul rising to its 'Orient.' " (167–8) It is the very idea of an "oriental knowledge" conceived as a knowledge obtained without any discursive mediation and as a "presence" which, as we shall see, Khatibi's work challenges.

29. Cf. Francis Bertin, "Corps spirituel et androgynie chez Jean Scot Erigène," in "L'androgyne," *Cahiers de l'Hermétisme* (Paris: Albin Michel, 1986).

30. Concerning the characteristics of the celestial being in the mystical epic, see Bertin: "Made in God's image, the androgyne is an idea (*idea*), a gender (*genos*), or a mark. It is intelligible (*noetos*), incorporal (*asomatos*), uncorruptible by nature (*aphthartosphysei*)." (77) These are precisely the "characteristics" Khatibi subverts when he replaces the "Adamic" figure of the mystical androgyne with the paradoxical and carnal figure of the Cupbearer.

31. Cf. Francis Bertin, Ibid.

Chapter 7
The Cartography of the Nation

1. Mouloud Feraoun, *Le fils du pauvre* (Paris: Éditions du Seuil, 1954).

2. Christiane Achour, *Mouloud Feraoun: Une voix en contrepoint* (Paris: Silex Éditions, 1986).

3. Ibid., 35.

4. I am thinking in particular of the importance of the letters that the father, who has emigrated to France, sends to his family through a public writer, and of the privileged status of the person who can read these letters and, especially, write responses. Feraoun writes: "In the village . . . he was given a certain importance, but Fouroulou was not vain because of this." Yet Fouroulou is proud to be able to read the letters from his father, and to be able to write back to him later." See also the beautiful passage in chapter 4 of the second part where Ramdane, Fouroulou's father, on returning from France asks Fouroulou to read the "documents" that he brought back and that are the living proof of what he has endured: "Here, read this, if you really are educated. Take a look at what your father has endured. . . . What he has suffered." (108) Is this a parody of the Koran, as is suggested by the words "read this"? What is certain is that "education," and eventually the "law," is linked here not to an oral knowledge of the Koran but to a written knowledge of French.

We can also refer to the "ethnographic" style in which the book opens: "The tourist who *dares* to penetrate the heart of Kabylia admires—from a sense of conviction or duty—*sites that he finds marvelous*, landscapes that seem to him full of poetry, and he always experiences a kind of indulgent fondness for the customs of the inhabitants." (8) Throughout the entire book, Feraoun works steadily at rewriting these "sites" and "landscapes," thus both surveying and archiving them. In a way, he also establishes what could be called the "ethnocultural cadaster" of Kabylia: a "country" that colonial France had attempted to set in opposition to the "Arab" country, and whose difference independent Algeria would tend to obscure.

5. This is a phenomenon that, along with the writing and sending of letters, we have already pointed out in Nabile Farès, with his

references to identity and registration cards in *L'état perdu*, but it can also be found systematically in the work of most of the writers we are studying here. No one has shown better than Assia Djebar the importance of the circulation and exchange of letters during the colonial and postcolonial periods. Whether letters written by conquering generals to their families or the many secret, mysterious, censured, or stolen letters written by the female narrators in *L'amour, la fantasia*, they all tell the same story of a failed encounter (between colonized and colonizer, men and women, and also between the cultures involved, French and Algerian as well as Arab and Berber!).

The letters of these forgotten captains, who claim to be worried about their supplies and careers, also sometimes reveal their personal philosophy; at bottom, they speak about an *Algeria-Woman* impossible to tame, as Djebar has so clearly shown: "The fantasy of a subdued Algeria: each struggle further delays the exhaustion of revolt," she writes, and the least we can say is that she takes this metaphor of *Algeria-Woman* most seriously. If indeed the French had something against this *Algeria-Woman*, the challenge must be taken up and one must show who these women were, what they did, what one owes to them, and so on.

With Feraoun, the letter is transformed into an "emigrant's archive," but it also aids the discovery of the self and true communication with others: "The teacher *was surprised not to have recognized his pupil's handwriting* and told him that he thought he was capable of writing to his father. But two weeks later, Fouroulou gave a second letter to his schoolteacher. On the envelope the father's address was written *like a sample of his finest handwriting*: Menrad Ramdane, 23, Rue de la Goutte-d'Or, Paris 18. The teacher glanced at it, and understood that Fouroulou was expecting something. 'Good work!' he said, and Fouroulou left!" (My emphasis)

As Derrida has said, the letter always runs the risk of not arriving at its destination; it is the signifier that is always deferred (*décalé*) in relation to the present of the writer; but it also runs the risk of coming back and producing unexpected "aftereffects." This is certainly true of the letters from the French captains and generals, the "aftereffects" of which reveal the horrors of the conquest for the autochtones/indigenous people and haunt them afterwards. And this is true as well of the letters that the women write or receive; afterwards, these letters allow them to better understand what they had repressed in order to survive, what they had to do in silence in order to continue to live. Finally, there are the letters (but this list is not exhaustive) that are lost or stolen, like the letter stolen from the female narrator of *L'amour, la fantasia* by a beggar at the market, and that winds up in the hands of someone other than the one for whom it was intended!

The letters exchanged in *Le fils du pauvre, L'amour, la fantasia, Un passager de l'occident*, etc., are also "Letters," in the sense of belles lettres, that is, literature. Through them our writers provide us with an "allegory" of the situation of Algerian women and emigrants and of the condition of Algerians and colonial Algeria. It is not by means of an epic "grand narrative," for example, that the actual history of (the conquest of) Algeria can be revealed, but by means of these small letters that, on the surface, are the most insignificant of signifiers. On the subject of these small letters, see François Paré's wonderful book, *Les littératures de l'exiguité* (Montreal: Le Nordir, 1994).

6. Geneviève Mouillaud-Fraisse, *Les fous cartographes: Littérature et appartenance* (Paris: L'Harmattan, 1995), 11.

7. With her usual flair, Achour underscored the importance of the rift that structures the text. But since she is focused on trying to extricate Feraoun's work from the ideology to which it has been subject since Feraoun's brutal death at the hands of his OAS murderers, she does not reach the conclusions that I do here. "The only *declared* autobiographical discourse that Feraoun conceived is that of the *Journal*," she writes. "The 'I' here merges with the writer, and expresses itself with no other screen than that of the writing (which is already an important screen). In the rest of his production, there is a subtle shift from a narrator who is *internal* to the fiction to an *external* narrator: a documentary and lyrical realism that becomes the more classic realism of a narrator who is omniscient, but absent from the narrative." (36; my emphasis) It is the unique nature of this subtle shift from one type of narrative to another and the absence that it conditions that interests me here and that is not, it seems to me, problematized

as such by Achour. For Achour, who nevertheless points to the idea that Feraoun's cultural dissidence is linked to the narrative structure and to the distribution of voices and gazes, this subtle shift to an omniscient narrator only exists to allow for a more detached tone. We shall see that it is a matter of much more than a simple psychological detachment.

8. In fact it is in this sense that one cannot say that the book is merely a veiled autobiography, as Achour would have it. (Achour, 37) The veil is, as I have attempted to show, also a screen, a ruse, and a becoming-imperceptible. Behind this veil, if it is indeed a veil, there are yet other veils.

9. I am trying to transpose, for the purposes of my analysis, the thesis that Mouillaud-Fraisse puts forth in the introduction to her book. See in particular the conclusion to her argument: "In a sense, I am using the mad cartographer as metaphor; it is not true that all the paradoxes of belonging are geopolitical in nature. But in another sense, *it is not pure metaphor*. It is a figure of thought; *the counterterm to a thought that would have belonging as a complex figure on several levels that cannot be superimposed on a single plane*, and which the reading of certain literary works develops, and which is the object of this book." (11)

What I am trying to put into perspective here may also be compared to what Amin Maalouf analyzed so well in the book he wrote on the conflict between our "identity" and our "belongings": *Les identités meurtrières* (Paris: Grasset, 1998). "Each of my belongings links me to several people; nonetheless, the more numerous the belongings I take into account, the more specific my identity becomes." (27) In his cartography, Maalouf does not take into consideration the "dehiscence" I am trying to describe here. "Linguistic alienation" is not at all taken into account.

If we wanted to push the question outlined here to its limits, we would take a detour through the blurring of identity (*trouble d'identité*) that Derrida describes in his book on the relation to language and the impact of colonial schooling. I will simply refer to what Derrida specifies regarding colonial alienation: This alienation begins by the subjection to a language—a single language—that itself refers to a single map, a single language, and, eventually, a single law. "The monolingualism of the other would be that sovereignty, that *law* originating from elsewhere, certainly, but also and primarily *the very language of the Law*. And the Law as Language. . . . The monolingualism imposed by the other operates by relying upon a foundation, here, through a sovereignty whose essence is always colonial, which tends, repressibly and irrepressibly, to *reduce language to the One, that is, to the hegemony of the homogenous*." Derrida, *Monolingualism of the Other or the Prothesis of Origin*, trans. Patrick Mensah (Stanford: Stanford University Press, 1998) 39–40; my emphasis.

10. Ibid., 29.

11. Ibid., 31. In this willfully (?) amphigoric but always fascinating text, Derrida assumes that only Jewish *pieds-noirs* have experienced the "alienation" he analyzes. I hope to have demonstrated that the "situation that cannot be found" he describes is shared by everyone and anyone who suffered the colonial "steamroller."

12. The Franco-Algerian word *mtourni* contains the idea of a person who is a "turncoat" and also someone who is a traitor who has "converted" (to the culture and customs of the other).

13. On the notion of the "spectral," see Derrida, *Monolingualismu*, 73ff, as well as Jean Baudrillard and Marc Guillaume, *Figures de l'altérité* (Paris: Descartes, 1994).

14. I am referring here to the well-known passage in chapter 4 where Fouroulou reveals the origin and etymology of his name: "Since I was the first viable boy born in my family, my grandmother peremptorily decided to call me Fouroulou (from *effer*, to hide). This means [Feraoun adds maliciously] that no one in the whole world will be able to see me, with his good eye or his bad, until the day that I shall cross, on my own two feet, the threshold of our door." (21)

Chapter 8
By Way of a Conclusion

1. Ania Loomba, *Colonialism/Postcolonialism* (New York and London: Routledge, 1998), 256.

2. For Ahmed Aijaz, for example, postcolonial intellectuals are no more than "radicalized immigrants located in the metropolitan

university," who are marked by a "combination of class origin, professional ambition and a lack of prior political grounding in socialist praxis." We find the same kind of apprehensiveness and the same sort of point-blank refusal and mistrust in the work of intellectuals as diverse as Gayatry Spivak, R. Guha, A. Dirlik, Angie Chabran, Rosandra Sanchez, and Stuart Hall. In each case the debate turns around whether the postcolonial intellectual is capable of avoiding the hold that the colonial education system had on him or her or whether he or she can, in the end, escape the destiny that would make of him or her a simple "native informant" of the (European) Center.

An excellent critical summary of these questions can be found in Leela Gandhi's book, *Postcolonial Theory: A Critical Introduction* (New York: Columbia University Press, 1998). See especially ch. 3, "Postcolonialism and the New Humanities," 42ff. The quote from Aijaz above is on page 58.

3. See Etienne Balibar and Immanuel Wallerstein, *Race, Nation, Classe: Les identités ambiguës* (Paris: Éditions La Découverte, 1997). Indeed, as Wallerstein shows in the chapter "La construction des peuples: Racisme, nationalisme, ethnicité," whereas the concept of nation "is linked to the political superstructure of the historical system, in the sovereign States that form the inter-state system and are defined by it," the concept of ethnic group is linked to "the creation of structures of domestic households that allow a large proportion of the labor force to remain non-salaried during capitalist accumulation," while the concept of "race" appeared as a "means to express and consolidate the center-periphery antinomy." (106, 112) For Wallerstein, this thesis on race, ethnicity, and nation relies in the end on an axial division of labor within the world economy that leads in its turn to a "spatial division of labor." (107) Intellectuals obviously are part of this division, and it becomes even more absurd to try to attribute to them an origin or a space of labor that would make their critical discourse more effective and more valid. The question we asked in the chapter on Khatibi remains: Should the writer/intellectual belong first of all to a *nation?* And in which *state?*

4. "To live the totality-world ["Tout-Monde"] from the place that is one's own, is to establish a relation and not to consecrate exclu-

sion." Glissant, *Introduction à une poétique du divers* (Paris: Gallimard, 1997), 67.

5. Quoted in Loomba, *Colonialism*, 255.

6. I am also thinking here of the work that has been done by historians such as Mustapha Lacheraf or Benjamin Stora on Algeria, as well as that of Lahouari Addi, Ali Merad, Hélé Béji, and many others for everything that deals with the conceptualization of the specificity of the work of the so-called postcolonial historian. But we must also include the work of writers, teachers, and scholars who, *from home* or from the outside, have produced a monumental work of marking out new historical and cultural configurations of their countries.

As far as Algeria is concerned, for example, it is impossible today to separate the work of intellectuals in exile from that of their national counterparts. A journal as important as *Algérie littérature/action* was founded by Algerian intellectuals in France and plays an essential role between the two countries today. Slimane Benaïssa, for example, published his *Théatre en exil* in France, yet this doesn't prevent it from being staged and studied in Algeria!

7. The same problematic turns up in Christopher Miller's excellent article "Nationalism as Resistance and Resistance to Nationalism in the Literature of Francophone Africa," *Yale French Studies* 82 (1993), 62–100. See in particular the passage in which he states: "By attacking particular regimes, these publications contribute to an emergent 'universe of discourse' that is specific to the nation-state. . . . The critique of a regime will in the long run contribute to a nationally specific universe of discourse. What any writer says about the nation matters less than the fact that he or she is addressing the question of the nation and thereby contributing to a national discourse. This is but one way in which nationalism legitimates itself and makes itself inevitable: the harder you pull, as in Chinese handcuffs, the tighter is its grip." (95) To that we can add that it is not necessarily within the framework of pure nationalism that these texts are produced. Sow Fall, for example, said precisely that she did not have much to do with African literature. I think this needs to be read as a symptom of a radically new situation that breaks completely with what preceded

it: nationalism of resistance, postindependence nationalism, critical nationalism, etc.

8. Another element that must be taken into consideration regarding Francophone literature and the question of nation: the analysis by theorists like Wallerstein and (especially) Balibar of the emergence of nation, race, ethnicity, people. If the era of nations is already a thing of the past, shouldn't we begin to think in terms of a literature that is not only postcolonial but postnational as well? What we see occurring in Algeria, for example, and in Morocco and Tunisia as well (Khatibi, Meddeb, Béji, Farès, Ben Jelloun, and many others), gives us a good idea of the direction to be followed. But to speak of postnational literature—and perhaps we should say "postnationalist" literature—does not mean for all that that considerations of nation or people are no longer valid. The current history of countries like Algeria, Morocco, and Tunisia—to remain within the realm of the countries dealt with in this book—makes obvious that any serious study of the culture of these countries *must pass through* the most detailed analysis of what is going on every day, in the present and in the long term, in economics, politics, and culture. What kind of government is in power in these countries? What institutions? What educational systems? What political parties? In addition, what relation do they have to the global world? What relation and kind of exchange with former colonies? What civil rights? What status for women? Children? Freedoms (of speech, of the press, of movement), and so on?

Once again, those who are concerned with knowing whether exiled or diasporic postcolonial intellectuals make up a *compradore* intelligentsia or simple informants fail to understand that the world in which these intellectuals live and move today is not the world that Fanon, Memmi, and others had in mind when they produced their analyses of colonial and postcolonial situations. As the sociologist of culture Zygmunt Bauman, for example, argued, the era of "globalization" no longer authorizes "positions" as clear-cut as those for which one could militate even ten years ago. See Zygmunt Bauman, *Globalization: The Human Consequences* (New York: Columbia University Press, 1998), specifically the chapter "After the Nation-State—What?" 55ff.

Appendix
Le Dépays: On Chris Marker's Lettre de Sibérie

1. See André Bazin, *Le cinéma français de la libération à la nouvelle vague* (Paris: Éditions des cahiers du cinéma, Éditions de l'étoile, 1983), 179–81.

2. Henri Michaux, *Plume, précédé de Lointain intérieur* (Paris: Gallimar, 1983), 75.

3. I am using a concept from Abdelkebir Khatibi's *Maghreb pluriel*. Also of interest in this context is Khatibi's *Figures de l'étranger dans la littérature française*, specifically the chapter devoted to Victor Segalen entitled "Célébration de l'exote," 17–59.

4. Marker, *Coréennes* (Paris: Éditions du Seuil), 15.

5. I am thinking in particular of the passage where Marker shows us the same sequence—a street in Irkutsk on a workday—three times with three different commentaries: the first is procommunist and "orthodox"; the second is frankly anticommunist (denouncing the inhuman conditions under which Soviet workers live and the sinister character of the city); and the third is seemingly entirely informative or supposedly objective.

No doubt this procedure essentially aims to show the totally arbitrary nature of the ideological anchoring of the images by the commentary and to denounce the falseness of the pseudo-objectivity of the images. But as the rest of the film clearly shows, this specific passage mostly provides Marker with the opportunity to break the rules of documentary filmmaking and to clue us in to his real project: making a film about the other, Marker seems to be saying, is more than simply filming what the other lets us see; making a film about the other should always involve not only a knowledge of his or her culture but also a sensitivity to his or her imaginary. Better yet: to brush up against the imaginary of the other is also to fight against the "degradation of the Diverse" (Segalen's expression), against reducing the diversity of beings and things in this world. As Marker himself puts it: "Objectivity is not true either. It does not deform Siberian reality, but it arrests it, for the time it takes to judge, and in so doing deforms it anyway. *What matters is momentum* [l'élan] *and diversity.* Simply strolling down the streets of Irkutsk will not help you understand Siberia. *What you need is a film of imaginary events, captured in the four corners of the country.*" (Marker, Commentaires, *Lettre de Sibérie*, 58; my emphasis)

6. I quote and emphasize here for my argument the wonderful pages that Deleuze devoted to hysteria in painting in his book on Francis Bacon. See *Francis Bacon: Logique de la sensation*, vol. 1, *La vue/le texte* (Paris: Éditions de la différence, 1981), in particular: "Painting proposes directly to disengage the presences beneath representation, beyond representation. . . . Abjection becomes splendor, the horror of life becomes very pure and very intense life. 'Life is frightening,' Cézanne said, but in this cry one could already hear all the joys of line and color." (37) Marker follows a movement of intensity very similar to that of the painter and much more systematic and rigorous in his 1982 video *Sans soleil*, where within the violence and the shouts that are deformed by electronic synthesizers, an infinite joy and affirmation of life nonetheless can be felt.

See also my article, "Du photogramme au pictogramme: A propos de *La jetée* de Chris Marker. Pour une analytique future des fondus enchaînés et des fondus au noir," *Iris* 78, Special issue on "Cinema and Narration II" (1989), 9–39. I analyze Marker's affinities with Francis Bacon, which are even more obvious in *La jetée*.

7. See Marker, *Coréennes*, ch. 4, "Les cinq sens," 70.

8. The word *exot* was coined by Segalen to account for a very specific category of traveler. The *exot* is first defined negatively, in contrast to two figures who represent his opposite: the colonizer and the tourist. The colonizer is not an *exot* and has nothing to do with the authentic traveler in that, for him, the Diverse and the Other exist only "in so far as [they] provide him with the means to dupe others" (35) or to make him rich. The tourist, for his part, is not an *exot* either because "amid the greatest speeds and the greatest distances," he only wants to be able to find his "woolen stockings," his "savings," his "armchair," and his "nap." Finally, the colonizer and the tourist are not *exots* because of the "changes they bring in their wake. The damages they cause. Their leavings." Segalen, *Essay on Exoticism*, trans. Yaël Rachel Schlick (Durham: Duke University Press, 2002), 39ff.

We can now see what Segalen and, it seems to me, Marker as well expect from the *exot* and the traveler. In a first stage it is less a matter of putting oneself forward or exalting one's own self than of being attentive to the reaction that one produces on one's environment: "To express the effect that the traveler has on the living milieu rather than the milieu's effect on the traveler." (Ibid., 15) In a second stage, however, one must become sensitive to the "call of the milieu to the traveler, of the Exotic to the Exot who penetrates it, attacks it, reawakens it, and agitates it." (17)

For the problem of "exoticism" as conceived by Segalen, see Marc Gontard, "Théorie de la différence chez Segalen," in *Imaginaires de l'autre. Khatibi et la mémoire littéraire* (Paris: L'Harmattan: 1987), 65–79, and Henri Bouillier, *Victor Segalen* (Paris: Mercure de France, 1986).

9. See Marker, *Le dépays*. At the beginning of this book, we find the following "note to the reader": "The text does not comment upon the images any more than the images illustrate the text. Each is a series of sequences that evidently comes in contact with the other and acknowledges it, but it would be pointlessly tiring to have them confront one another. They should be taken in no particular order, in simplicity and doubling, like all things should be taken in Japan."

(The words *dépaysement* and *dépays* have no literal translation in English. While *dépaysement* is a word that exists in French, and can be translated as "disorientation," or "feeling of strangeness," or even "change of scenery"—none of which are adequate here—the word *dépays* is Marker's coinage, and I would translate it in this instance as the "un-home," for there is, too, a sense of Freud's *Unheimlichkeit* here. —Trans.)

10. I am borrowing this word from Montaigne. For a more detailed analysis of its status in Montaigne's work, see my *Barthes Effect: The Essay as Reflective Text* (Minneapolis: University of Minnesota Press, 1987).

11. See Marker, *Commentaires* 1, 49.

Monolingual reader, 115, 120
Montage, 59
Morganatic, 109
Morganatic projection, 114
Mosaic, 126
Mtourni (the postcolonial intellectual as a), 154
Multilingualism, 99
Multiple centers, 47
Mutation of thought, 120
Mystical *Epos*, 145
Mystical narrative, 140
Mystical writer, 143
Mythical self-fictioning, 23
"Mythic fiction," 23
Mythic language, 18
Mythiing thinking (*Pensée mythante*), 23
Myth of origin, 24
Mythological realism, 24

Narrative bipartition, 151
Narrator-*trekker*, 75
National allegory, 68
National borders, 130
National character, 14
National conscience, 15, 26
National culture, 2, 15
National entity, 13, 22, 103
National feeling, 19
National Front, 43
National identity, 38, 42, 47, 57
Nationalism, 19, 26
Nationalist power, 26
National language, 103
National liberation, 2
National literature, 7, 18
National myth, 25
National theater, 19
National trait, 13, 99
Nation building, 23
Nation formation, 22
Native subject, 155
Neocolonialism, 7
Neutral, 132, 137, 155
Neutrality, 26

Neutral language, 61
Neutral space, 29
Never-ending narrative, 146
New man, 23
Nomad, 58
Nomadic writing, 132
Non-hierarchical systems, 56
Non-identity, 26
Non-locatable center, 114
Non-signifying system, 56
Nostalgeria, 42, 44
Nuit blanche, 137, 139, 144–47

Onirism, 21
Opacity, 163
Open space, 30
Operator of analysis (the city as an), 29, 33
Oral enunciation, 150
Orality, 18
Order of things, 29
Organisation de l'Armée Secrète (OAS), 2
Oriens/Origo, 142
Orient, 140, 142
Orientalism, 140
Orphic, 155
Osmosis, 104
Otherness, 145

Paganism, 51
Palindrome, 64
Panoptic city, 37
Panoptic eye, 32
Panoptic power, 37
Paper language, 118
Paradisiacal harem, 139
Paradoxical experience, 47
Paradoxical mourning, 41
Para-grammatic interplay, 120
Paraliterature, 132
Paranoid, 151
Parataxis, 92
Paredre, 134
Parisian culture, 1
Patriarchy, 50

Pensée autre, 118, 122, 140, 141, 163
Pensum, 69
Periodization, 22 ff.
Phalanx, 62
Phenomenology, 89
Philosophic complement, 59
Pied-noir, 39, 42–44, 118
Place of memory, 81
Plurality of tongues, 5
Plural universality, 127
Pluri-langue, 105
Poetical allegories, 67
Poetical imagery, 28
Poetic of relation, 132
Political allegories, 67
Populist novel, 155
Postcolonial city, 38
Postcolonial historians, 161
Postcolonial nation, 67
Postcolonial text, 69, 76
Postindependence, 21
Postmodern condition, 8
Poundian ideogram, 62
Primitives, 59
Primordial atomization, 94
Primordial chaos, 92
Professional foreigner/stranger, 126, 134
Professional traveler, 124, 131–33
Promenade, 28
Prosopopeia, 44
Protocol of knowledge, 160
Psychic experience, 60
Psychological identity, 47, 90
Punctum, 92
"Pulsion scripturale," 31

Reappropriation (cultural), 6, 122, 131
Rebeginning, 64
Recollection (*anamnesis* as), 43
Reductionism (critical), 68
Referential language, 17, 18
Registered identity, 57
Repression (political, cultural), 41, 42
Repression of language, 55
Reterritorialization, 12, 13, 15, 18, 21, 33, 50, 52, 107, 112

Rhetorical imagery, 28
Rhetorical strategy, 72
Rhétorique habitante, 37
Rhizome, 30, 31, 102, 133
Rhizosphere, 102

Scheherazade, 137, 139, 146
Schize, 152, 153
Schizophrenia, 101
Scotoma, 39
Seduction, 137
Self-identity, 123
Self-mutilation, 2
Sexual difference, 93
Signifying interiority, 54
singular identity, 45
Site of memory, 12, 38, 39, 43, 44
Site of speech, 43
Social time, 28
Sociolinguistics, 16
Space of thought, 30
Space of writing, 104
Spacing, 107
Stalker, 77, 78, 81
Stigmata (writing as), 55
Stochastic logic, 62
Strangeness/foreignness, 134
Stranger's eyes, 2
Strategy of the performative, 73
Strobophonic, 120
Stroboscopic, 120
Subjective interiority, 54
Supremacy (cultural and/or political), 50
Sur-reality, 89
Syllogistic knowledge, 62
Symbiosis, 144
Symptom, 55
Synchronic time, 28
Syntactic (logic), 115

Technonarcissism, 106
Temporalization/Temporization, 110, 120
Terrain, 11, 12, 13, 14, 16, 18, 26